Women's Violent Crime in Uganda

... essential reading for lawyers, law-enforcement agents, judicial officers, social workers, and students.'

— Lady Justice S. B. Bossa of
the High Court of Uganda

Women's Violent Crime in Uganda

More Sinned Against than Sinning

Lillian Tibatemwa-Ekirikubinza

Fountain Publishers

Originally published as MORE SINNED AGAINST than sinning: Women's violent crime in Uganda.

Fountain Publishers Ltd
P.O. Box 488
Kampala, Uganda
(256) (41) 259–163

© Lillian Tibatemwa–Ekirikubinza 1995, 1999
First published by Fountain Publishers 1999

All rights reserved. No part of this publication may be reproduced, stored in a retrieval system, or transmitted, in any form or by any means, without the prior permission in writing of the publisher, nor be otherwise circulated in any form of binding or cover other than that which it is published and without a similar condition including this condition being imposed on the subsequent purchaser.

ISBN 9970 – 02 – 166 – 4

Cover photo © 1997 *The New Vision*

Typeset in 11/13.2 pt Times New Roman
Printed in Kenya

04 03 02 01 00 99   5 4 3 2 1

Cataloguing in publication data

Tibatemwa-Ekirikubinza, Lillian *1961 –*
    Women's violent crime in Uganda: more sinned against than sinning / Lillian Tibatemwa-Ekirikubinza.—Kampala: Fountain Publishers, 1999.
         262 p.   cm.

    Originally published as More sinned against than sinning: women's violent crime in Uganda. Author's Ph.D. thesis, Institute of Criminology and Criminal Law, University of Copenhagen, 1995.
    Includes bibliographical references and index.
    ISBN 9970 02 166 4

    1. Female offenders—Uganda   2. Homicide—Uganda—Psychological aspects   3. Women murderers—Uganda.

364.374'09761 – dc20

Dedication

To my husband Paul, whose endearing love and support brings out the best in me, and to my three sons: Emmy, who after months of separation could only call me 'Aunt Mummy'; Joshua, the only family member who was present at my dissertation defence, albeit in the womb; and Elisha, who has crowned my joy.

Contents

Dedication   *iii*
List of tables   *vii*
List of abbreviations   *viii*
Acknowledgements   *ix*

Introduction: Why a Book about Women's Violent Crime in Uganda?   1
The objective – The problem – The justification – Definition and scope – Background literature – Research methodology – Chapter summaries

1. Women's Violence: A General Profile   27
   Who are these women?

2. Husband as Victim   39
   Physical abuse – The role of alcohol in marital violence – Other forms of abuse – Resistance against double oppression – Land conflicts and domestic violence – Far from women's liberation – Conclusion

3. Marriage, Divorce, and Separation   79
   Introduction – Social barriers to divorce – For the sake of the children – The economic trap: nothing other than marriage – Legal barriers to divorce – The need to be free

4. Child Victims   99
   The offender's child as the victim – Other child victims – Stepmothers as first suspects – Conclusion

5. Polygamy and Women's Violence   122
   Patrilocality and violence between co-wives – Threats to women's socio-economic status: Natukunda's story – Choice of the victim: husband versus co-wife – Predominance of junior wives as victims – Polygamy and societal change – Cultural change – Mistresses – Conclusion

6. Reactions to Victim Precipitation   159
   The battered woman – Legal recognition of victim precipitation – The doctrine of self-defence and the concept of 'reasonableness' – Accumulated violence – Threats of future injury – The use of weapons – Provocation as a defence – Witchcraft as both motive and defence – Provocation and sentencing – Accumulated violence and sentencing – Verdicts under Section 182 of the Uganda Penal Code – Conclusion

7. Consequences of Imprisonment   211
   Separating categories – Far away from home – Children of women prisoners – Clothing for the children – Prisoners' children left outside prison – Child delivery in prison – Counselling – Life after prison – Ill-prepared for the outside society – Conclusion

Conclusion: Where Do We Go from Here?   229

List of References   *239*
Further Reading   *246*
Index   *254*

Tables

1. Demographics of prisoners interviewed   29

2. Relationships between co-offenders: court records   31

3. Relationships between co-offenders: interviewed inmates   32

4. Age categories of accused women: court records   33

5. Relationships between victims and offenders   34

6. Results of cases in which women had men as co-offenders: court records   35

7. Weapons used: court and prison records   181

Abbreviations

A.C. – Appeal Cases
AIDS – Acquired Immune Deficiency Syndrome
All E.R. – All England Law Reports
d/o – daughter of ...
D.P.P. – Director of Public Prosecutions
E.A. – East African Law Reports
E.A.C.A. – East African Court of Appeal
FIDA – (Uganda) Association of Women Lawyers
H.C.B. – High Court Bulletin
H.C.C.S. No. – High Court Civil Suit Number
H.C.C.S.C. No. – High Court Criminal Session Case Number
HIV – Human Immunodeficiency Virus
K.B. – King's Bench
M.C.A. – Magistrates' Courts Act
M.M.A. – Chief Magistrate's Court of Masaka
M.M.B. – Chief Magistrate's Court of Mbarara
RC – Resistance Committee
PMS – Premenstrual Syndrome
S. – Section; Senior
s/o – son of ...
T.I.D. – Trial on Indictments Decree
U.L.R. – Uganda Law Reports
U.P.C. – Uganda Penal Code
w/o – wife of ...

Acknowledgements

This book began as a postgraduate thesis which I submitted for a Ph.D. degree in Law at the University of Copenhagen, Denmark, in 1995. The thesis was published in its original form by the Institute of Criminology and Criminal Law, University of Copenhagen under the title, *MORE SINNED AGAINST than sinning: Women's violent crime in Uganda.*

For purposes of the present publication, some amendments have been made to the original work. The introductory chapter has been recast to exclude details which are of no immediate interest to the general reader. A chapter that included an extensive description of the Ugandan legal and judicial systems has been dropped, as has a chapter on women's experiences in court, where the detailed analysis did not throw light on the question of the involvement of women in violent crime.

I still feel obliged to express gratitude to the many people and institutions whom I mentioned in the original publication and to the Danish Development Agency (DANIDA) for the fellowship which enabled me to conduct the research. Special thanks to Professor Holger Bernt Hansen, who ensured that all I needed was in place. I am also grateful to the Uganda Science and Technology Research Council for allowing me to carry out research in Uganda. My thanks also to the Uganda Prisons Headquarters in Kampala, without whose cooperation I would not have had such easy access to various prisons. To the staff at the prisons I visited, for allowing me to disrupt their routine.

My appreciation to the Institute of Criminology and Criminal Law, University of Copenhagen, for availing me with the facilities that opened the doors into the field of criminology. Rie — thank you for your constant concern and for being a friend. Annika, Britta, Annalise, Margaretha — thank you for your precious time which enabled me to have proper focus of the study within months of arriving at the Institute. Vagn, your constructive criticism often helped me see the law in a new perspective.

Profound gratitude to Dr Annika Snare for academic supervision. For your untiring guidance and keen interest in my work, right from the moment I arrived at the Institute. Thank you for your critical eye, for encouragement and for making me feel at home.

Many thanks to Mr Sansa Matende, the LC 1 chairman, and to the elders of Bugono village, who took time off to share with me their knowledge about polygamy. Special thanks to the women and men within polygamous families who allowed me access to the very personal details of their marital relationships.

I am indebted to the 66 women prisoners who trusted and shared with me the secrets of their often very agonising life experiences.

And to God, without Whom nothing could have ever been so right.

Introduction

Why a Book about Women's Violent Crime in Uganda?

The objective

The objective of this study was to examine the interface between Ugandan society, the law and women's violent criminality. I examined the phenomenon of women's violence through an analysis of homicide[1] and assault offences created by the Uganda Penal Code Act,[2] the country's major criminal legislation. The specific purpose of the study was to explore the circumstances under which women get involved in homicides and assaults, and to determine what common patterns (if any) contribute, precipitate and advance a woman towards homicide in particular and violence in general. According to Bohannan (1960a:27), 'homicide is, no matter what else it may be, [e.g., a crime], a social relationship. It is therefore necessary to study situations which may predispose women to commit the crime more than studying the individual offender's personal characteristics.'[3]

Similarly, writing on criminal law in Africa, Seidman (1966:xi) said:

> Every human being is a product of his society. The acts of the accused persons in the cases reported ... must be viewed not merely against an abstract ethical or moral framework, but also against the society of which the actor is part.

The focus of the study was not so much on the perpetrators of the offences but rather on the circumstances within which they acted. My study involved a discussion of the lives of specific women in particular situations and I have, through their own voices, given detailed accounts of these specific situations. I have, in addition, attempted to place the accounts in the context of the wider society. I assumed that the violence was a rational act by the woman after she had reflected on her situation. This assumption is a direct contradiction of 'society's' view of women who do not fit the conventional image of womanhood and femininity. It is also a contradiction of theories which contend that '... when women do commit criminal offences they do so for pathological or irrational reasons.'[4]

It is important to remember the essential rationality of most women who commit crime, for to label them irrational or more specifically mad, as 'society' would want us to do, is:

> ... more complex and dangerous [than labelling them] bad, more damaging in its restrictions, more wide-ranging in its implications. Not 'bad'? Then definitely 'mad'. [Such label] ... is a smear, a dismissal of the women underneath (Bardsley 1987:95,115).

It is important, however, to note that recognising a person's action as rational does not necessarily imply premeditation, and thus rob her of the legal defences of self-defence and provocation. I agree with Sommers and Baskin (1993:138) that 'for behavior to be rational, it does not have to be carefully preconceived or planned, nor does it require hierarchical, sequential decision making.'

Homicide (and violence in general) is assumed to have a particular meaning in relation to the offender and her situation. The act is preceded by conditions, circumstances, events and processes that make her behaviour a probable consequence. This necessarily entails a consideration of her past experiences since these determine how she defines her situation. It is my hope that this study has been able to throw light on the question: What 'provocations' are likely to induce a Ugandan woman — who has a subordinate[5] and largely passive role in society — to act, to kill her husband or any other person?

Feminists may object to the use of adjectives such as passive and submissive in reference to the role of women in society. For example, Meena (1992:10) said:

The African woman who carries heavy loads on her head and a baby on her back, who tills the land with the crudest tools, and grinds the grain, who walks kilometres to fetch firewood and water for domestic use, is far from being docile, humble or dependant. It takes a lot of courage to do what the rural African women are doing for the survival of their families.

In referring to a woman's role as passive, I in no way intend to be derogatory. Neither do I imply that women in Uganda are idle or that they waste time doing nothing and are dependent on men. The term is used to refer to the fact that many women experience suffering at the hands of men, for long periods, without opposition. This has not only been revealed in my study but is evidenced by studies on 'battered' women in other societies. Furthermore, even if one may be convinced that women suffer oppression without opposition, this is not to say that women are naturally passive but rather that they are brought up and expected to be passive. In other words, they are culturally conditioned to be passive.

This study has also clearly revealed that women can act; women sometimes retaliate against specific kinds of oppression. For example, in killing their abusers, women are actively dealing with the abuse they have suffered. This would be an answer to Meena's (1992:26) complaint that:

> ... most of the studies which have been focusing on women have tended to emphasise their being victims of oppressive patriarchal ideologies. Little has been done to unveil the degree and nature of women's resistance against oppressive gender relations.

The problem

There has been no effective reporting system on crimes in Uganda for a considerable time but the general opinion, often sounded in the media, is that female criminality is on the increase in the country. The phenomenon is reported as true more or less on a global scale. The problem, however, is that crime and criminality were for a long time, and almost universally, regarded as male phenomena and, consequently, the nature and extent of female criminality were neglected. Causes of crime among women were hardly analysed and Morris (1987:2) observed that 'theories of criminality have been developed from male subjects and validated on male subjects.' Therefore, the assumption is that the theories are gender neutral and will apply to all criminals, women inclusive. According to Morris:

> Theories of crime should be able to take account of both men's and women's behaviour and to highlight those factors which operate differently on men and women. Whether or not a particular theory helps us to understand women's crime better is of fundamental, not marginal, significance for criminology.

The same criticism has been thrown at theories of violence. As Warren (1979:3) has observed, 'theories of violence have been based on research carried out mainly by men using male subjects. This obscures the sex differences in aggression.'

Wilson and Daly (1992:207) contended that there are large qualitative differences in husband versus wife killings, even in societies like the USA where women kill their men almost as often as the reverse. The reasons for wives killing husbands differ from the reasons for wife killings. Research on men who have killed their wives can therefore not fully elucidate the dynamics of husband killing; it should therefore not be presented as an explanation of intramarital homicide in general. The significance of gender on criminality is very crucial to a full understanding of criminology since:

> Age and sex remain the best predictors for crime and delinquency — better than class, race or employment status. It follows that any adequate theory of crime and delinquency must include an explanation of sex differences in crime rates. Most theorists take the sex differential for granted and do not develop adequate analysis. Thus theorists who locate crime causation in the social environment of the city, the structure of the society or the interaction process between public, police, courts and offenders need to make clear why these factors operate so much more effectively on males than females (Heidensohn 1985:143).

Gender must be given a central place in the understanding of female (and of course male) criminality because 'gender appears to be the single most crucial variable associated with criminality... [since] the crime statistics of *all countries, despite considerable legal and cultural variations, tell the same story: that women have lower crime rate than men'* (Heidensohn 1987:22) (my emphasis). Moreover, the trend is not just a contemporary phenomenon 'because *over long periods of time* and in *many differing judicial systems,* women have a consistently lower rate of officially recorded crimes than men' (Heidensohn 1985:2) (my emphasis).

We should not take Gelsthorpe and Morris (1988:98) lightly when they say that 'gender blindness is not a trivial oversight; it carries social and political significance. Moreover, theories which do not address gender are not merely incomplete; they are misleading'. They correctly maintained that:

> Theories are weak if they do not apply to half the potential criminal population; women after all, experience the same (sic) deprivations, family structures and so on that men do (1988:103).

Naffin and Gale (1989:154) are also in agreement with Gelsthorpe and Morris on the fallacy of gender-blind philosophies:

> Criminologists have often based their theories on total crime figures in which the female contribution, being relatively small is obscured by the sheer volume of male crime. Others have developed their ideas abut crime using specifically male figures and assumed that females could be simply added later to the final result. While criminologists persist in developing general theories of crime using evidence which is insensitive to the effects of the sex of the individual, they will continue to produce bad scholarship... When the behavior patterns of females are taken into account supposedly gender-neutral criminological theories are thrown into doubt.

And they have been doubted since the mid-1970s.

There is, therefore, a case for studying the aetiology of female crime. This is not necessarily a call for the development or formulation of a separate feminist criminology but rather an effort to reconsider and make a re-appraisal of the relevance of established criminological theories to women. We must not fall prey to Lombroso and Ferrero's (1895) fallacy of treating women as a species different from men and, consequently, explaining women's behaviour as fundamentally different from that of men. But gender must play a part in any such explanation, for alongside other factors such as age and class, gender roles do have an effect on one's behaviour, criminal and non-criminal. As Smart (1977b:398) stated: 'The material conditions under which women and men ... exist are not identical and these structural factors need to be accounted for in analyses of ... deviant behavior.'

However, to consider gender necessitates the inclusion of women in samples studied if any resultant theory is to apply to both men and women. Rafter and Natalizia (1981) specifically called for 'women only' studies if the vacuum of crucial information is to be filled, studies which will focus on women without necessarily excluding comparative data on men. As early as 1968, Heidensohn (171) called for 'a crash programme of research which telescopes decades of comparative studies of males'. It also requires validating the existing theories on women subjects. Criminologists should pause and think what it would mean, for their studies, if a theory of crime causation would be exclusively based on female criminal subjects.

The justification

It is the goal of every society to prevent the commission of crime among its citizens.[6] This is irrespective of age group, social class, race or gender, for criminals are a liability to society.[7] But the problem of crime among women should have a central place in all crime-prevention strategies. Ugandan society has made women the primary guardians of the nation's children: it is a woman's societal duty to tender and nurture children. A child of a delinquent mother may, therefore, become a delinquent, not only because the mother is often the first and, consequently, a very important teacher but also because a convicted mother may be imprisoned, leaving her children uncared for and thus delinquents for the sake of survival or for lack of motherly guidance. An infant of a convicted and imprisoned mother may for lack of any alternative guardian have to endure prison life with its mother, and so may a child born to a female prisoner.

Underscoring the mother's role in bringing up a child does not, however, imply that a father plays no role or that his role is of no significance. What should be acknowledged is that society differentiates between women's and men's roles. For, as Mbilinyi (1992:50) said, 'Women and men's lives are experienced differently, because we live in differently structured lives, arising from the intersection between gender, class ... [and other] relations.'

There is also need to point out that a woman's contribution to society should not be exclusively valued in terms of motherhood. Society has a duty to ensure that a woman whether mother or not does not get involved in anti-social behaviour. It follows therefore that the prevention of crime in any society necessitates knowledge of, and consequently investigations into, the causes of criminal behaviour.[8]

In my attempt to understand women's violent criminality, I considered several variables. This arose out of the expectation that crime, to paraphrase Mannheim (1960), is the result of multiple causes; the causes constitute anthropological/individual characteristics such as sex, age, status and social class, as well as social variables such as public opinion, custom, religion, family, economics, legislation, etc. These causes are interlaced in an indissoluble net.

Since the concept of crime is a creation of the law,[9] the study investigated whether Ugandan law and legal institutions in any way contribute to women's violent criminality. A fuller understanding of the criminality of any particular group in society requires a critical analysis of its position vis-à-vis the law in order to determine whether the group in question stands in a significantly different position from those of other social groups. That is why I treated the law itself as a topic for analysis. Are Ugandan laws sensitive to the needs of women, or do they relegate women to an inferior socio-economic status and thus 'force' women to resort to crime as a means of fighting legitimatised inequality and oppression? In this regard, the effects of family and property laws on women's position and status were analysed to find out whether these laws create social situations in which women may be driven to violent behaviour within the family. I also analysed the extent to which Ugandan laws apply different legal categories according to gender. This involved analysis of how women fare in the criminal justice system.

In their introduction to *Gender, Crime and Justice*, Carlen and Worrall (1987:9,11) are in agreement with the contention that in Britain 'some women choose to break the law under ideological conditions that, incorporated into both statute and judicial decisions, reinforce women's dependency upon, and regulation by, men; ... some women's lawbreaking is in part provoked by legislation and forms of economic regulation that discriminate against women by reinforcing their dependency upon men ....'

Although this statement referred to prostitutes and to women guilty of defrauding the social welfare system; crimes easily recognised as simple crimes for economic benefit, the present study explored the extent to which it can be applied to women's violent crimes in the family context in Uganda.

I also analysed the effect of gender on women's criminality. Are violent crimes committed by women specifically due to women's gender-specific roles as wives, sexual objects, child bearers and minders, unpaid family workers, etc.? What does it entail to be a wife, a mother — a woman in Uganda? How do these roles inform women's violence in the family?

In addition to analyses of gender and of the law, I also evaluated the relationship between socio-economic status and women's violence. Is classlessness a myth, or is the frequency and severity of women's domestic violence related to socio-economic class? It was necessary to categorise women in terms of socio-economic status in order to arrive at a viable understanding regarding the phenomenon under study. This is because focusing on gender per se, to paraphrase Morris (1987:15), blinds us to the different experiences resulting from socio-economic class and 'to the significance of the interaction of gender' with class.

I proceeded on the assumption that, as Morris said (Ibid), 'being a woman' is not a clear, single conceptual category; prospects, situations and experiences differ. Mbilinyi (1992:35) also correctly observed that gender relations which oppress women vary according to class, race–ethnicity, and imperial–national relations.

Tanner (1970:82,83) doubted whether socio-economic class is a guiding variable in explaining crime patterns in Uganda since:

> The dominant class in Uganda has not developed over a long period of time — most of its members have had less than a decade to experience and develop a set of social behaviours identifiably different from social groupings in which they originated. Upward mobility has been very quick and rarely demonstrates the value of upholding non-violent virtues. [In Uganda] there is no subculture of violence which is totally different from, and totally in conflict with, the national society of which it is a part.

Although even today the notion of socio-economic class may not exist in Ugandan society in the mode it presents itself in Western societies, the level of education and the nature of employment may affect an individual's 'readiness' to use violence as a means of conflict resolution. Thus Mushanga (1978:484) explained the prevalence of violence by husbands against wives in Uganda in the following words:

> A woman who stages an argument with her husband in front of other people ... stands a good risk of being a victim of violence. This is especially true among the less educated or uneducated and those who are unemployed or who are employed in the traditional sector of the economy, as cultivators, herdsmen, porters, cleaners and the like ....

Mushanga's observation is consistent with a comment made by Stahly (1978:600) that, in Gelles' (1974) study of intrafamily violence in American society, there was an inverse relationship between a husband's level of education and conjugal violence. I therefore used the level of education and the type of occupation as indicators of socio-economic class and considered illiteracy (or low levels of education) and peasantry background as demographic characteristics of the low socio-economic class in Uganda.

Definition and scope

Violent crime
I defined the concept of violence as any act which involves the use of force, or a threat to use force, against the person of another. In addition, any act which is done with the intention to cause fatal consequences for, or injury against, the person of another was also taken as a violent act. I have limited my study to the use of violence with the primary purpose of inflicting physical injury on the victim. Therefore my analysis is, in the words of Mushanga (1976), limited to 'acts of outright violence'.[10]

The present study discusses the offences of murder,[11] manslaughter,[12] infanticide,[13] attempts to murder,[14] conspiracy to murder,[15] and several types of assaults.[16] It has often been argued that whether or not an act is prescribed as a crime is a political question.[17] Similarly, Wilbanks (1982:154) said that whether a particular type of homicide is designated as murder or manslaughter or something else (e.g., abortion, justifiable or excusable homicide) is a political decision too. The present study analysed what is legally defined as murder and manslaughter and was not concerned with the political undercurrents that determine why one type of homicide belongs to one category and not the other, except insofar as such a discussion throws light on the effects of gender on the criminalisation of women's actions.

Homicide and assault
The decision to deal with homicides together with assaults is partly because I agree with Marshall's introduction to Mushanga's *Criminal Homicide in Uganda* (1974:5) that 'if there were sufficient medical services, as well as rapid transportation and communication, many of the victims of violence would survive, resulting in offences of assault rather than murder.'

This background was supported by Mushanga (1974:34) when he reported that:

> ... comparative studies of homicide and aggravated assault carried out in other cultures have revealed that the patterns for the two crimes are similar, and that the difference between the two is of chance and accident rather than of degree and typology.

He continued to say that:

> ... sociologically, homicide and aggravated assault are one and the same phenomenon; the difference being that in the former someone gets killed while in the latter, he recovers. The concept of 'malice aforethought' that differentiates murder from other degrees of homicide could exist in aggravated, even in simple assault; but depending on intervening circumstances, a homicide does not take place. In this respect, the assaulter is no less an offender than a murderer (Ibid: 36).

Manslaughter and murder

Homicides defined as murder are punishable by a mandatory sentence of death, whereas those defined as manslaughter call for a maximum sentence of life imprisonment. Unlike the law, I have made no differentiation in accounting for the interface between society and women's involvement in murder, on the one hand, and manslaughter, on the other. I have frequently referred to both acts merely as homicides. I agree with Tanner (1970:10) that the actions in question involve occurrences which cannot be separated sociologically in the same way they are legally.

Marriage

Ugandan marriage law recognises as valid various kinds of unions governed by different legislation. However, many people live together (cohabit), without undergoing formalities under any marriage legislation, who genuinely believe themselves, and are considered by other members of society, to be husband and wife. Society is likely to base its judgement on the existence and number of children between a couple, the frequency of interaction, the length of the period since the couple's relationship commenced, cohabitation, and the man's financial contribution to the upkeep of the children and/or the woman. Even without legal sanctions, a couple will bear children and consider themselves a family.

For purposes of the study, therefore, I considered as married any two people who regarded themselves as married irrespective of their legal status. Marriage was regarded as a social rather than a purely legal relationship.

Polygamy
I have used the term polygamy to refer to situations in which a man treats two or more women as his wives. It will include instances in which the said man lives with all the wives under the same roof/in the same homestead (patrilocality) as well as instances in which each wife has a separate home and the man rotates from one home to the other.

In Uganda, legal polygamy can only exist if a man marries the various women under either customary or Islamic law. This is because marriages under Islamic or customary law are potentially polygamous. Many men, however, enter into legal monogamous marriages but then go ahead and take (marry) other women under customary law. Alternatively, a man who is already married under customary law may decide to marry another woman under the monogamous marriage statute. In law, the latter marriages are invalid and the man concerned and sometimes the second woman are guilty of criminal bigamy. The concerned parties are, however, usually oblivious to the invalidity of their marriages and thus consider themselves husband and wife. For purposes of the study, a man in any of the above situations was treated as polygamous. This is consistent with the given definition of monogamous marriage.

Patriarchy
Smart (1983:174) stated that 'the concept of patriarchy has become controversial within feminist discourse. Its meaning is frequently unclear and its relationship to capitalism has posed apparently intractable theoretical problems.' Central to the debate is the problem of definition. According to Evans (1983:1) 'for while all

feminists would accept that women are universally subordinate to men, the degree and means of this subordination are matters of debate.'

It has not been an aim of this research to pursue, in any depth, debates on the definition of patriarchy or on the origins of patriarchy in Ugandan societies. It is, however, acknowledged that Ugandan societies attribute a higher status and give more power and privileges to men than it does to women, merely on the basis of sex. Men, consequently, have power as men. For example, as Tanner (1970:82) observed, beating a wife who has failed to conform to her husband's expectations is permitted or at least tolerated in Uganda. Yet beating a husband in similar circumstances is incomprehensible, as interviews I conducted on 'battered' women-turned-killers in prison clearly revealed. The same attitude prevailed among both the men and women within polygamous unions. It is also to be noted that, in all Ugandan societies, descent is through the male line and, consequently, a child, whether born within or outside wedlock, belongs to its father.

The term patriarchy is used here to indicate that in Uganda there is one sex (the male) which dominates another (the female) which is subjected. It denotes the institutional structure of male domination. This book does not, however, discuss whether or not the promotion and maintenance of patriarchal relationships has been conscious and intentional, or merely a reflection of structure. It has, nevertheless, been assumed that patriarchal relationships within the family are on the whole oppressive towards women.

Gender

The concept of gender refers to the social relations between and among women and men (Mbilinyi 1992:49). As Mannathoko (1992:72) contended, gender is a relational concept that denotes the manner in which women and men are differentiated and ordered in a given socio-cultural context. I have used the concept of gender to refer to the fact that, in Uganda, different rights and privileges, duties and obligations, and roles and status are attributed to both men and women by virtue of their sex.

Background literature

Ugandan sources on crime and criminology in general as well as on violent crime in particular are sparse and I did not come across any study which had women's violence as the centre of focus. Criminology as an academic discipline is still in relative infancy. Consequently, it was necessary to begin with a selective review of Western theories concerning female violent criminality.

Women's contribution to violent crime on a more or less global scene is still substantially lower than that of men. In Uganda, the same pattern has been revealed by several studies edited by Bohannan (1960), Tanner (1970) and Mushanga (1974).

Exponents of the role theory of crime (e.g., Wolfgang 1958; Hoffman–Bustamante 1973) have found low female criminality in Western industrialised countries. It is contended that women do not generally commit crime because they are socialised to comply more with societal values and standards than men. These theorists argue that women do not commit violent crime because they are socialised to be gentle and that, 'in all classes of society the socialisation process is such as to place stronger inhibitions against the exercise of physical force and violence on females than on males' (Harlan 1950:740, cited in Totman 1978:6).

The role theorists go further to state that in the relatively few instances where women are violent, the method of involvement and the victims of such women offenders still reflect women's gender role and socialisation. The crimes will take place within the offender's home and the victim will be a relative or a lover — factors which are indicative of domesticity. But before gender was ever considered to have an effect on criminality, theories of crime attributed female homicides to physiological factors peculiar to the female sex, while male homicides were explained in terms of either poor socialisation or economic need.

For example, Lombroso and Ferrero (1895) considered women to be 'congenitally' less inclined to crime than men and contended that the few women who are criminal are abnormal; they are genetically more male than female. They insisted that the true, biologically determined, nature of women is antithetical to crime and if a woman is a 'true criminal type', she is biologically like a man.

Pollak (1961), too, fundamentally stressed biological and physiological factors, albeit in association with social factors, in order to explain female criminality. He asserted that there is some biological, psychic or social imbalance which induces women to commit criminal offences. He contended that the 'generative' phases in a woman's life such as menstruation, pregnancy and menopause, are 'frequently accompanied by psychological disturbances which may upset the need and satisfaction balance of the individual or weaken her internal inhibitions, and thus become causative factors in female crime' (Ibid:157).

As a result of the sexist attitudes towards female offenders in the Western world, mental instability is more often regarded as the cause of female homicide than is the case for male offenders. Sickness rather than criminality is more often attached to a female than to a male killer.

As recently as the 1980s, biological explanations for women's criminal behaviour were still encouraged. These explanations diminish women's ability to make rational decisions. In the 1980s there was a resurfacing of the theory that there is a link between criminal behaviour and menstruation: an increased criminal tendency in some women during certain phases of the menstrual cycle. The advocates of this theory assert that hormonal changes that take place in a woman's body just before and during the first days of menstruation cause some women to commit crime.

Violence is the most frequently mentioned behavioural change associated with premenstrual women. Dalton (1961), who has produced the most direct and most widely cited evidence for a relationship between the menstrual cycle and criminal behaviour, labelled the symptoms of the hormonal changes: the 'premenstrual syndrome' (PMS). The PMS was later interpreted as a sign of mental disturbance or disorder. Consequently, in a number of cases, British courts acquitted women of murder charges, and convicted them instead of the lesser offence of manslaughter on the grounds that the PMS had lessened the women's responsibility for their actions.

Similar to other biological explanations of crime, the PMS implies that female crime is a product of individual rather than social forces and influences. Such explanations seem to suggest that the solution to female criminality lies in treating individual cases rather than overhauling the social order which perpetuates the social imbalances of power that generate crime. They isolate the crime from the social context and help maintain the existing social order.

Although we cannot dismiss biological facts like menstruation, we must nevertheless question how it is interpreted within patriarchy (Kendall 1992:97). A woman's actions should be understood within the social context within which she has acted. Rather than interpreting anger and frustration as symptoms of hormonal changes in women, we should connect them with women's oppression.

It is also imperative to note that the existing criminological theories were developed in, and validated on, Western societies. Yet the people of Africa differ racially, culturally and sociologically from people in the Western societies. Clifford (1974:14) correctly maintained that there is need to undertake criminological research in Africa. He further argued that even though the methods and tools of investigation used in the West may be used in Africa, the content of criminology may be conditioned by the diversity of the socio-economic (and cultural) factors in different societies. Moreover, Tanner (1970:75) was surely right when he wrote:

> The main factors attributed to promoting crime in Europe and the United States are variables which have to be completely assessed and redefined. It may well be found that such variables as broken homes, working and inadequate mothers, low educational and intelligence levels, transiency, overcrowding and poverty cannot be directly related to the Uganda situation.

One of the purposes of this study was, therefore, to find out whether the Ugandan woman is violent for the same reasons and in the same situations as her European and American counter parts and, if not, to find out how and why the conditions differ. As Bohannan

(1960) observed, 'homicide [and violence in general] ... is everywhere, set firmly into the social background where they occur ...' and must, like all other relationships, take place and therefore be studied and understood in terms of culture.

Avison (1974:236) too observed that homicide [and violence in general] is not only a social relationship but is also 'a *human* relationship which takes place within a particular social and cultural context' (emphasis original). Mahfooz (1989:37) also agreed that:

> ... cultural context and cultural environments are too important to be ignored in studying the murderous or any other violent assaultive behavior. Cultural context shapes all human behavior including criminal behavior. ... The social processes involved in the development of criminal behavior are components of the same social structure that produces law-abiding citizens.

It is, therefore, imperative to recognise that violence, like any other social phenomenon, must, if it is to be meaningfully understood, be analysed within its social and cultural setting. That is why studies of female homicide in Western industrialised societies may[18] have only limited significance to an understanding of female homicide in Uganda.

As already mentioned, studies on crime and criminology in Uganda are sparse. Furthermore, the available studies on violent crime did not have female offenders as the focus of analysis. For example, in La Fontaine's study (1960) of homicides among the Bagisu of eastern Uganda, only nine percent of the 99 offenders were female. In Beattie's study (1960) of homicides in Bunyoro, among 34 cases of 'intentional' homicide, only nine percent of the cases involved women as the killers. Fallers and Fallers (1960) carried out a study on homicides among the Basoga and reported that only two percent of homicides were perpetrated by women. Southall (1960) analysed 47 homicides among the Alur and reported only that four percent of the offenders were women.

Even later studies by Tanner (1970) and Mushanga (1974, 1976) did not specifically focus on women. Mushanga (1974), who dealt with a much larger number than the other researchers (569 offenders), still reported an overwhelming involvement by men; only 63 (11 percent) were women.

As already observed, women in Uganda appear to commit far less violent crimes than men, but why do they commit them? The fact that women's violence is still very low in comparison to that of men does not lessen the need to investigate its causes. The gravity of the problem must be judged from the social injury caused by female violence rather than by its frequency. Women are apparently most violent within the most treasured institution of society — the family — and they are sometimes violent towards the most vulnerable members of society — children. These are compelling reasons for analysing the causes of such behaviour. It is also worth noting that apart from Tanner's study (1970), most other studies of Uganda have concentrated on particular ethnic groups. In contrast, the present study has been national in character. Moreover, it is the latest empirical study on violence in Uganda since the last one was published more than a decade ago.

Research methodology

This book is based on extensive and in-depth interviews of women offenders in Uganda, supplemented by court and prison records. In all, 66 women convicted or suspected of various violent crimes drawn from prisons in Uganda — Mbarara, Fort Portal, Jinja, Mbale, Masaka and Luzira — were studied. In addition, information was collected from husbands and wives as well as senior citizens in a select village in eastern Uganda. The conduct of these interviews was inspired by Heidensohn (1985:23) who wrote:

> The search for the authentic voices of women and girls involved in crime is difficult. So often those voices have been ... more concerned to demonstrate their lack of criminality than to illuminate their actions, although these attitudes are, of course, enormously revealing about the status of deviant women in our society and societal reactions to them (Heidensohn 1985:23).

During the course of the interviews, each offender was given the opportunity to give her own perception/definition of the homicide or other violent situation. The interviews shed light on the more personal dynamics of each woman's violent behaviour. In-depth accounts describing the interpersonal dynamics of these women's lives helped to shed light on the antecedents to their violence — those rooted in personality as well as role structures. Since any act is preceded by conditions, situations, events and various processes, I am of the opinion that insight into an offender's history would also shed light on her interpretation of particular circumstances that 'led' to the violence.

This approach was considered pertinent, especially in view of the fact that:

> Criminologists interested in women have rarely approached their subjects for their account of their experience. They appear thus to have assumed women are unable to shed light on the reasons for their own actions. That they possess no critical insight. Pity rather than empathy characterises the new work on women (Naffin 1987:83).

Moreover, I share Box's view that 'an understanding of crime and criminal justice from the offender's standpoint is a prerequisite to the reduction of crime' (1983:29).

I have found it necessary to reproduce large parts of the stories of some women in order to clearly illustrate the interface between a particular variable and the violent situation in which a particular woman was involved. In choosing the stories I was guided by the ability of a respondent to articulately describe her life situation before the homicide event or, to put it more bluntly, the circumstances that eventually led to the homicide event. The women's stories are told in their own words but translated from their vernacular into English. In presenting the women's personal accounts, I have used fictitious names in order to protect their identities. It is also pertinent to note that the stories of the less-articulate women were not different in substance from the stories I have reproduced in this book.

Given that Uganda is composed of a heterogeneous population, it was necessary that as representative a sample as possible should be studied in order for the results and conclusions to be applicable to the general population. I thus visited Mbarara and Fort Portal prisons in western Uganda, Jinja and Mbale prisons in eastern Uganda, and Masaka and Luzira prisons in the central region. All the interviews conducted were with women in prisons located in these southern regions of Uganda. This limitation was as a result of the fact that, at the time I carried out the research, there was insecurity in several parts of northern Uganda. Therefore, I did not venture into those regions.

I am, however, convinced that despite the above-mentioned limitation, the results of my research may to a great extent be applicable to the north. Indeed, some of the women interviewed in Jinja, Mbale and Luzira prisons were from northern Uganda. Furthermore, the High Court records which I perused pertained to cases from all over the country including the northern region. Of 91 court records perused, 36 (40 percent) of the cases involved women from northern Uganda.

Although the perusal of court records could not fully clarify the offenders' perception of violent situations, the information contained therein was, on some occasions, adequate enough to reveal the nature and patterns of women's violent criminality insofar as relationships between the victims and the offenders, the weapons used, the sex of the victims and sometimes even the existence of histories of conflicts between victims and offenders were concerned. The patterns revealed thereby were similar (if not identical) to those from the interviews. Consequently, this study is a fair and balanced reflection of the state of women's violent criminality in Uganda.

All women inmates, whether on remand or already convicted, were potential units of analysis. The total number of women interviewed was 66. It is worth mentioning that among the 66 women interviewed, 47 (71 percent) were in for completed acts of homicide, five were in for attempted murder, four were in for causing grievous bodily harm and three were in for doing acts intended to cause grievous harm.

Earlier interviews with prison authorities, reports in newspapers, court records and public opinion in general, all indicated that women are often violent towards co-wives and stepchildren. I therefore set out to interview husbands and wives in polygamous families in a selected village in Uganda for the purpose of throwing light on the conflicts inherent within polygamous unions. The specific object of the interviews was to reveal the influence of the family structure (polygamy), and women's subservient role within that structure, on women's violent criminality.

I interviewed members of polygamous families in Bugono village, Iganga district, which is one of the districts with the highest number of polygamous marriages in Uganda. (Kaijuka et al 1989). This, and the fact that I am conversant with the local language of the area, made the district an appropriate choice for the research.

A 1993 visit to Luzira prison had revealed to me that most women imprisoned for violence were rural residents and so I carried out the research in a rural area. I specifically selected Bugono village basically because of its rural character and because I was already familiar with that village. Acceptability and cooperation of the people were thus guaranteed.

The village had 45 polygamous men and a total of 104 women within such marriages. At the end of the survey, 38 of the 45 men (84 percent of the potential respondents) had been interviewed. I was able to interview 65 (63 percent) of the 104 potential female respondents. I interviewed at least one wife in all except four homes. In some of the homes I interviewed all the wives.

The nature of polygamy was addressed in a developing social framework and this necessitated an insight into the changes which may have taken place in the practice and the probable consequences arising from such changes. I interviewed senior citizens in the village in order to throw light on the differences between polygamy in traditional societies and polygamy in contemporary Uganda: Did violence exist in traditional polygamous unions? If not, why has the incidence of violence in polygamous families increased? Some of the respondents had experienced polygamy either as children brought up in polygamous families and/or as men and women who had at one time been husbands or wives within such marriages.

I also undertook to compare the stories of the women prisoners whom I interviewed with their court records — the legal perspective of their criminality.

This analysis was also important because although interviewing female prisoners may bring out the women's perspectives about their crimes, it is the law which condemns such women with the label of criminal.

Insofar as the women prisoners were concerned, my aim was to answer the question: Did the courts understand these women's perspectives? Furthermore, court documents, where possible, were also used to corroborate information obtained from the prisoners. Apart from specific court records pertaining to the case studies, I perused other relevant court records relating to women's criminality. At the end of the research I had perused 91 court cases.

Chapter summaries

Chapter I presents the general profile of the women involved in violent crime, their partners in crime, and the victims of these women's violence. Chapter II is an analysis of the circumstances under which the victim is the husband. In this chapter, I present the voices of the women interviewed in prison, giving accounts of their specific situations which led to the violence. Chapter III is a discussion of the socio-economic, cultural and legal barriers faced by a Ugandan woman who wants to put an end to a conflict ridden marital relationship.

Chapter IV is an analysis of child homicides by women. The first part of the chapter discusses the circumstances that may drive a woman into killing her own child. In law, women who kill their own children aged under 12 months are treated as a category separate from other women who kill their own older children. Is this distinction justified? The second part of the chapter discusses a wife's enforced role as caretaker of her husband's children born to other women, and the probability that such children may be exposed to violence at the hands of such a caretaker.

Chapter V is a discussion of the conflicts inherent in the practice of polygamy. Noting that the practice is not new in Ugandan society, I address polygamy in a developing social framework. I analyse the socio-economic and cultural changes which have taken place in Ugandan society to see the extent to which these changes may explain the existing animosity between co-wives in contemporary society.

Chapter VI discusses the reaction of the law to women who commit violent crime. It exposes the reasons for the near-total inapplicability of the defence of self-defence to women's acts of violence, and the courts' failure to incorporate women's social reality in the interpretation of the concept of self-defence. The chapter also discusses the operation of provocation as a partial defence to a charge of murder, and a mitigating factor in sentencing. In addition, the chapter discusses how leading Ugandan courts handle threats of witchcraft as legal provocation.

Chapter VII deals with the effects of imprisonment on women, an experience which often culminates into a 'fear of the outside world'. It discusses the suffering endured by the children of women prisoners, whether brought into prison with their mothers or left outside in the custody of other persons. In the concluding chapter I expose women's violence for what it is — an attempt at self-preservation.

Notes

1. The term 'homicide' refers to the killing of a human being by another. It covers both criminal and non-criminal (justifiable, excusable, etc.) killings.

2. Chapter 106 of the Laws of Uganda.

3. The study has left to the psychologists the question of why other women living in situations similar to the offenders' do not react by committing similar acts as have the offenders: the differentiation of deviants and conformists who occupy similar social positions.

4. See for example Jones (1980:286), who said of American society: 'Traditionally women who killed had been seen as insane, unnatural, or aberrant.' Smart (1976:147) also reported that in England, there

is a pathological model of female criminality, and ' ... women fit more easily into the model provided by the sick analogy.' See also Morris (1987:52), where she discusses how mental illness is either presented as an explanation of women's criminal behaviour, or as an alternative to criminal behaviour for women.

5. Subordinate because in a patriarchal society such as that of Uganda, the gender relations support men's domination of women and the women are expected to defer to male authority.

6. Suffice it to say that the question whether crime can ever be entirely wiped out of society or merely reduced has not been a subject for this study.

7. This is not to deny the philosophy that law breaking is, under certain material and ideological conditions, a rational and coherent response to societal injustices. It is also noted that crime may even be considered desirable under certain circumstances. As Clifford (1974:6) said: 'It may be that crime is useful. ... It may be that crime is an outward expression of other social, economic or psychological problems and that its presence forces the authorities to focus attention on these. It could be that the protest, which is embodied in crime, against present restrictions and values is a subtle but dynamic factor in the whole process of social change and development.'

8. I am aware of the works of scholars like Rosenfeld (1968) who believe that 'knowing the forces that contribute to a social evil tells us nothing about how to eradicate the evil'. See also Smart (1995:33, 34) who said: 'The problem of positivism ... lies in the basic presumption ... that we can establish a causal explanation, which in turn will provide us with objective methods for intervening in the events defined as problematic.'

9. This is so in the sense that it is the law which specifically outlines actions which will not be tolerated, actions which will be officially punished. Crime is dependent on a legal definition.

10. See also Marshall and Quinney (1973:24).

11. Section 183 of the Uganda Penal Code: Any person who, of malice aforethought, causes the death of another person by an unlawful act or omission is guilty of murder.

12. Section 182(1) of the Uganda Penal Code: Any person who, by an unlawful act or commission, causes the death of another person is guilty of the felony termed manslaughter.

13. Section 206 of the Uganda Penal Code: Where a woman by any wilful act or omission causes the death of her child being a child under age of twelve months, but at the time of the act or omission the balance of her mind was disturbed by reason of her not having fully recovered from the effect of giving birth to the child or by reason of the effect of lactation consequent upon the birth of the child, then, notwithstanding that the circumstances were such that but for the provision of this section the offence would have amounted to murder, she shall be guilty of the felony of infanticide, and may for such offence be dealt with and punished as if she had been guilty of the offence of manslaughter of the child.

14. Section 197(a) of the Penal Code: Any person who attempts unlawfully to cause the death of another is guilty of a felony and is liable to imprisonment for life.

15. Section 201 of the Penal Code: Any person who conspires with any other person to kill any person ... is guilty of a felony and is liable to imprisonment for fourteen years.

16. Criminal assaults created by the Penal Code are: common assault (Section 227); assaults causing actual bodily harm (Section 228); acts intended to cause grievous harm (Section 209); wounding and similar acts (Section 215); maliciously administering poison with intent to harm (Section 214); attempting to injure by explosive substances (Section 213); and the offence of causing grievous bodily harm (Section 212).

17. For example, by propounders of the Marxist theory of crime.

18. Cultural differences are likely. but they do not always produce different homicide patterns. In their study of suicide and homicide

in Ceylon, Straus and Straus (1952–53:463) noted the cultural differences between Ceylon and the Western countries and said: 'Because of these cultural differences, it might also be expected that the reasons for homicide would differ from those of the Western world.' However, after analysing the public statistics of homicides in Ceylon they came to the conclusion that: 'Insofar as can be determined from the public statistics, the pattern of ... homicide in Ceylon is essentially similar in this Eastern culture to that found for Western countries. It is significant that, in spite of the wide differences in culture, there should be such a similarity' (Ibid:467).

1

Women's Violence: A General Profile

Who are these women?

Level of education[1]
The court records did not have information regarding the educational level of accused persons. Information regarding the women I interviewed in prison is indicated in Table 1. The highest level of education attained was senior secondary 4 (eleven years of formal education), whereas the least educated of the women never attended formal school at all. Thirty-four of the 66 women (52 percent) never had formal education, 23 dropped out of school at various levels within the primary section and only three went up to the end of the primary section. Thus, 35 percent of the women were of very low education, beyond the 52 percent who had none at all. Among the nine women who went beyond the primary level, none reached the advanced level of secondary education (senior 5 and 6). The majority of women imprisoned for violent crime at the time the study was carried out were therefore illiterate.

Occupation
Forty-four (67 percent) of the respondents were peasant farmers by occupation at the time of arrest; 52 (78 percent) of these women were resident in rural areas at the time of the alleged offences (see Table 1). Among the 66 women interviewed, 43 were married at the time of the offence. The husbands of 28 (65 percent) of these women were peasant cultivators.

The results of my research are similar to Goetting's (1988:186) observation that women arrested for killing fellow women in Detroit, Michigan, were deprived, disadvantaged and with little education. The results also give support to Totman's (1978:29) contention that women killers are likely to be persons with little success in vocational or educational experiences, women who had 'all their eggs in one basket — a marital and/or parental relationship' and to Blum and Gary's (1978:190) assertion that 'most of these women (murderesses) are poor, living in very specific socio-economic situations, exposed to very specific frustrations and specific options.'

However, a high rate of illiterate or poorly educated peasant women in a studied sample may not necessarily prove a link between either illiteracy or peasantry on the one hand, and violent, (or indeed any type) of crime, on the other, in a country like Uganda where only a small minority of the women (and indeed men) are educated and the majority of the population are peasants.[2] The high representation may merely be symptomatic of the trend in the general population. The observations should therefore be interpreted with caution.

Age

The eldest woman among the interviewees was 60 years old and the youngest was aged 15 years. The age group between 20 and 24 years inclusive had the largest number of women imprisoned for violent crime at the time of the interviews (fourteen), followed by the 15 to 19 year-olds and 35 to 39 year-olds, which had ten women each. The 55 to 59 and 60 to 64 age groups had only one woman each. Information regarding age in the court records is similar to the pattern revealed in prison, in that offenders are concentrated in the age group 20 to 34 years (See Table 1)

Partners in crime

Some women's acts of violence were committed jointly with other persons. Among the 91 court records accessed, 30 (33 percent) of the cases involved more than one offender, for a total of 101 women, since some women acted jointly with fellow women. Twenty-two out of the 66 women interviewed (33 percent) acted in concert with other persons in their acts of violence.

A glance at the relationships between the women and their co-offenders lends credence to the contention that homicides by women are family-based; where a woman had a co-offender such other offender was usually a relative. Table 2 indicates the

Table 1: Demographics of prisoners interviewed

Age group	Number of women	Percent
15-19	10	15
20-24	14	21
25-29	09	14
30-34	09	14
35-39	10	15
40-44	03	5
45-49	05	8
50-54	04	6
55-59	01	<2
60-64	01	<2
Total	**66**	**100**
Level of education		
None	34	52
P.1-P.7*	23	35
S.1-S.4**	09	14
Total	**66**	**100**
Occupation		
Peasant cultivator	44	<67
Beer seller	04	6
Housewife***	05	<8
Market vendor	01	<2
Farm labourer	01	<2
Clerk	02	3
Petty trader	01	<2
Shop assistant	03	<5
School girl	03	<5
Unemployed****	02	3
Total	**66**	**100**
H/occupation+		
Peasant cultivator	28	42
Mason	02	3
Head teacher (primary school)	01	<2
Invalid*****	01	<2
Trader	02	3
Security guard	02	3
Businessman	02	3
Driver	04	6
Cattle trader	01	<2
N/A******	23	35
Total	**66**	**100**
Urban	15	23
Semi-urban	04	6
Rural	47	71
Total	**66**	**100**

categories of relationships between women prosecuted with other persons as co-offenders among the court records accessed. There was no information regarding the relationship between eight women and the persons they acted with. In regard to another eight women, the information in the records merely indicated that the women and their co-offenders were not related.

The relationship of mother–daughter was the most frequent between co-offenders (eight women) followed by mother–son (seven women) and then by wife–husband, on the one hand, and sister, on the other (six women each). Five women acted with a friend and five with a brother. In one particular case, which involved four men and three women as accused persons, the judge merely commented that the accused persons were all 'somehow related to one another'. It was only 22 women who acted with non-relatives and, in some of those cases, where the non-relative was not the sole co-offender, the case involved other persons related to the woman.

A similar pattern was revealed among women prisoners who acted in concert with other persons. Table 3 shows the relationships between women prisoners and their co-accused persons, on the

---

Notes to Table 1

* P stands for primary education.
** S stands for Senior Secondary education.
*** These five women were not involved in any income generating activity. They lived in urban areas and were not involved in any cultivation. Asked as to what they did for a living, their response was that they were housewives.
**** The women who are indicated as unemployed were urban residents but were not involved in any income-generating activity. They had no land to cultivate for a living. They were unmarried and could not therefore respond in a way similar to the group mentioned above.
***** The husband in question was an invalid and thus incapable of engaging in any employment.
****** The said 23 women were either unmarried, widowed or estranged from their husbands.
+ H stands for husband.

Table 2: Relationships between co-offenders: court records

Relationship between woman and co-offender	Number in particular category
Son	7
Sister	6
Husband	6
Brother	5
Friend	5
Daughter	4
Mother	4
Employee	4
Lover	3
Neighbour[3]	2
Father, aunt, niece or cousin	1 each
Not related	8
Not indicated	8
Total	**66**

one hand, and the relationship between these women and the victims of the crimes, on the other.

Among the court records accessed, a total of 101 women were involved as accused persons. In 34 of the cases, the records available did not mention the age of the offenders. Information in the court records is, as already noted, similar to the pattern revealed among the prisoners in that offenders are concentrated in the 20 to 34 years age group (see Table 4).

Twenty out of the 22 women who had co-offenders (91 percent) acted with family members which means that only two cases involved women acting solely with non-family members. In one of these two cases the woman acted with villagemates and even the victim of the offence was a villagemate.

Husbands were the most frequent co-actors; seven (32 percent) of the women acted with their husbands.

We also noted the predominance of men as women's co-offenders. Among the 30 court cases in which women acted with others, a total of 48 men were involved as co-offenders. Among the 22 women prisoners who acted with other persons, 18 (82 percent) acted with men and a total of 28 men were involved as the women's co-offenders. Only four women acted with fellow women to commit the alleged crimes. Moreover, this pattern involved only two cases; two of the women (sisters) acted with a friend against the co-wife of one of them, and the other two women (mother and daughter) were also involved in one homicide incident.

Table 3: Relationships between co-offenders: interviewed inmates

Name of prisoner	Number of co-accused	Sex of co-accused	Relationship between prisoner and co-accused	Relationship between prisoner and victim
Natukunda	1	M	cousin	co-wife
Mukandori	1	M	husband	stepdaughter
Nakyanzi	1	M	husband	nephew of husband
Nalinya	2	F, F	sister, friend	co-wife
Kayaga	2	F, F	sister, friend	co-wife of sister
Mukoda	2	M, M	brother, cousin	cousin
Naisikwe	2	M, M	son, son	husband
Nalwoga	2	M, M	nephew, nephew	nephew
Nambi	3	M, M, M	villagemates	villagemate
Nabafu	1	M	husband	clansmate
Namadaya	1	M	husband	brother-in-law
Masika	1	M	husband	villagemate
Nasijje	1	M	son	husband
Nabalayo	2	M, M	son, son	husband
Abwoli	2	F, F	sister, mother	stepbrother
Farida	2	F, F	daughter, daughter	stepson
Kabatangale	2	M, M	villagemate, husband	villagemate
Bonabana	1	M	brother	maternal aunt
Kyaligonza	2	M, M	husband, son of husband	nephew of husband
Birungi	2	M, M	son, son	husband
Mukisa	1	M	husband	co-wife
Bagonza	2	M, M	brother, brother	mother

Table 4: Age categories of accused women: court records

Age group in years	No. of women prosecuted	Percent
15-19	8	8
20-24	10	10
25-29	12	12
30-34	13	13
35-39	8	8
40-44	6	6
45-49	5	5
50-54	4	4
55-59	0	0
60-64	1	1
Age not indicated	34	34
Total	**101**	**100**

Victims

Out of the 96 victims in the perused files, 62 (65 percent) were male, 31 (32 percent) were female, and in three cases (3 percent), the sex of the victim was not indicated. Among the 66 women I interviewed, there were 69 victims; 41 (59 percent) were male, 25 were female, and in three cases, the sex of the victims was not known.[6] The predominance of male victims is in line with other studies which have indicated that in the rare cases where women kill, their victims are usually male; see, for example, Wolfgang (1966), Schneider and Jordan (1978) reporting about American society; Mushanga (1974) on Uganda.

A perusal of the 91 court files indicated that among the 96 victims, 63 (66 percent) were within the accused's family, 25 (26 percent) were outside the accused's family and the relationship between the accused and eight victims (8 percent) was not indicated. Of the 66 women prisoners interviewed, only ten (15 percent) directed their violence against non-family members

Table 5: Relationships between victims and offenders

Relationship	No. of interviewees	No. from court records
Husband	20	26
Co-wife	9	13
Villagemate/nbor.	9	14
Offspring	7	9
Stepchild	6	4
Niece/nephew	3	1
In-law	3	5
Cousin	2	0
Mother	1	0
Stepmother	1	0
Aunt	1	0
Stepbrother	1	0
Grandma	1	0
Lover	1	4
Relative	1	3
Not related	0	9
Employer/employee	0	3
Sister	0	2
Not revealed	0	8
Total	**66**	**101**

(though one did so against a male lover), and nine against neighbours. As in the case of court records perused, therefore, family members were the predominant victims of the women prisoners (see Tables 5 and 6). The strong predominance of family members as victims suggests that familial violence is the key to women's criminality in Uganda.

Table 6: Results of cases in which women had men as co-offenders: court records

Case No.	No. of females	No. of males	Result for female accused	Result for male accused
166/92	1	4	nolle prosequi	escaped arrest
249/92	1	1	no case	no case
171/92	1	1	pending	pending
462/87	1	3	no case	no case
261/69	1	2	2 y imp	2 y imp
66/76	2	3	no case	no case
123/67	1	2	M/S	1: M/S; 1: no case
23/77	1	2	M/S	1: M/S; 1: nolle prosequi
59/77	1	5	insufficient evidence	insufficient evidence
178/77	1	1	pending	pending
102/75	1	2	insufficient evidence	death penalty
116/75	1	1	cautioned	no case
25/76	1	1	insufficient evidence	4 y imp
24/76	1	1	3 y imp	3 y imp
108/91	3	1	no case	death penalty
263/92	2	1	death penalty	death penalty
22/69	1	2	7 m imp	7 m imp, 3 m imp
703/69	1	1	18 m imp	18 m imp
729/69	3	4	1: acquitted; 2: 2 y imp	3: 2 y imp; 1: 4 y imp
567/70	1	1	insufficient evidence	insufficient evidence
331/71	1	1	6 y imp	6 y imp
77/73	1	3	2 y imp	insufficient evidence
496/71	1	2	M/S	M/S
447/71	1	1	insufficient evidence	insufficient evidence

The most predominant group of family members in the studied court files were husbands, who were 26 in number and thus constituted 27 percent of all the victims and 41 percent of family members. Even in the prison cases, husbands were the largest group of victims of women's violence; 20 (29 percent) out of a total of 69 victims.

Another significant group of victims were the 'husband's other woman'/co-wives. Among the court records they constituted 14 percent of all the victims and 21 percent of family members. Among the 66 women I interviewed in prison, nine directed their violence towards their husband's 'other woman'.

In the court records accessed, twelve of the victims were natural children of the offenders, but the homicides involved nine women, since one of the women killed four of her children in one homicide act. Among the 66 women interviewed in various prisons, seven directed their violence against their own offspring.

Among the 66 women interviewed, 16 women were violent against children, and among these, six were violent against stepchildren. court records revealed four cases in which the victims of women's violence were stepchildren of the offenders.

The offender–victim relationships revealed in this study give credence to Totman's (1978:15) observation that when women kill

---

Notes to Table 6

'Nolle prosequi' means the state opts to discontinue its proceedings against the accused but may at a later time take them up again. It is usually entered in cases where the prosecution fails to produce key witnesses.
'No case' means the prosecution failed to prove a prima facie case against the accused.
'Imp' means imprisonment.
'y' stands for years, 'm' for months
'M/S' means the accused was convicted of manslaughter but the court record available did not indicate the punishment given to the offender.
'Insufficient evidence' means that the accused was acquitted on the basis that the evidence available did not prove the prosecution's case against her/him beyond reasonable doubt.

they mostly kill those who are physically and emotionally closest to them. In her study, Totman presented a sociological analysis of murder based on interviews with 50 female offenders who were in prison for killing either their mates or children. The pattern also lends credence to the contention that women usually commit crime in their gender-specific roles, that is, as wives, child-bearers and child-minders.

On the basis of studies of homicides and suicides among seven African societies; one from Nigeria, two from Kenya and four from Uganda, Bohannan (1960:253,255) reported that African women kill co-wives, and that except for the Bagisu, the killing of a husband scarcely occurred in the sample analysed. He also reported the killing of offspring but said that it was usually in a state of emotional stress following the breakup of the family or contravention of important norms. According to him, such murders of children are often followed by suicide attempts.

Contrary to Bohannan's observation, the evidence of the women prisoners I interviewed, as well as of the court files I perused, show that husbands are the most predominant single group of women's victims. The killing of husbands thus seems to have become more common than was the case when Bohannan and others carried out their research. And it is worth noting that in the present sample, only three of the husband-killers are Bagisu and whereas one of these admitted the homicide, the other two completely denied responsibility for their husbands' deaths. Just as Bohannan has noted, co-wives are also still common victims of women's homicides.

Notes

1. Formal education in Uganda is organised under a four-tier system. It begins with the primary section, which takes seven years and is referred to as P.1 to P.7. After the purposes of selecting students who qualify for the next stage referred to as the 'secondary school' stage. For pupils who do not qualify for further education, one cannot realistically talk of chances of job training. The secondary stage consists of two levels; the 'ordinary level' of four years (S.1 to S.4)

and the 'advanced level of two years (S.5 to S.6). At the end of the first four years of education, a national examination is conducted. One's results in the examination determine whether one qualifies for the two years of the advanced secondary level or for a tertiary institution. Most of the tertiary institutions at this level offer diploma courses which normally take not less than four years training. At the end of the advanced secondary level, national examinations are conducted to determine who qualifies for university and other higher-education colleges. It needs to be mentioned that as a result of the last 20 years of political turmoil and social discord which Uganda has gone through, the quality of education has been negatively affected. Consequently those who drop out of school at the lower stages of education easily relapse into illiteracy after a few years out of school.

2. Results of the 1991 Population and Housing Census indicate that 55.1 percent of females aged 10 years and above are illiterate. According to the same sources, the illiteracy level among rural women is 59.4 percent. It was also reported that 11 percent of women in Uganda live in urban areas whereas 89 percent reside in rural areas. (Source: Statistics Department, Ministry of Finance and Economic Planning, April 1994.)

3. The question of who is a neighbour is difficult to determine. According to Mushanga (1974:89), '... neighbourhood in sociology denotes more than spatial proximity. There is an element of *gemeinschaft*-like affective orientation that characterises members as neighbours.' In other words it refers to persons who have common tastes, sentiments and attitudes. In describing relationships between different persons, I have not distinguished between neighbours and villagemates.

II

Husband as Victim

The most predominant group of victims in the studied court files were 26 husbands who constituted 27 percent of all the victims and 41 percent of family members. Even in the prison cases, husbands were the largest group of victims of women's violence; 20 out of 69 (29 percent) victims. This pattern is consistent with Mushanga's (1974:164) observation that 'the most likely victim of a female slayer is her husband.' In his study of the Bagisu of eastern Uganda, La Fontaine (1960:105) had made the same point when he wrote that: 'it seems that the marital relationship is more prone than any other to drive women to murder.' The question is, what provocations induce women to kill or otherwise act violently towards their husbands?

Physical abuse

Several of the women interviewed in prison justified their actions either on grounds of self-defence or at least as a reaction to a provocative act by the victim. This was especially common among women who killed men and more specifically those who killed husbands. Among the 66 women I interviewed, 20 directed their violence against husbands. Fifteen of these 'husband assaulters' reported a life history of extreme physical abuse from their husbands. Their violence was a reaction to physical abuse. The law may not consider their acts as self-defence, but the women believed they acted in self-preservation. It should be mentioned that all five women who reported the absence of physical abuse by husbands denied having committed the alleged homicides.

The information available in several of the court records also indicated that the homicides by women often occurred in circumstances which suggest that the women's acts were either in self-defence or a reaction to provocation. According to these files, although many of the women were prosecuted for murder, only one was convicted of that offence. The majority were convicted of manslaughter, and in light of the definition of manslaughter,[1] this is an indication that the courts, too, sometimes considered the homicides to have been provoked by the victims. A ruling of manslaughter, however, is evidence that the law (read courts) did not consider the women's acts as self-defence since self-defence leads to an acquittal.

The results of this study further support Mushanga's (1974:164) observation that in Uganda most women kill husbands 'when the latter are in the habit of harassing and beating them for unspecified reasons *over a long period of time'* (my emphasis). In his *Crime and Deviance,* Mushanga (1976:65) also commented on the acceptance of the use of violence by a man against his wife in western Uganda:

> Violence is widely used in different situations by different people; both in criminal and in non-criminal behaviours. In a non-criminal situation, violence is very often used as means of obtaining conformity as when parents beat their children or *when a man beats his wife* for minor infractions of marital or sexual obligation (my emphasis).

In his survey of homicides in Uganda, Tanner (1970:37,47) commented that 'in the relationships of husbands and wives, violence is socially permitted and a wife who does not submit to a husband's wishes can expect to be *beaten'* (my emphasis). The findings on Uganda are similar to the pattern reported in regard to American society, e.g., by Schneider and Jordan (1978:8), who found that 40 percent of the women incarcerated in Chicago's Cook County Jail for homicide had killed their husbands or lovers as a result of physical abuse.

In my survey on the existence of violence in polygamous marriages, 21 of the 34 interviewed husbands answered the question: 'What is your opinion of a woman who leaves her marriage as a reaction to a husband's physical abuse?' Among these 21 men, only seven saw physical abuse by a husband as a justification for a woman's leaving her marriage. Out of the fourteen men who were against divorce, one argued that a woman's duty was first and foremost to mother her children, and consequently, a woman should tolerate the abuse for the sake of her children. The rest of the men were of the view not only that a man has a right to chastise his wife but also that it is only a woman who does wrong that will be beaten by a husband. In the words of one of them: 'Physical abuse is for wrong doers' and 'the purpose of the beatings' is 'to correct the wife'. Summed up, the general view was that there must be a reason why a husband beats a wife, so the solution does not lie in divorce. The woman should improve her ways and discard that which provokes the husband in order that the marriage stabilises. A woman who is beaten for doing wrong has no justification for leaving her husband. If she provokes her husband, she should endure the abuse.

In fact, one man compared the need to chastise a wife to the duty of a teacher to correct a pupil. Asked what women usually do to deserve beatings, the general view was that such women are beaten either for promiscuity or insubordination to their husbands. Only one man submitted that there are 'better' ways in which a wife can be made to play her rightful, subordinate role in the family. According to him, 'physical abuse is a way of correcting a wife. But I have better ways of disciplining my wives. Just deprive such a woman of sexual pleasures and she will surely and quickly reform.'

Wife-beating is a norm accepted by the women as well. I was often told by the women that a disobedient wife deserves chastisement by her husband. This is a reflection of the fact that the opinions and ideals of the dominant sector in society (read men) become the ideals of society. Justification of wife-beating or chastisement is a reflection of the gender power relations within Ugandan society. A woman is subordinate to a man and the duty of a wife is first and foremost to please and obey her husband. Society expects a woman to sacrifice self-interest to the needs of others.

However, there is need to emphasise the fact that wife assault transcends cultures. For example, Morris (1987:182) reported that wife assault is institutionalised. He referred to the fact that 'until the nineteenth century, English law gave husbands the right to beat their wives.' Writing of Sierra Leone, Thompson and Erez (1994:29–30) also reported that:

> [I]n the tribal communities in Sierra Leone, ... as a rule, neither physical nor sexual abuse of wives by their husbands is viewed negatively by tribal members. Apart from homicide, the physical handling of wives in tribal communities is viewed as the prerogative of the husband. Under customary law, a husband has the right to administer 'reasonable chastisement' to his wife for her misconduct.

It is nevertheless significant to note that several of the men interviewed submitted that where the abuse becomes habitual and extreme, the woman may divorce and that it is not every wrong that calls for physical chastisement of a wife.

Although society's 'permission' does not extend to homicide, (it falls short of 'extreme abuse'), a husband's violent action may, in fact, produce fatal consequences. This is because 'the outcome of an aggressive interaction ... is not predetermined. It is, at least partially, a function of events that occur between the parties *during* the incident' (Sommers and Baskin 1993:139) (my emphasis). Just as the outcome is not predetermined, neither is the eventual victim. Block (1993:189) thus said:

> In reality, most violence ending in a homicide involves a confrontation in which either person *could become the victim* or the offender. In fact, at the outset of the confrontation, it may be difficult to distinguish between the person who will later become the victim, and the person who will become the offender (my emphasis).

Consequently, in subjecting his wife to violence, the husband risks retaliation by his wife, whereby he, the original assaulter, may end up as the victim of homicide.

Insofar as the women who killed husbands after a long time in a violent relationship were concerned, the homicide event was only the last straw in a load of domestic quarrels. The reason for the killing seemed to me to be not so much a reaction to an immediate threat of death but a step taken to put an end to routine suffering, an act of self-preservation.

Twelve of the 20 women who were in prison for violence against their husbands admitted responsibility for the fatal assaults, but they justified their acts as retaliation against assaults by the husbands. Perhaps these women would endorse what Firdaus said:

> I am a killer, but I've committed no crime. ... I kill only criminals: ... men who subjugate, humiliate, and terrorise women.[2]

Karugaba was 42 years old and was serving an eight year prison sentence for killing her husband. By the time of the interview she had been in prison for almost eight years (six on remand) and had so far served close to two years of her sentence. She had committed the offence at the age of 34 years. Although charged with murder, she had been convicted of manslaughter. Karugaba was educated up to senior secondary two and had married the victim at the age of 21 years. The homicide occurred after 13 years in marriage; a marriage which had originally been a consequence of 'mutual love'. Karugaba was the only wife in the home and the marriage had been consecrated in church. Karugaba related the homicide incident thus:

> My husband came back very late (around 2:00 AM). When I opened the door for him he slapped me and scolded me for having taken long to open the door. But I had gone to sleep very late and that is why I took long to hear him knock. ... I left him eating and went to bed again. On entering the bedroom, where I was lying with my daughter, he ordered me out and said he did not want me to sleep with his daughter. He started insulting me and said I had earlier on in the day given his guests bad eyes, that the food I had prepared had been hopeless. We started fighting and he tore my night dress. I escaped to the kitchen but he came after me and banged my head against the wall. I escaped to the dining room but he followed me. He had meanwhile locked the children's door. This is because whenever we fought I would run to their bedroom

and once the children started to scream he would stop assaulting me. I sometimes used to hold on to my children so that if he were to push me I would fall with my child. This would stop him from assaulting me further. Having locked the door this particular time he said; 'Your children have always saved you, but today I am going to kill you. And then I would buy you.'
Interviewer (Hereafter Lillian): What did he mean by saying he would buy you?
Karugaba: That he could buy his way out of prison. After all, he had so much money. [Karugaba went on to say] I escaped to the kitchen and hid under the sink but he followed me and started slapping me continuously. He hit my head against the wall. At the time we were building a pit latrine outside and we kept instruments like machetes and pickaxes in a corner in the kitchen. ... I ran to the corner where they were kept and I stretched my hand towards the implements. He came at me and said, 'Do you want to kill me?' He kept on hitting me. I got hold of a cutlass and hit at him; as he turned to escape the cutlass cut him at the nape of the neck. He ran and fell in a chair in the living room. He died that very night.

In reaction to the question on the frequency of her husband's assaults, Karugaba said:

> Once he got drunk, he would abuse me and beat me up. On one occasion he had thrown acid on me, towards my vagina, saying that since it was useless to him, it could as well be burnt.

Karugaba had a scar on her thigh which she said was a result of that acid attack. She showed me scars on her back as well as one on the forehead resulting from beatings by the husband. She also had a scar on her shin caused by a knife which her husband once used to attack her. She attributed her husband's violence to the fact that 'he used to drink almost every day of his life.'

Lillian: Had you ever before the homicide retaliated against your husband's assaults?
Karugaba: When the assaults had just began, I never used to hit back, but when it turned into a routine, I started hitting back.
Lillian: Did you ever use a weapon against him?

Karugaba: He used to hit me with anything he could lay his hands on: chairs, sticks, anything. I used to hit him back with whatever I could get from him. If he had a stick and hit me with it, I would fight to break off a piece and would hit him with it.
Lillian: Did you ever go to hospital as a result of your husband's assaults?
Karugaba: Only once. He never allowed me to go out of the house after his assaults on me. But one day he beat me severely and left me in the house. I escaped and went and boarded one of my father's buses which was on its way to Ibanda. He followed me, but on reaching the bus park, he realised that some of my brothers were on the bus so he could not force me to go with him. I proceeded home but later on ended up in hospital because I had a miscarriage.
Lillian: What did you dislike most about your marriage? Was it the physical assaults, was it the verbal abuse, was it your husband's refusal to buy home-necessities or was it his extramarital affairs?
Karugaba: It was the physical assault. When a woman does wrong she should be punished by being denied something but never with physical assault. *Touching one's body is tantamount to touching one's life* (my emphasis).

Agaba's story is in many ways similar to that of Karugaba. During her 33 years in marriage, she was persistently subjected to physical assault by the husband whom she eventually killed. In one particular incident, he threw a spear at Agaba and when he missed her and she managed to escape, his wrath was turned against a neighbour's cows. He speared and slaughtered the neighbour's cattle. On this particular and only occasion, he was sentenced to prison (four months) not for assaulting his wife but for malicious damage to property. This clearly shows that whereas society could tolerate the man's regular assaults on his wife, his destruction of a neighbour's property was unacceptable. Apart from imprisonment, he was also made to pay for the animals when he left prison.

Agaba was at the time of the offence aged 48 years. She was convicted of manslaughter of her husband. Agaba was the only wife and their marriage had been solemnised in a Catholic church; both parties were Catholics. She had at the age of 15 years married a 20-year-old man. They had been introduced to each other by a mutual relative. The two liked each other and got married. They belonged to the same tribe. Both Agaba and her husband never went to school, and at the time of the offence, Agaba used to sell a local brew, *tonto*, in addition to peasant farming.

The couple had three children aged 12, 16, and 20 years respectively. The eldest child is a girl and the other two are boys. At the time of the offence, her daughter was already married; she, too, had married at the very early age of 15 years. Agaba believed that the daughter had married early in order to escape from the violence in her parents' home.

Agaba pleaded guilty in court and also admitted to me that she had killed her husband. On the frequency of her husband's assaults Agaba said, 'as long as he was drunk, I would expect him to beat me and he was a habitual drunkard.' About the fatal day she said:

> He came back very drunk and wanted to beat me. This was nothing new. He had been a drunkard for a long time and we had often fought as a result. He would come back home and for no apparent reason beat me up.

She then continued to say:

> I remember one particular time when he found me lying down breastfeeding my baby, and he just hurled an iron bar at me. I was as a result unable to move for a long time.
> *Lillian:* Did your husband ever threaten to kill you?
> *Agaba:* Almost every time he beat me. The time he slaughtered (speared) the neighbour's cattle he had threatened to kill me. ... Even on the day of the homicide he threatened to kill me.
> *Lillian:* Did he usually use weapons in his assaults on you?
> *Agaba:* Yes, he used to use anything he could get his hands on. On several occasions some of the weapons he hurled at me were handed over to the RC.

Like Karugaba, Agaba showed me several scars which she attributed to her husband's assaults with the iron bar, an assault with a machete, and teeth bites.

> *Lillian:* What would his justifications for the constant assaults be?

> *Agaba:* As long as he was drunk, anything could make him pick a quarrel with me and then he would beat me. When sober he was quarrelsome but would not fight. Either way we never had peace in the home. But even the quarrels were nasty. He would refer to me as a failure as a mother and as a wife.
> *Lillian:* Were you ever treated in hospital for the injuries sustained from his beatings?
> *Agaba:* Only once and that was when he cut my finger with a machete. [Agaba showed me a large scar between her left thumb and the index finger.]
> *Lillian:* How long after the marriage did the beatings start?
> *Agaba:* Within two years of our marriage. When we had just got married we stayed in a home of my relatives for two years, and while there he never was violent towards me. As soon as we moved to our own home, he started being violent towards me. He even told me that the only reason he had not been violent before was because we were living with my relatives, but now the end of my 'pride' had come, he said.

Agaba's story is the story of a woman who endured only so much violence against her person until she retaliated with a fatal blow.

Asaba too was in prison for killing her husband. At the time of the offence, she was 36 years old. Asaba was educated up to primary six. She was basically a housewife though occasionally she brewed and sold *enguli,* a local brew. Asaba told me:

> I killed my husband. *We fought, as was the case every other day.*[3] But I did not intend to kill him. How could I have intended to kill him? After all, this was not the first time that we had fought. He used to beat me every time that he drank and I had with time learnt to retaliate. When he fought he would hit me with anything he could lay his hands on. For this reason I made sure that nothing dangerous was kept in our house (my emphasis).

Asiimwe, aged 40 years, was on remand for the murder of her husband. She related her marital life-history thus:

> We had fought for years and by the time I reported him to the authorities I was fed up. He would go out to drink and then come

back and accuse me of having been with other men and then beat me up....

Lillian: Did he ever use weapons against you or was the fighting with bare hands?

Asiimwe: He would use weapons as well as bare hands. There is a time he used a spear and injured my back. [Asiimwe showed me scars on her back.] He had often said, 'If I do not kill you with poison, I will kill you with something else.' That time, I was lying down breastfeeding when he woke up. I thought he was going out to urinate and then I just felt something hurting me. He had spent three days drinking and quarrelling but since he had been in such a mood for all those days I had no reason to suspect he would do anything more than quarrelling.

Lillian: Did you ever go to hospital as a result of injuries sustained during such fights?

Asiimwe: The time he used a spear on me, I went to hospital.

Lillian: Is there any other particular incident of violence you remember?

Asiimwe: There is a time he beat me excessively when I was eight months pregnant. I as a result had a miscarriage. I escaped to my brother's home and it was my mother who buried the child[4] and nursed me. My husband feared I would die so he sold off some land and escaped to Rwanda. When he heard that I was all right, he came back and then brought two jerrycans of local beer and a goat to my brother. My brother chased him away — it was this time my brother approached the RC and demanded that the land be divided so that I and my sons get our share. My husband begged the RC to let him have 'his wife' back but I resisted; I wanted to live separately from my husband. The RC however said 'we have created a way out for you; you will have your own land, so go back to your husband.' I went back to him.

Byarugaba, aged 41 years, also admitted she killed her husband. Her marriage was a story of constant physical and other abuse by her husband. On one occasion, he even attempted to burn her in the house at night but she escaped through a window. The homicide took place at a time when he had abandoned Byarugaba for another woman. He had spent almost a year without coming to her, but:

> On that day my husband came in the night and called my name. I got up very frightened but decided to open the door. I was frightened and said to myself, 'This person has taken so long without coming to me, what could be the reason for this visit?' We greeted each other and I gave him a chair to sit on but he carried the chair and threw it against the wall. I then said to him, 'Is this the hour you have decided to kill me?' He slapped me and said, 'There is no surviving this time.' He pushed me and I fell down. He started strangling me and I tried to free myself. We rolled over fighting, he trying to strangle me and I trying to free myself. I was able to get near a hoe and I thought to myself, 'Since I am also dying, why don't I save myself?' I hit him with a hoe and cut him on the neck. After that his hold over me loosened and all I could hear was groaning. I immediately realised what I had done; he was dying. I immediately decided to look for poison to kill myself, for it occurred to me that it was better that I be dead rather than being a killer....

Thirty-nine-year-old Byamugisha was on remand for the murder of her husband. Their marital conflicts were so intense that she believes that her husband had once put poison in food which he knew was being prepared for their children. Two of the children had died.

When Byamugisha killed her husband, the couple were no longer staying together. The husband had moved into another woman's house. About the fatal night Byamugisha said:

> On the night of the homicide he came to my shack [house] and entered without announcing his arrival. The house had no door and a mat was what served as a closure. At that time, I was very heavy with my youngest child. I was asleep on the bed and was surrounded by my children. It so happened that on that very night I was experiencing slight labour pains [Byamugisha in fact delivered the child a day after her arrest], but in my sleep I felt somebody touching me. I sensed the presence of someone but when I asked who it was there was no answer. The intruder just went on feeling for me. The person then held me tightly and started pulling me away from the children. He then spoke and I realised that it was my husband. He lighted a match and I attempted to

escape through the mat door. I shouted out to the children that I was about to be killed and then my husband said, 'I am being forced to build a house for you but you will not live to sleep in it; you are soon to follow your children.' The reference was to the children he had poisoned. Since I was very heavy I was too slow and the man managed to stop me from escaping. I told the children that they should make an alarm but the children were trapped in the house since the father was standing at the entrance. It was a very small house and manoeuvring was almost impossible. The kids remained trapped under the bed. The man tried to throw me down so that I could burst with my eight-months' pregnancy and we kept on struggling. I eventually managed to trip him onto the floor and I escaped towards the door. He then got a hoe and aimed it at me but the hoe hit the wall. He managed to grab me back and said he wanted me dead with the child in my womb. He kept on swearing that I would die that very night. I struggled and managed to get the hoe and threw it away from him so that he could not use it against me. In the struggle my husband tripped and fell against the door, among jerrycans and other implements. I managed to escape and ran to the RC chairman's home. I pleaded with the chairman to go and see what was happening in my house because I was afraid that my husband could be killing my children. When I arrived with the chairman, the chairman called out to my husband and told him to come out but he answered only twice and then there was silence. He died that very night. It was because when I pushed him and he fell, he hit his head against the hoe.

Lillian: Was this the first time you had fought?

Byamugisha: He used to beat me so often and many times I would leave him but would have to come back because in my absence my children would suffer a lot. It was because we could not stay together that he had been ordered by the elders of the village to build a house for me. One time he had fractured my chest. There is a time when he beat me when I was pregnant and at delivery time I failed to push the child. Many times I would be treated by herbalists after his assaults on me. Everybody knew about our constant fights.

These women's experiences reflect Chimbos' (1978:67) observation that 'inter-spouse homicide ... is rarely a sudden explosion in a blissful marriage,' but is rather an end point of an ongoing series of bitter quarrels between parties. Chimbos' observations were based on his interviews of 34 men and women in Canada who had killed their legal or common-law spouses. From the interviews, Chimbos analysed the social conditions and marital conflicts that led to the homicide.

Similarly, in his criminal-homicide studies in Uganda and Kenya, Mushanga (1978:481) reported that:

> ... in general, ... violent homicide involving people who are related to each other tends to be the culmination of a series of episodes over a period of time rather than an abrupt eruption of violence, as is common among friends during a drinking session.

With regard to intramarital homicide, Mushanga (1978:482) said that 'it is unlikely that the homicide was the result of single outbursts, it rather is usually an end to prolonged conflicts.' Commenting about homicides, Tanner (1970:50) also noted that 'since motives do not exist in a social vacuum, the role of the killer to the victim should explain the homicide.'

My study revealed patterns similar to what Duncan and Duncan (1978:172) said of family murders in the USA:

> Except in infanticide, murder within the family depends as much on the interpersonal relationship between the perpetrator and victim as on the psychopathology of the murderer. ... After-the-event data often indicate that the victim contributed significantly to his own demise.

The stories given by the above-mentioned women are not rare and unique to Uganda. It is now widely acknowledged, in almost all societies in the world, that domestic violence is widespread among spouses of all social and economic backgrounds and very often it takes the form of wife battery. Women, in almost all the world societies, are regularly beaten, tortured and, in some cases, even killed by their spouses or cohabitants. This then implies that wife battery is not reducible to the Ugandan or, indeed, any single culture but is rather an issue of male–female domination.

Sometimes, however, battered women kill their assaulters. For example, in her historical analysis of homicidal American women, Jones (1980:xvii) said:

> Today in the United States the typical pattern of women's homicide is this: a woman's husband or boyfriend beats her up and sexually assaults her, again and again. She tries *again and again* to get away. He won't let her go, and he won't let up. *At last she defends herself, and either by accident or design, she kills him* (my emphasis).

While acknowledging the fact that British women kill far less frequently than their American counterparts, Jones observed that 'when a British woman kills, it's likely that she too is defending herself against physical or sexual assault at home. She too is likely to kill a husband, a boyfriend, or a father.' Stories told by many of the women I interviewed confirm Ewing's (1987:23) observation that 'there is ... good reason to believe that many females who kill are, in fact, battered women who kill their battering mates.'

Moreover, true to Totman's (1978:46) contention:

> Every woman in the mate-murder study denied entertaining consciously the notion of murder except in the last few moments prior to the victim's demise. ... I just wanted to frighten him. ... I didn't even realize I had pulled the trigger....

Thus, after Karugaba had narrated the incident in which she killed her husband, without any prompting, she said: 'I never intended to kill him, I never planned to. After all, this was not the first time we had fought. It had become routine and I was used to it.' Similarly, Agaba said:

> I only hit him out of anger. ... It was when I saw him lying down and helpless that I realised what I had done; ... I said to myself, 'What is this that I have done?'

Asaba, too, said she had not intended to kill her husband. They fought as was the routine when he was under the influence of alcohol, and went to sleep. She woke up in the night and felt her husband's body cold against her own. She put on the light and then realised that her husband was dead. After narrating her story, without prompting, she said: 'I had stood his violence for years and even thought it cruel to leave him since he was a sick man; ... out of my kind heart, I have ended up in trouble.'

Nafuna, aged 50 years, was on remand for the murder of her husband. She admitted killing her husband but said she did so to save her life. Moreover, her action was not intended to kill him. Her aim was to free herself from her husband's grip on her throat. On the night before the homicide, she had run away from her home because he wanted to beat her. She took refuge in a friend's house in the neighbourhood, but:

> The following day, while my friend was out and I was still sleeping, my husband knocked on the door. I first told him to leave me in peace and that I did not want to talk to him but he went on knocking. I realised that he would not go away so I opened for him. He entered the house and I immediately noticed that he was very drunk, he even had a bottle full of alcohol in his hand. On entering he started abusing me, ... insulting me. He then came after me and in the process the bottle he had in his hands fell down and broke. The room was tiny and as I tried to keep him at bay, we both fell down and then he reached out and held me by the throat. I felt that he was suffocating me but I saw a piece of wood broken off a chair and I picked it up and hit him on the neck. I hit him just so that he could let go of me. ... His grip on my neck immediately relaxed and I got up. It is then, there and then that I realised what I had done, ... that he was dead....

As already mentioned, Byarugaba admitted killing her husband but said it was not a premeditated homicide. It was an impulsive reaction to her husband's attempt to strangle her. Byamugisha too said that it was only after she arrived home with the village authorities that she realised, that when she pushed her husband away in order to escape his violence, he had hit his head against the very hoe he had wanted to use against her.

It is also worth noting that interviews with the offenders consistently revealed that, quite often, the men they killed had a history of violence towards persons other than their wives, including non-family members such as drinking mates. Similarly, in her analysis of 18,482 homicides which occurred in Chicago from 1965 to 1989, Block (1993:187) reported that 20 percent of the victims of spousal homicide had prior arrest records for violence. Speaking of family violence, Roberts (1993:112) reported that studies conducted in both the United States and Great Britain show that, in most families in which the father batters the mother, the children are also battered.

As already mentioned, Byamugisha claimed that she killed her husband after years of abuse. He was also allegedly responsible for the death of two of her children, several years before his own death. Byamugisha said that her husband had put poison in the children's food. He used to beat the children. Asked whether his parents knew about his extreme violence she answered: 'He once tried to kill his own mother.'

Kansiime, who also killed her husband, was 59 years old. Her husband too used not only to beat her but also to beat the couple's children and his other wives, as well as fight with other people at drinking places. According to Agaba, her husband 'was as violent to the children as he was to me. Many times the children would spend nights at the neighbours in order to avoid his violence towards them.' About his relationship with other people, she said:

> He used to be violent towards his relatives; that is why they stopped coming to our home. He was not violent towards my relatives because when he tried to assault them they would beat him. He was quarrelsome even in the drinking joints but since people knew how fast he was with weapons; ... he easily resorted to weapons: whenever he started quarrelling, many of his drinking mates would leave the place.

Similarly, Asiimwe said that her husband used to beat anybody as long as he was drunk. Quite often Asiimwe and the couple's children had to spend nights in the bush because of his violence.

Asaba's husband, who was violent whenever drunk, used to fight with anybody, and by the time of his death, he had been chased from almost all drinking clubs.

The role of alcohol in marital violence

Several studies have established that alcohol is often present in either the victim, the offender, or both parties in a homicide incident.[5] However, in studies based on Uganda, the cases in which alcohol has been present in homicide situations has been low. Tanner (1970) and Mushanga (1974 and 1976:74) attributed the apparently insignificant role of alcohol in the Ugandan homicide situations to inadequate or non-existent medical facilities for proper serological analysis of the offenders' and victims' blood to determine alcoholic content.

In my study of court cases there was hardly any information to indicate whether or not alcohol was present in the homicide situations. From the prison interviews, however, I was able to get information regarding the possible role of alcohol in the violent incidents. In 19 such cases (29 percent), there was evidence pointing to the presence of alcohol. In six of these cases, both the victims and offenders had taken some alcohol.

The stories of many of the women I interviewed revealed that where husbands were the victims, the history of wife abuse which preceded the homicide was often attributed to alcohol. Some of these women, in fact, blamed alcohol rather than their husbands. Many times the homicide or other violent incidents occurred in circumstances where the husband was under the influence of alcohol. In very rare cases, the women, too, were under the influence of alcohol.

After Karugaba had narrated her history of abuse, I asked her: 'Did he behave any differently when he was not drunk?'

Karugaba said that 'when sober he used to be all right. In fact, it is even possible that some people did not believe me whenever I told them of his intense abuse towards me.' During the homicide incident, Karugaba's husband was under the influence of alcohol but she was sober.

Although Agaba told me that her husband was nasty to her even when he was sober, she attributed the physical abuse to alcohol. Unfortunately, Agaba's husband used to drink from the very beginning of their marriage. And yet, like Karugaba, Agaba was a teetotaller.

Asaba's story was not very different:

> *Lillian:* Were you at the time of the homicide experiencing any marital problems?
> *Asaba:* My husband used to drink a lot and this was a constant source of quarrels and fights. Whenever he drunk he used to fight. He would fight with me, fight with his brothers, with drinking mates, with anybody, he used to beat up his own sisters. By the time of his death he had been chased from almost all drinking clubs as a result of his quarrels and fights.
> *Lillian:* Was he any different when sober?
> *Asaba:* He never fought when sober; as a sober man he was very agreeable. Several times he was laid off from work due to his drinking problems. ... He was drunk on the fateful day. He wanted money for more drink and I refused to give it to him. This was a frequent source of quarrels and fights.

At the time of the homicide incident, both Asaba and her husband had taken some alcohol.

Asiimwe's marital history was also tainted with abuse of alcohol by her husband. Even on the night of the homicide, he had taken excessive amounts of alcohol.

> *Lillian:* Were the fights frequent?
> *Asiimwe:* Every time he drunk, we would fight. ... He had often promised to leave alcohol and that he would never beat me again but would soon resort to alcohol *and then* become violent (my emphasis).
> *Lillian:* Was he any different when sober?
> *Asiimwe:* When sober he was not a problem, but once drunk he would become a madman. When sober he would be a good parent; we would live like people, like human beings. He would beat anybody as long as he was drunk. The day he assaulted me with a spear, he had spent three days drinking and quarrelling.

> *Lillian:* What would be the source of the constant quarrels?
> *Asiimwe:* Main problem was drinking....

Kansiime too attributed years of physical abuse and suffering at the hands of her husband for years to alcohol. She said:

> At the time of marriage, he used to drink just like any other youth but it was after the 5th child that he began dangerous drinking. It was also then that he started to beat me. [I noticed numerous small scars on her chest and she said they were the result of her husband's assaults on her.]

Later on Kansiime continued:

> He was perpetually drunk, and whenever drunk he would come and fight me. When sober he would never be violent but when drunk he would be like a madman. Unfortunately he was almost always drunk. Sometimes he would come back drunk and as soon as I opened the door for him, he would beat me up without saying much. At times he would fight the whole night.

On the night she inflicted the fatal wound on her husband, he was very drunk.

Nafuna said of the homicide incident in which she killed her husband:

> He entered the house and I immediately noticed that he was very drunk. I then knew there would be no peace. ... He was always picking quarrels with me over the slightest excuse. He used to beat me over small things....
> *Lillian:* Was his violence always when he was drunk?
> *Nafuna:* He was quarrelsome even when sober. He never spent even two days without beating me. But anyway, he used to drink every day. He was violent towards me even when sober, but it was worse when he was drunk.

Rwanyarare, on the other hand, blamed her husband's 'other women' rather than alcohol, despite the fact that her husband was a habitual drunk. Rwanyarare was serving a 24-month prison sentence for assaulting her husband. She said that whenever her husband came from one of his concubines, he would pick a quarrel with Rwanyarare and beat her. In her opinion:

> ... the problem was not with alcohol as such, but with his women. If he was drunk but did not visit another woman, he would not be nasty to me. But as long as he got involved with other women he would fight me. Women were more of a problem than alcohol. ... But I hated his daily drinking sprees all the same.

Similarly, Byamugisha was of the view that her husband's violence had nothing to do with alcohol. Although her husband was a habitual drunk, she said that even when sober he would assault her. On the day she killed him, he had not taken any alcohol.

Alcohol was, however, not exclusively limited to cases of spousal violence. In the crime committed by Nalwanga against her co-wife, both the victim and the offender were under the influence of alcohol.

> *Lillian:* But what actually led to the fight?
> *Nalwanga:* We just quarrelled and then fought. Both of us had taken some alcohol; in such circumstances it does not take much to make one fight.

Similarly, Biteete and Bwire both killed men who were attempting to sexually assault them. Although neither women had taken any alcohol at the relevant times of homicides, the two victims were under the influence of alcohol.

Other forms of abuse

In her broad historical presentation based on crime records in the United States, Jones (1980:254) said that:

> Husband-murder reflects a profound social malaise and murder is but 'the last act in a long, sordid history of *family obligations* betrayed and common decencies violated' (my emphasis).

Wilson and Daly (1992:206,207) also correctly contended that understanding the nature of marriage is a prerequisite for understanding spousal homicides. According to them:

> Marriage is thus a particular kind of intimate relationship, ... to which people bring particular conceptions of their entitlement and obligations. These conceptions must be identified if researchers wish to know what will be perceived as betrayals of the relationship and what will elicit violence.

It is, however, important to note that 'expectations within relationships are socially and culturally constructed and modified by an individual's previous experience' (Rodriguez and Henderson 1995:46).

What does a Ugandan woman expect from a husband? The expectations of a Ugandan woman are that her husband would give her financial support if he is formally employed, and if not, give her a hand in cultivation. It is also the duty of a husband to clothe his wife and, as a symbol of this duty, it is the cultural requirement among many societies in Uganda that when a groom comes to pick his bride on the day of marriage, he must come along with a *busuti* (the traditional attire for women), which the bride puts on before leaving her father's home. Where the couple go through a Westernised marriage ceremony, it is still the duty of the man to buy a wedding gown for his bride. It is also the duty of a husband to provide his wife with farming land, since women do not as a rule own land. A man who financially depends on his wife is given no respect in traditional Ugandan society.

The stories of several women I interviewed indeed reflect the violation and betrayal of marital and family obligations. Rwanyarare said of her relationship with her husband:

> After some years (maybe ten) in marriage my husband started moving around with several *malayas*.[6] He developed a habit of taking my money and other property and giving them to his mistresses. I would cultivate crops, sell them and buy property; my husband would spend money drinking and then take my property to his mistresses. This was a source of constant quarrels and conflicts.

Later on Rwanyarare continued to tell me:

> On one occasion, he took two of my *busutis* and gave them to his mistress — *busutis* which I had bought myself. We fought, [so] I quit the home and went back to my parents. When my people intervened, the man was forced to bring my attire back and I agreed to come back to my marriage.

Of the incident which led to her imprisonment, Rwanyarare said:

> On that day, after 19 years in marriage my husband took my 3,000 shillings, and in addition sold two of my goats. He gave all the money to his mistresses. When he came back and I asked him for money to pay for one of my children's school dues, he refused and just went off to drink. On coming back from his drinking spree, he started beating me. I also got a stick and hit him on the head, as a result of which he sustained an injury. He raised an alarm and the people who answered the alarm found me still armed with a stick and my husband ... bleeding.

Asiimwe, whose husband, as already narrated, used to beat her, also suffered non-physical abuse. She said that whenever she bought anything for herself (clothes for example), the husband would accuse her of getting them from other men and would burn the clothes.

> *Lillian:* Was your husband an otherwise responsible man? Did he contribute to the family's economic needs?
> *Asiimwe:* Never, and whenever my crops were ready he would 'steal' the produce, even food crops, and sell it and buy alcohol

Byarugaba, too, suffered more than physical abuse. In her words:

> ... he went off and started staying with another woman, a woman who had her own house. Earlier on in the marriage he used to contribute to family property; he would buy goats, cows, etc. but that had long stopped. I had nevertheless continued cultivating the land and increasing the family property, the flock. When he married that other woman he came for all the animals, including

those I had worked for on my own. He sold all the land except the portion where the house was located. He built a house for that woman. He also ordered my four eldest children to leave his home and that if they insisted on staying with me he would burn the house. He often came to harass me. Many people advised him against sending his own children away but he never took heed; he was like a madman. But he continued to come to my place and one time he even came and stayed for a week with me. I became pregnant with the current baby, the one I am with in prison. When he realised that I was pregnant he was really mad with me. He swore never to sleep with me again and said that would indeed be my last pregnancy. 'I will never sleep with you again; that is your last pregnancy,' he said. He shifted all his clothes, everything of his to the other woman's place and went away. All through the pregnancy he never came back to me, ... not until the fatal night.

Byamugisha's story is not very different. Her husband not only regularly subjected her to physical abuse but she said that:

At one time he burnt my clothes and he was arrested and kept at the police for two weeks. He paid the police 20,000 shillings and was released. Earlier on he had sold off all the land we had and just left the portion on which the house stood; he took the money to one of his mistresses. When my father heard about the sale of the land he gave me a cow so that I could purchase land for his grandchildren. After I had bought the land, my husband attempted to sell it. Yet the land was still on credit; the cow fetched 12,000 shillings less than the purchase price. ... When the elders made it clear to my husband that the land was not his, he went and started living with the other woman. But he kept an ear towards what was happening with me. When the coffee on the land was ready for harvesting, I started harvesting it; I would dry it and pack it in bags. I used to keep it on my veranda but every morning I would find it gone. After a short time some elders found my husband carrying coffee bags and they told him to bring it back. They blamed him for selling off his children's coffee, the proceeds of which were supposed to enable them acquire land, acquire a home.

Kansiime, aged 59 years, was on remand for killing her husband during a fight that he started. And yet: 'By the time of his death he had walked out on me and everybody knew that he was no longer staying with me. But even then he would come and harass me, he would come just to beat me.'

In Uganda, the oppressive patriarchal order gives the male absolute superiority over the female in the ownership of family property. Although the husbands of these women had abandoned their duty to acquire property for the family, educate their children and dress their wives, they still exercised their rights over the property that the wives acquired and subjected them to psychological and physical abuse if they questioned that right.

What La Fontaine (1960:106) observed about the Bagisu more than three decades ago is still true of most societies in Uganda:

> In marriage a man gains full rights over his wife's labor, and any economic gains she makes. ... A woman may have considerable de facto control over the domestic economy, but she has no jural right to it. ... There is, moreover, a potent source of conflict in the fact that husband and wife both utilise the same resources, but with different ends in view. She is primarily concerned with getting the best she can for her children; his aim is to use his economic resources to improve his own status in society. His advancement necessitates the use of property which she considers reserved for her and her children. Where this property is used by the husband to acquire another wife, the situation is fraught with interpersonal tensions....

In his Canadian study, Chimbos (1978) discovered that some victims of interspousal homicides were killed because they presented a social threat to the slayer, and that the likelihood of violent reaction was stronger if the threat related to the slayer's role expectations and gender identity. For example, if a husband says or does anything which throws into doubt his wife's capability, such wife may react violently towards such husband. As Totman (1978:16,18) has said:

> To fail at marriage (or male relationships) and/or motherhood. ... to have fewer other possibilities for success or acceptance ... may contribute to an overwhelming personal situation. ... She reacts

> in terms of values.... When a woman obliterates her mate or child, it may perhaps be assumed that ... she thinks she is not succeeding in her primary purpose and activity in life [wifehood and motherhood]. In combination with other predisposing factors in her particular life experience, like ... lack of other supportive relationships, ... etc., the resolution of her sense of failure becomes an act of murder.

Totman (Ibid:93) also observed that: 'When being a wife and/or mother is a total activity and commitment, and the person fails at it, and other outlets are either not available or conceived of, family trouble seems inevitable.'

An ideal wife in Uganda is a woman who, among other duties, cooks and cleans for her children and husband. To say that a wife neither knows how to cook nor how to keep a home clean is to say that she has failed in that role. And yet a woman's social status depends so much on her marital respectability that any threat to that status may lead her into violent behaviour. Perhaps this may, among other things, explain some women's violence: women like Agaba and Karugaba, whose husbands constantly accused them of being poor cooks, poor wives and poor mothers.

Karugaba said that for a long time her husband had abandoned his duty to buy food for the home. Karugaba's needs were met by her own father and her father-in-law. And yet the husband had told her to stay home and not to look for paid employment. In addition, Karugaba recalled:

> He would abuse me as a bad cook and throw the food in my face. He used to say that I was filthy dirty and that my bedroom stunk. He had even prevented me from sleeping on his bed. Together with my youngest child, I was permanently sleeping on a mattress on the floor of our bedroom, while my husband was using the bed. Before this he used to bring women in the house and I would have to leave my marital bed for him and his concubines. By the time of his death we had spent more than a whole year without sexual intercourse.

Karugaba mentioned sexual deprivation as one of the several abuses she suffered at the hands of her husband. As I listened to her story, however, I did not give sexual deprivation any more thought than I did to the other deprivations. From the way she mentioned it, it appeared that her intention was to emphasise to me the intensity of their marital disharmony. This was not, however, the interpretation attached to this revelation by several members of the criminal justice system. For example, when I visited the court where her case had been heard, to peruse the court proceedings, I talked to one lady magistrate about the Karugaba case and her immediate reaction was:

> Oh, that woman! She caused so much embarrassment in court here; she really is a scandal. Imagine she told a whole packed court that she had killed her husband because he had sexually aroused her and then refused to have sex with her.

Furthermore, on one of my visits to the prison headquarters in Kampala, I was introduced to the officer in charge of one of the prisons that I intended to visit. When he learnt that I was seeking permission to conduct research on women who had committed violent crime, he reacted thus:

> Oh, you will certainly meet them; women are capable of the unimaginable; ... there is this woman who killed her husband just because he refused to have sexual intercourse with her....

He was referring to Karugaba.

Karugaba's case was reported in the *New Vision* newspaper, and although the reporter mentioned the several abuses the accused had suffered at the hands of her husband as she had testified in court, her mention of sexual deprivation was emphasised. Karugaba reportedly told the court that her husband had been a habitual drunkard and a womaniser who subjected her to a lot of humiliation. On the fateful night, he had sexually aroused her and then refused to make love to her, saying she had a foul smell. When he started beating her, she 'picked something from a dark corner and hit him' in self-defence. Karugaba may have suffered sexual deprivation but she attributed her assault against her husband to his beating her. Yet the newspaper's article about her story was entitled: 'I was Sexually Starved.'

In most African societies, it is a taboo to openly discuss sexual matters, and whereas a man may be forgiven for doing so, it is abominable for a woman not only to break that rule but also to dare demand sexual satisfaction. Insofar as sexual relations are concerned, the woman's duty is to satisfy her man's sexual needs and she has no right to expect satisfaction, let alone to voice her dissatisfaction or needs in public. This is the very opposite of instances in which a woman has no interest in having sexual intercourse with her husband.

For example, in their research on 'Gender Bias in the Zambian Court System', Sampa et al (1994:15) reported a matrimonial case, heard by a local court, in which a woman refused to have sex with her husband for two weeks in protest against his ill-treatment. She was consequently warned by the court justice that a woman has no customary right to deny her husband sex. She was lectured that the husband is the head of the matrimonial bed. Just as the Zambian court failed to sympathise with the said woman, it is highly unlikely that a woman like Karugaba could get the sympathy of the judge who presided over her case. Karugaba's utterances clearly did not fit the conventional image of womanhood or femininity. She thereby paid heavily for her image. Having stayed on remand for six years, Karugaba was given an eight-year prison term.

The women's stories are evidence that women are abused in ways other than physical abuse. They are subjected to humiliation, ridicule and other kinds of emotional violence. This psychological abuse also assaults a woman's self-esteem and may, together with other circumstances, lead a woman into violence.

Resistance against double oppression

It has been said by several sources that many women in Uganda today are no longer financially dependent on 'their' men. On the contrary, many women have become the major breadwinners in their families. The stories of some of the women confirm this observation. Despite this 'fact', however, women's status in the family remains subservient to that of the men. The women's great contribution to the family welfare has not brought them marital equality, let alone supremacy, in the home. Consequently, a wife who is the major financial support for the family can still be subjected to multiple forms of oppression by her husband: he can exercise his traditional right to acquire another wife without the consent of the breadwinning wife; he can bring a child he has sired outside marriage to live in 'his' home without his wife's consent; he can subject the wife to physical violence. The wife's domestic position is thus one of responsibility without authority or privilege. Her heavy responsibility, on the one hand, and her subservient status on the other, amount to double oppression.

This situation is not peculiar to Ugandan women. Among the Yoruba of Nigeria, for example:

> ... women may control a good part of food supplies, accumulate cash, and trade in distant and important markets (Lloyd 1965); yet when approaching their husbands, wives must feign ignorance and obedience: *kneeling to serve men as they sit* (Gelsthorpe 1989:138; emphasis original).

Similarly, Carlen (1983:27) described the social position of the Scottish working-class women as follows:

> ... the social position of Scottish working-class women has turned upon a contradiction; ... on the one hand, they have been given heavy responsibilities as breadwinners and homemakers; ... on the other, they have suffered ... familial repression at the hands of ... husbands.

Could this be a cause for some women's violent reactions towards either the husband or the husband's 'other woman'? As Jones (1980:xxix) pointed out, 'we can learn a good deal about woman's changing position in social life by considering whom she killed, when, and why, and how her community regarded her crime.'

It may be that wives in traditional society were 'willing' to accept subordination because they were at the receiving end: the men provided for the material well-being of the family, and thus merited supremacy. In contemporary society, the wife may shoulder heavier responsibility, but sooner or later realises that her heavier responsibility has given her no extra standing in her husband's eyes This recognition may partially explain the woman's violent reaction, since as Gelsthorpe (1989:149) stated, '... women see the defining features of oppression differently at different historical times.'

On Uganda, Tanner (1970:83) reported a possible connection between changes in women's roles and inter-sex homicide in the following words:

> There is some evidence that a developing change in women's roles may lead to homicide, ... [in areas outside Buganda] where such changes in role have not worked and changes in the role of women are anticipated on the side of women and resented by men, there is more inter-sex homicide.

Straus (1978) reported that in families where a woman is 'the head of the house', the level of violence is significantly high. Similarly, Stahly (1978) contended that the ensuing violence is due to the fact that the husband, lacking other resources, is more likely to use violence in an attempt to regain his superior status position. According to Roberts (1993:114), 'a man's inability to fulfill the patriarchal ideal of manhood by providing for his family or exercising authority ... may lead him to attempt to restore his power through physical abuse.'

Besides, as Straus (1977-8) has shown, the wife-to-husband violence is the wife's reaction to the husband's violent attempts to reassert his authority. It is a woman's struggle against male domination within the family. The presence of many women de facto heads of households among the husband killers I interviewed supported Straus's assertion. Violence between husband and wife may, therefore, be a form of power struggle.

Agaba's story is that of a woman whose husband much exercised his traditional patriarchal right to supremacy in the home without contributing to the family's economic needs. She said that when they had just got married, they used to till the land together but after a few years the husband had left all the work to her. All he used to do was drink. To make matters worse, he used to help himself to the money which she earned by selling *tonto*.

> *Lillian:* Did you ever fight over the money you used to get from the sale of *tonto*?
> *Agaba:* There was no need. He just used to steal my money, go and drink and then come and tell me that he had stolen it for his drinking. What could I do, he was my husband.
> *Lillian:* Apart from physical assaults, did your husband ever say or do anything to you that was really humiliating?
> *Agaba:* Inevitably. Oh, he was so violent! At times he would find me preparing food and he would just remove it from the fire and pour it away.
> *Lillian:* Did your husband have extramarital affairs?
> *Agaba:* Too many. Sometimes he would even bring his girlfriends to the home for a night.
> *Lillian:* Did he ever marry another wife?
> *Agaba:* Several times he actually brought women for purposes of marriage. One particular time the woman stayed for eight months but due to her bad habits the neighbours chased her away. She used to beat my children, used to destroy my property, and there was no peace in the home. She at one time ganged up with my husband and beat me up. ... On another occasion he had brought a woman in the home with the intention that she become a wife but the woman had insisted she would only stay if bride price was paid to her parents. My husband and I used to keep cattle in the same kraal but each of us knew what belonged to either. My husband had in my absence decided to use my cows to pay bride price for the woman. But my children had resisted the move. When I came back I removed my cattle from the kraal and took them to my uncle's place. My husband did not pay the bride price and the woman left.
> *Lillian:* Why did he not go ahead and use his own cattle to pay bride price after failing to use yours?
> *Agaba:* He always wanted to do things to hurt me. Always looked for something to hurt me, that was him. He did not want to use his own cattle.

In an attempt to resist her husband's abuse, Agaba committed a homicide.

As already mentioned, Rwanyarare's husband had long abandoned looking after his family but he nevertheless had no respect for Rwanyarare, who had taken up that duty. He would thus take Rwanyarare's hard-earned income and buy presents for his other women as well as use the money for his drinking sprees. He would also physically chastise her for questioning his authority.

Asiimwe, Byamugisha and Byarugaba were in similar situations. Byarugaba's husband exercised a further right, the right to decide who would live in 'his' home. Although he had completely abandoned Byarugaba, he decreed that Byarugaba's four eldest children should leave the home or face consequences. He also still exercised the right to enter Byarugaba's house whenever he wanted to, and when he came in on the fatal night, Byarugaba, as is the custom among her people, offered him a chair even though it was late in the night.

Byamugisha's husband had not only stopped contributing to the family financial needs, he had even sold off the land that Byamugisha depended on for survival. When her father came to her rescue and enabled her to purchase lad — the only asset she knew how to exploit — her husband regarded the land as his and he attempted to sell it off. In his opinion, a woman had no right to own land; whatever she purportedly owned belonged to him.

Nabalayo's interview revealed a similar trend. In reply to whether she had ever been subjected to physical assault by her husband, she replied in the positive, and when I asked her what the reasons for the abuse would be, she said:

> He would disappear from home with the chicken and goats that I had reared, sell the animals off, spend the money and then come back. Before I could even say anything, he would attack me and beat me up.

In several of these cases, therefore, whereas the men did not hesitate to abandon their onerous patriarchal duty to financially cater for their wives, they were not ready to discard their patriarchal privilege of controlling family income and property. When the women challenged their husbands' rights, the latter resorted to physical violence in order to maintain their control and to ensure that the women remained subservient to men. It seems true that:

> ... marital violence can be understood only in the context of the hierarchy within the marital relationship. Violence is not simply the result of a quarrel, it arises in situations where the husband feels the need to assert his dominant status. A minor incident may provoke a ferocious attack when the husband perceives such an incident as a challenge to his authority or a neglect of his wishes (Eaton 1986:92).

It is also noteworthy that most husbands not only physically assaulted their wives, they were flagrantly involved in extramarital affairs (not necessarily polygamy). Women like Agaba and Karugaba were of the view that once a man gets another woman, he mistreats his wife. Komugisha, who killed her co-wife, and Natukunda, who conspired to kill her husband's 'other woman', were also of the same view. Likewise, in his study of some thirty intramarital homicides in Canada, Chimbos (1978) revealed that the predominant complaint by the slayers was their spouses' promiscuity.

Women's violence can consequently be seen as a reaction against the contradiction between their role and their status in the contemporary Ugandan family; it is a form of resistance against double oppression. On the one hand, they occupy a subservient position within the family with all its attendant denials and repressions. On the other hand, they carry the heavy responsibility of catering to the multiple needs of that institution.

Land conflicts and domestic violence

In Uganda, agriculture supports over 90 percent of the working population. Thus, the majority of the people depend on farming for survival. Among the 66 women interviewed in various prisons, 44 were peasant farmers by occupation at the time of arrest. One woman was a vendor of local brew but her husband was a peasant farmer. In 45 (68 percent) of the cases, therefore, land was the basis of survival. It should also be noted that among the 66 women, only 14 women (21 percent) resided in urban areas.

In several of the cases of husband killing, marital conflict and endless bitter quarrels revolved around the constant sale of portions of 'family' land by the husband until the only remaining land was the piece where the 'family' house was located. Often the husbands had abandoned their duty to take children to school, to feed their families, etc., and the wives had struggled to fulfill these duties through tilling the land. Yet the husbands had persisted in selling off this land which the wives needed to cater for family needs. Although none of the women gave the sale of land as the direct reason for having killed a husband, conflict over land was nonetheless one of fundamental causes of marital conflict and disharmony.

In his study on homicides in three districts in Uganda, Mushanga (1974:121) reported that in Kigezi, a district with serious land scarcity, disputes over land featured prominently in homicide cases and that among the three societies he studied, Kigezi showed a larger number of victims of land wrangles.

Although Asiimwe denied killing her husband, when asked whether she was experiencing any marital problems at the time of the alleged offence, her immediate response was:

> My husband used to sell off bits of our land and I was against it. He would then spend the money drinking. This was a constant source of marital conflicts and in fact, not long before the alleged offence, I had left him and gone to my brother.

In contrast to the above response, Asiimwe only mentioned her husband's physical assault after I had directly asked her whether her husband had ever beaten her. Yet her body had several scars which were a result of her husband's assaults. The husband had even used a lethal weapon against her: a spear.

It is probable that Asiimwe could have forgiven her husband for the physical assault but not for the sale of land. In response to whether she had ever reported her husband's assaults to any authority, she replied that she was fed up with reporting him. Yet, shortly before the homicide, she had reported her husband to RC authorities for the sale of family land. She may have endured her husband's physical assault, but his unilateral sale of 'family' land was completely unacceptable. She had, in fact, left her marriage shortly before the homicide and gone against her brother in protest to her husband's sale of land. She had only come back after her brother had advised her to present her complaints to the RC so that this local authority could share out the land between her and her husband. The RC had allocated part of the land to her and her sons and the husband was forbidden to sell that specific piece of land.

Byamugisha's husband even went further than Asiimwe's in what amounted to an obsession to sell land. He even attempted to sell off land that Byamugisha had acquired through her father's efforts. Similarly, although Byarugaba's story was mainly centred on her husband's physical violence, she, too, was bitter that her husband had sold off all the family land except the portion where the house was located.

The sale of the land without the consent of the wife, and in spite of her resistance, is possible because land is according to custom the property of the husband. Mushanga's (1974:48) lucid description of the status of women in western Uganda is to a large extent true for most parts of Uganda:

> Culture, especially in Ankole and Kigezi, gives the male absolute superiority over the female in the domestic matters of economics, politics, religion and the ownership of livestock, land and other movable property; *the female takes a risk if she questions the legitimacy of the male's position* (my emphasis).

In Uganda one can acquire land either through direct purchase or by means of a gift of deed or through inheritance. There is no legal provision that prohibits women from owning land or indeed any other property in Uganda.[7] The High Court has, in fact, recognised the right of a woman, whether married or unmarried, to own property in her own right.[8] But although the legal possibility exists, very few women own land. According to the 1991

Population and Housing Census figures, Uganda's population was 16,582,700 and 51 percent were female. But only seven percent of privately held land was in the hands of women.[9] This is because the system of ownership has largely been based on customary tenure. The basic law of inheritance is governed by statutory law; the Succession Act, a law which recognises testamentary freedom and, implicitly, customary practices. Most societies in Uganda are patrilineal and, as a result, it is extremely difficult for a woman to inherit her father's land. In most societies in Uganda, upon marriage, an ordinary bride carries very little with her to her new home. Yet the husbands are often owners of land inherited from their fathers.

When women challenge their husbands' supremacy in the domestic matters of property ownership, the women might be subjected to physical violence. In reaction against this weapon of subjugation — physical violence — women sometimes kill their tormentors.

Far from women's liberation

In Western societies a relationship between the women's liberation movement and female criminality has been presented. In particular, Adler (1975) asserted that there is an association between the women's movement and female criminality, that the women's movement has led to the rise of the 'New Female Criminal'. Adler contended that the women's movement has led to the masculinisation of female behaviour and that this is partly reflected in the fact that women are no longer passive: the contemporary woman is assertive. She further averred that women's assertiveness has led to their involvement in violent crime, an area hitherto dominated by men.

Contrary to Adler's assertion, the majority of women prisoners I interviewed did not belong to the 'liberated' group. They still subscribed to the supremacy of a man in the home. This is evident in their ideas about the proper role of a wife in relation to her husband. For example, Agaba's replies to several questions clearly indicate such views.

> *Lillian:* Are there any circumstances in which a man is entitled to physically assault his wife?
> *Agaba:* Yes. If a woman is lousy, e.g., the husband comes back home and meals are not ready, or she fails to keep her home clean, or has affairs with other men; then a husband would be entitled to physically assault such a wife.

Even before answering my question, Agaba put on a face indicating that the answer to my question was very obvious.

> *Lillian:* Supposing a man has extramarital affairs and the woman as a result also decides to get involved with other men, would such a husband be entitled to beat the wife?
> *Agaba:* Yes, such a woman should be beaten because she would be equating herself with the man.
> *Lillian:* What is your opinion on the issue of equality between men and women?
> *Agaba:* Attainment of such a status quo is impossible and will only remain verbal. It is difficult for men to accept it.

Karugaba's replies too revealed that she believed that a husband's position is superior to that of his wife.

> *Lillian:* Would you have accepted to look after your husband's illegitimate children if they had been sired after your marriage?
> *Karugaba:* I would have looked after them. ... [E]*ven if you refuse to look after your husband's child, time comes when the child turns up to claim what is due to him or her as a child of its father*. It is better to accept a child and get used to it (my emphasis).
> *Lillian:* In your opinion are there any differences in the roles of a husband on the one hand and a wife on the other in a home?
> *Karugaba:* Yes there are. A man is the boss and the wife must fear him. Once a man puts you in his home you must fear him.
> *Lillian:* Is it fear or respect?
> *Karugaba:* It is the same thing; you must ensure that you do not wrong him. A husband must be your boss.
> *Lillian:* Are there any circumstances in which a man should get another wife? [Karugaba hesitated to answer this question but later said:] If a woman is careless, irresponsible — yes. Supposing a man has wealth, he buys food in the house and you cannot prepare

meals for him, you cannot wash his clothes, you do not welcome visitors in the home, he comes back home and meals are not ready, what then would be the use of such a wife?
Lillian: And supposing the wife is barren?
Karugaba: Well in that case you should not let the man die without a child, you let him get a woman to bear children for him. You cannot let somebody's son die childless.
Lillian: Supposing a man is barren; should the wife get another man in order to get a child?
Karugaba: A woman cannot do that; she must keep her honour, she has a duty to maintain her respect. There is even no way your husband can allow you to do that; if you have an extramarital affair a husband would kill you.
Lillian: Are there circumstances in which a woman is entitled to physically assault her husband, e.g., if he is unfaithful to her?
Karugaba: I have never heard of a woman who physically assaults her husband. You would be afraid to do so.
Lillian: Are you afraid because of his physical strength? After all, some women are stronger?
Karugaba: Out of respect for your husband, you would not do it even if you are physically stronger than him.
Lillian: Where do your children live?
Karugaba: They are with their paternal uncle.
Lillian: Why did you not leave them in the custody of your own people?
Karugaba: After I had been arrested I had no power to decide anything. *In any case children belong to their father's side. It is their blood. It is only proper that they remain where they belong* (my emphasis).
Lillian: But I thought children belong to both the man and the woman!
Karugaba: Well, in a way yes. But they really belong to their father's side, that is their blood.

I asked Nalwanga, who was in prison for assaulting her co-wife, why the anger she felt towards her husband for neglecting her in favour of her co-wife had been directed against the co-wife, and she replied, 'Of course a woman cannot start a fight with her husband... Even when he used to beat me, I never hit back....' The reason was because a husband is 'one's master'.

As already mentioned, although Byarugaba's husband had abandoned her for almost a whole year, when, on the night of the homicide, he knocked on her door, she not only opened for him (despite the fact that he was in a foul mood), but she also offered him a chair to sit on, as would any wife who respects her husband.

These and other women's answers indicate that they did not subscribe to the notion of equality between the sexes. Nevertheless, they had acted violently. What Eaton (1986:6) observed about women who were processed through a magistrate's court on the edge of London can also be said about the women in Uganda's prisons: '... these women are usually those least affected by the ideas or the material benefits of women's liberation'.

But perhaps the answer to the apparent contradiction is found in Smart's (1976) contention that:

> The influence of 'emancipation' is extremely complex; it affects the material being and consciousness of not only the women who become 'emancipated' — but also those women — who reject the principles of liberation.

Furthermore, to be liberated is not necessarily a conscious effort and belief. For to paraphrase Adler, the women's movement is not an organised movement with identifiable membership. Rather it is an all-pervasive consciousness, a consciousness of self-determination. This self-determination may take the form of a struggle for autonomy of action. The need to be free is sometimes articulated, sometimes not. Since women's role in society is greatly restricted, it is no wonder that self-determination for most women entails taking part in activities considered a male monopoly by society.

Conclusion

The analysis of the circumstances within which women kill husbands supports Gelles' (1983:158) recommendation to American society that 'there is a need to change the existing power structure, which is based on inequality between members of the family, thereby ... allowing husbands who have higher status ... to use violence against their wives.'

In Ugandan society, men have higher status than women by virtue of being male and consequently husbands are, to paraphrase Mushanga (1974:48), given absolute superiority over their wives in all family matters. As Gelles (1983:158) has pointed out, a woman who questions her husband's authority takes a risk of being subjected to physical violence, since patriarchy does not only demand that power be vested in men to dominate and control others (women) but also allows men to use whatever means (violence) necessary to maintain their authority. But, as already noted, a man who subjects his wife to abuse also takes the risk of becoming a victim of the wife's retaliation.

Why do some women who go through similar experiences as the women who kill, opt for actions other than homicide? According to Ewing (1987:61), the answer to this question may lie in the degree of abuse to which the two categories of women are subjected and their relative lack of resources. Ewing may be right, but what is most important to realise is that each individual perceives options differently. Thus, in her study of the special problems, needs and contributions of women in the criminal justice system, Morris (1987:186) said that 'the women need not actually be as helpless as they perceive themselves to be; it is *their* perception of what they can and cannot do which is crucial' (my emphasis). Moreover, in the case of battered women,[10] it is important to remember that '... *even where options of escape exist, the woman may be unable to act or even perceive the existence of such options*' (Cipparone 1987:431) (my emphasis).

What however is highly evident is that socio-cultural values and norms within patriarchal society and the family increase the chances that women will resort to violence. This is, among other things, because legitimate means of marriage dissolution are often not viable options to a woman who desires to bring to an end a conflict-ridden marital relationship.

Notes

1. Given by Section 187 of the Uganda Penal Code and cited in Chapter VI, note 46.

2. Bardsley (1987:155), quoting an Egyptian prostitute hanged in 1973 for killing her pimp. Her statement was published in *Woman at Point Zero* by Nawal El Saadawi (Zed Press, 1983).

3. Asaba was one of the few husband killers who admitted that she and her husband used to fight, most of them talk about being constantly beaten rather than fighting. This may have implications for the definition of the concept of victim precipitation to be discussed in Chapter VI.

4. In many Ugandan societies it is believed that burial of a person should be done at the ancestral grounds of maternal grandparents, and where it must be done, a lot of rituals are performed in order to keep away the misfortune.

5. Wolfgang (1958) reported that alcohol was present in the homicide situation in 64 percent of the 588 cases that he analysed.

6. Local term for prostitutes, but also often used in reference to mistresses.

7. In using the term 'ownership', one must note that the Land Reform Decree of 1976 purported to abolish absolute rights in land such as those held under the freehold land tenure system. The legal effect of the Decree is that all land in Uganda is public land and is held by the Uganda Land Commission in trust for all citizens of the Nation. Individuals therefore only have an interest in using the land and in the developments they make on the land. In practice however the people of Uganda operate in total disregard of the Decree; they purport to sell and purchase land. Consequently one can get money from another person for a piece of land on which there is no development.

8. See e.g., *Uganda v Kyanda* [1977] H.C.B. 111; *Moonlight Sengooba Salongo v Administrator General* H.C.C.S. No. 894 (1973).

9. Source: Ministry of Lands, Housing and Urban Development. Kampala.

10. The concept of battered women is discussed in detail in Chapter VI.

III

Marriage, Divorce, and Separation

'Give a woman a peaceable way to escape from a violent partner, they say, and she'll take it.[1]

Introduction

What legitimate and effective means of protest are open to a Ugandan woman faced with marital conflicts and various kinds of abuse? Mushanga (1978:481) postulated that the major factors of family conflicts are priority, frequency, duration and intensity. Expounding on the concept of priority, he said:

> Priority refers to how soon after the marriage the disputes and conflicts begin. This should show that the earlier the disputes begin, the more likely they are to lead to domestic disasters. ... *Disputes that start soon after marriage lead to either divorce, separation, or frequent fights which sometimes result in the death of either the wife, the husband, or other members of the family* (my emphasis).

I asked the women who had experienced physical abuse at the hands of their husbands, how soon the violence towards them had started. The answers were consistent with Mushanga's above observation: the abuse began very soon after marriage. For example, Agaba, who was in marriage for 33 years, said her husband started assaulting her within two years of their marriage. In Karugaba's case, her husband's assaults began in the third year of their 13-year marriage. Asaba's fights with her husband started as soon as they started to cohabit.

But if the women offenders are persons who for years had been subjected to physical and emotional assault, why had they taken so long to react? In answer to the question: 'What would a reasonable person do if she was subjected to regular torture?' the majority of people would readily say that she would either report the matter to the police, or at least flee the situation.

In her sociological study of women and imprisonment, Carlen (1983) interviewed 20 women incarcerated in Cornton Vale Prison, Scotland. Melissa, who was serving three years imprisonment for attempted murder of a husband that had subjected her to physical abuse for so long, may have the explanation:

> I was getting sick of it, you know. I didn't want the same thing to happen that had happened before. *You can take so much violence towards your own person, then you will retaliate.* I know ... I'm fedup with getting battered *and when you do get fedup with it you will retaliate.* You don't care what you've got in your hand and you don't care about the consequences afterwards (1983:43) (my emphasis).

Perhaps Melissa's words would be echoed by women like Karugaba, Agaba, Byarugaba, Asaba and others. After they withstood violence against their persons for years, they reached a point where they could not stand it any more; then they reacted. Homicide is one of the extreme means of conflict-resolution. According to Tanner (1970:25), it runs counter to human instincts.

Jones (1980:xv) explained that homicide is often an extraordinary response to ordinary conditions. In the nineteenth century, infanticide was a commonplace crime in Europe and America when women had little access to birth control or abortion and were faced with hard social consequences for producing illegitimate children. She furthermore noted that many women in Europe and America in past times poisoned their husbands but today they divorce them.

Ugandan law recognises divorce and separation as solutions to conflict-ridden marriages.[2] Cruelty and adultery are some of the grounds on which a woman can petition to court for divorce in a civil marriage. Even under customary law, cruelty, if excessive, may also provide a woman with grounds for divorce. In the present study, all the women who killed husbands had among other things, endured habitual and excessive violence from those husbands — clear evidence of cruelty. Adultery was also present. Why did they not opt for divorce or separation? Does society, in spite of the law, present any specific barriers to women's use of divorce and separation in Uganda?

In an attempt to understand a woman's conscious and semiconscious 'choice' of conflict-resolution, (e.g., her decision to divorce or not to divorce an abusive husband), it is important to acknowledge that the assessments and decisions she makes take form in specific contexts, and are shaped by the resources as well as the social controls within that context. In deciding to divorce, a Ugandan woman faces several interrelated socio-cultural, economic and legal barriers.

Social barriers to divorce

My interviews with members of polygamous families (see Chapter V) revealed that in Ugandan society divorce is not an easily acceptable solution to broken marriages. Even those women who admitted intense difficulty in, for example, having to endure co-wifeship and its socio-economic consequences did not see divorce as a realistic option. One particular woman who was extremely burdened with the risk of AIDS inherent (in her opinion) in polygamous unions said:

> I have never had peace since my husband got that other woman. At one time he sold my cow and gave her money to seek medical treatment. He said that he used my cow because I am the one who bewitched his wife ... In many ways he has neglected me. He buys his other woman whatever she needs, he buys booze for friends but says he has no money for me. My children have no clothes, he does not cater for their medical needs. He has money but is not willing to spend it on me. I have had to hand over two of my children to my relatives so that they can be cared for. But I have told him that if his aim is to make me leave his home, he had better give it up for I will never go away. After all, with this AIDS how many more years do I have to live?

But even for women like Karugaba, Kansiime and Agaba, who saw divorce as a plausible solution to their problems, it sooner or later became clear to them that society would not allow them to do so.

These women realised that society could not protect them. They had often deserted their husbands and gone to their parents only to be reminded of their place in society — marriage. They had once thought that they had options in life, but were constantly reminded that society only respected women as wives and mothers. It was hence their duty to ensure that they remained married.

Asiimwe, Agaba and Karugaba contracted civil marriages. But because civil marriages are not yet internalised in Ugandan cultures, it is common for people to mix those marriages with some customary rituals. One such ritual is the payment of bride price by the man to the family of the woman. The husbands of these three women paid bride price despite the fact that the marriages were solemnised in church.

Customary marriages are normally dissolved when the parents of the wife refund the bride wealth to the husband. The courts have taken cognisance of this custom.[3] In those civil marriages in which bride price has exchanged hands, the practice is that on divorce the husband is entitled to a refund of the bride price. On many occasions the father or other relations of the wife will have spent the bride price and may not be in position to refund it at the time when the wife desires to leave her marriage.

For Asiimwe, society used both the civil and customary aspects of her marriage to hold her at ransom. After Asiimwe had told me that her husband's abuse had started when she was newly wed, I asked her why she had never left such an unhappy relationship. Her answer was as follows: 'The brothers who took the bride price never wanted to refund it. And I was married in church; my brothers used to say that one cannot revoke a church wedding.'[4]

In answer to the question whether her parents were aware of her marital problems, Kansiime answered:

> Yes. I sometimes used to go back to my parents but my husband would come for me. My parents often offered to return the bride

price but he would reject it and say he wanted his wife. *My parents would then tell me to go back since the man had refused* to take his bride wealth (my emphasis).

Karugaba had often deserted her marital home and gone to her parents, only to be 'forced' to go back. According to her she had left her husband on several occasions but each time she was forced to go back by her parents.

> *Lillian:* Why then did you keep on going back?
> *Karugaba:* In no time my husband would come for me. He would beg me to go and look after the children. Whenever I left him, his own relatives would harass him and put pressure on him to apologise to me. They were worried about his changing wives; he had married four times before. His own parents and sisters would come with him to plead with me. ... But the most important reason for having stayed in the marriage was the pressure put on me by my own father. My father used to force me to go back and to be as patient as my mother had been in the face of marital problems. My father used to tell my mother that if I did not go back to my husband even my mother would have to leave his (my father's) home. How then could I refuse and thus spoil my mother's marriage? ... He (my father) also seemed very worried about my children; whenever I left my husband my father would ask me about my children; 'Where is A.B.? Have you really decided to turn your back on him?' he would ask. He knew my husband was incapable of looking after the children. ... My mother used to plead with and tell me that despite the fact that my father had brought two women after her, she (my mother) had persevered. 'I won the battle even though we were three wives,' she would tell me. And I could actually see that in their old age they were settled and satisfied with their relationship. ... My mother-in-law also used to advise me to be patient and to remain in my marriage. She would tell me that, after all, my father-in-law had married ten other women after her, but all had left and she (my mother-in-law) had, due to her patience won. 'Did I not see how close the old couple was now?' she (the mother-in-law) would ask. ... But it was my father's stand that made it impossible for me to leave. Even when he comes to see me in prison I tell him that it was because of him that I ended up in this trouble. He used to tell me

that he could not vomit the bride price. That the problem with my husband was his age and that once he matured all would be well.

Karugaba's narration of her family history indicates that her father was not a poor man. He was involved in the transport business and had several buses. I asked Karugaba why her father had attached so much importance to property at the expense of his daughter's happiness. In her reply she expressed the view that the bride price was not so much the problem. Rather it was because her father saw it as a disgrace to have a daughter who had failed in her marriage. He used to tell her that if she left her marriage, he would automatically regard her as a prostitute and he was not going to have a prostitute in his home. On one occasion Karugaba had left her husband and gone to live with her brother in another town. The father had told his son that, if indeed he was his son, he should tell Karugaba to go back to her man and to look after her children. Her father used to say: 'How can a woman married in church, a woman with children and whose husband has built a house leave her marriage? What you are going through is experienced by all women.'

From stories like Karugaba's, it is evident that unlike men, whose physical and emotional independence is — despite difficulties and differences arising from class, circumstances, etc. — a birthright, such a woman must fight for emotional and physical independence.

Lillian: Did you ever contemplate setting yourself up independently of your relatives since they were not willing to have you permanently in their homes? Did you ever think of getting employed?
Karugaba: Yes on one occasion I left my husband and set up a shop near my parents' home in Kamwenge.
Lillian: Where did you get the money from?
Karugaba: Before my husband had told me to sit at home I used to work in his shop. I used to set money aside and this is what I used to set up the shop. ... I set up a home in the same building; the front was the shop and the back was my living quarters. My shop was well stocked but my father sent me a message through

> one of my brothers that he would not have a daughter prostituting under his very nose. My aim was never to prostitute but my father made life so difficult for me that I left the stock with my brother to put into his shop and to buy a cow for me out of the proceeds. I told him to take my house hold property home, that is, to my parents' home. I went back to my marriage. ... On yet another occasion I went to a place called Saaka, rented a place for a shop and started business. When my husband learnt of it he went to the police and reported that I was a rebel wife. The police, after being shown the marriage certificate, came and threw me out. ... I had got the premises through a woman friend and my husband went and assaulted her, accusing her of making me wild.

The police's reaction supports the following observation of Schneider and Jordan (1978:10) in the context of American society: 'A marriage license is viewed as giving a husband permission to do what he wants with and to his wife.' This observation is equally applicable to Ugandan society. Unfortunately, and like Karugaba's father, many other people in Ugandan society believe that women have no value as individuals apart from their men, apart from marriage. Parents seem to think that daughters are only valuable if they are married, for marriage is the culturally approved goal for women. The reaction of Karugaba's husband gives credence to Jones' (1980:299) assertion that the question why a battered woman does not leave the abusive relationship may, in some circumstances, not be as important as the question: 'Why don't the men let the women go?'

In her study of women who kill, Jones cited many cases of wives in the American society who left their husbands only to be pursued and forced back into their homes. Likewise, despite the fact that Karugaba's husband no longer needed her sexually and no longer appreciated her cooking or her company, he could not let her go. As already said, whenever she left her husband, he and his relatives would plead with her to go back. Similarly, Kansiime's abusive husband used to reject the bride price and insist that he wanted his wife. Agaba's story also falls in this category. In her testimony she said:

> I could not re-marry because I was too old. Even if I had been young, *my husband would not have allowed me* to marry another man as long as he was alive (my emphasis).
> *Lillian:* What would your husband have done if you had taken such a move?
> *Agaba:* He would have come for me.
> *Lillian:* Did you have any close friends? Did you ever seek their advice in relation to your marital problems?
> *Agaba:* My friends used to advise me to stay, especially since I was wed in church. That I should protect my ring.[5] They also used to urge me to stay and look after my children.
> *Lillian:* Did you ever report the beatings sustained from your husband to any authority?
> *Agaba:* Yes. On several occasions when my husband severely assaulted me, the RC intervened and 'arrested' him.

Agaba said this with a smile, as if she recognised the futility, the emptiness in the mock arrests experienced by her husband, compared to her own arrest which landed her in prison. She then continued:

> ... but he would always negotiate with them and he would be released. You see in our custom it is all right for the husband to beat a wife; he is the boss. ... One time I decided to report him to the police and the RC gave me a letter to take to the police. On my way to the police I met a family friend, a man, who advised me not to go to the police. He was of the view that such a step would not augur well for the family. And how would it augur for the children that I had reported their father to the police? ... At one other time he had really beaten me and I ran to the RC 1 chairman for safety. I spent two days at the chairman's place and asked him for a letter to the police and he gave me one. I had however escaped in shabby clothes so I decided to sneak back home and to tell my children to secure some neat clothes for me. As I headed home, the RC chairman ran after me and told me not to report my husband. He said it would be a shame on the family; moreover my husband had been in prison before and if I reported him it was likely that he would be given a long prison sentence. We argued for a long time but he kept on insisting that I give him the letter he had written. I was eventually irritated, annoyed and I

tore the letter to pieces and threw them at him. He told me that I should go back to my husband and he then escorted me.

Agaba had thus gone a step further than Karugaba: reported her husband to authorities — the RC — but the authorities failed her. She had even attempted to report him to the police, but society reminded her of her duty to protect her marriage and family honour at all costs. As in Karugaba's case, society expected Agaba to put up with her husband's many faults. In other words, neither the husband nor the wider society was willing to let Agaba go. It was all these pressures from all around her that made her stay. The cases of many of the other women interviewed are also stories of women pressured to stay married.

In his study of criminal homicides in three districts in western Uganda,[6] Musanga (1974:80), who noted a lower rate of husband killing in Toro than in Ankole and Kigezi, contended that:

> This could be explained by the nature and structure of the marriage system and the degree of socio-psychological attachment of women (in Ankole and Kigezi) to their honour and to that of their husbands and of the family. In a society where domestic and marital altercations, desertions, separation, divorce and infidelity do not bring shame and dishonour to the individual and to the family in particular (as in Toro), the wife is not inclined to assert her rights even to the use of violence against her husband because there are other socially approved ways of overcoming such situations. Divorce, separation and desertion as ways in which to solve marital disputes are not socially approved in Kigezi and to a lesser extent in Ankole. A divorced woman is an unhappy woman. ... In Ankole and Kigezi, cultural values compel a woman to remain in her husband's house even when the latter marries another wife, and such a prolonged stay in a disharmonious domestic and marital situation increases the chance of using violence against a husband when a situation arises that is defined as requiring the use of violence. For it does appear that homicide will tend to follow prolonged ill-feelings between family members. ... In the domestic group, criminal homicide is an outgrowth of long-standing disagreements, threats, fights, altercations and strain in the domestic day-to-day interaction.

It is worth noting that among the 20 women I interviewed who had husbands as victims, ten of them came from Kigezi and Ankole. Eight of these women reported the existence of extreme marital conflict and disharmony at the time of the homicide. On the other hand, only one (Simba) came from Toro and she denied the offence. This pattern lends credence to Mushanga's foregoing argument that where a woman who is experiencing marital conflict has divorce/separation as plausible solutions, she is less likely to use violence against her husband. Where such solutions are readily available, she is less likely to use violence to resolve her conflicts.

It is true that, in law, some of these women could have sought divorce from the courts since their marriages had been solemnised in church, but the women had no idea that courts had power to separate married people — a consequence of the fact that in Uganda legal knowledge is largely a monopoly of the legal profession.

I asked Karugaba whether she had ever contemplated reporting her husband to any authorities and she answered: 'What I knew was that if a couple has problems in their marriage, it is the parents on either side who intervene.' Indeed, the parents on either side constantly intervened — intervened to ensure that she stayed married. To Karugaba, the idea of calling upon law authorities to intervene was out of question. This shows that the role of the law in solving family conflicts still evades many of our people. When asked why she had not at least reported the matter to the RC authorities she answered: 'If a man's parents cannot convince him to change, I cannot see how strangers can make him change. What I knew was that it is the parents of either side that can solve marital problems.' Karugaba told me that her in-laws had, on many occasions, intervened in the marriage and pleaded with their son to change his behaviour and he had promised them he would.

When the women tried to leave their broken marriages, they were consistently reminded that society regarded them first and foremost as women and therefore as wives and mothers, before acknowledging that they were human beings with any individual rights. The women were consistently showered with talk on the spirit of tolerance and forgiveness. Divorce and separation were not realistic options available to them. This was especially because the decision to divorce was not entirely (if at all) in the hands of these abused women; the decision to a large extent depended on the ability and the willingness of the male relatives to refund the bride price. In some cases, even where the family of the woman offers to return the bride price, the husband may decline the offer, and by so doing, block his wife's freedom. In some societies in Uganda, if a husband rejects the return of the bride price, it means that he still wants his wife. The woman's family then has a duty to tell her to go back to her husband. In other words, it is the feelings of the husband that matter when it comes to the survival or dissolution of marriage; the woman's feelings are more often than not irrelevant. Such was also the case of Kampikaho whose husband constantly subjected her to physical and other abuse. Asked whether she had ever left her marriage due to the abuse, she replied:

> I would run to my parents every other day. My parents offered him the bride price but he rejected it. ... After the death of my father, my brothers too told him to take his things but he refused and said it was 'the woman' and not the wealth that he wanted. Whenever he refused to take his things, my brother would say, 'You go, your man has refused to take his things.' Whenever he fetched me from my parents' place, cows would be put before him, would be offered to him so that he could leave me but he would reject them....

Kampikaho's reply confirms Mushanga's (1974:44) findings on divorce in Kigezi district, where he observed a high ratio of female violence:

> Divorce, in Kigezi, is a process which ... is not a question of one of the parties deciding to divorce. Before divorce can actually take place, there are established channels that will have to be followed. There are also attempts by kin, friends and neighbours to restore the marriage.

Evidence of these attempts was clearly revealed in the women's stories.

In contrast, in the Toro community, where the level of female violent crime is low, Mushanga found that:

> In Toro where the level of social involvement in the institution of marriage is low, and where marriages can be contracted as easily as they can be dissolved, ... disputes and altercations arising out of the families are brought to an end by separation. ... A married woman in Kigezi will define a family or any other social situation in which her rights or dues are infringed as requiring the use of violence, whereas a Mutooro woman will define the same situation as calling for separation.

Similarly, in the United States and other Western societies, Wilson and Daly (1992:206) observed:

> ... a large proportion of the spousal killings perpetrated by wives ... [occur] ... after years of suffering physical violence, *after they have exhausted all available sources of assistance,* when they feel trapped ... (my emphasis).

It follows, therefore, that husband killers in Uganda and, indeed, elsewhere in the world exhausted what they perceived as all the available sources of assistance before turning to their last option — homicide.

For the sake of the children

Most women interviewed said that if they had had no children they would have left their abusive husbands. For most women, the breakup of marriage meant leaving their children with the husbands. As already mentioned, Ugandan society is patrilineal and children 'belong' to their fathers, who have the right to custody of the children. In fact, in many battering relationships, men use children as blackmail — a man will declare that if his wife ever left him she would never be allowed even temporary access to her children.

After Rwanyarare had related to me the extreme physical and other abuse she had suffered at her husband's hands for years, I asked her why she had not left her husband and she answered:

> I have left him many times and gone to my parents but he has always come and begged me to remain married to him. He has always promised me to change, to improve. But the most important reason why I always went back was for the sake of my children — without me they would suffer.

Byarugaba too left her marriage several times due to her husband's abuse. She, kept coming back because: 'I lived for my children. Whenever I thought of my children, of whom I was mother and father, I would come back to my marriage.'

After listening to Byamugisha's story of the homicide event, I asked her: 'Was this the first time you had fought?' She answered: 'He used to beat me so often and many times I would leave him, but would have to come back because, in my absence, my children would suffer a lot.' The wider society also made it clear that Byamugisha had to remain in her marriage for the sake of her children. In her words, the village elders:

> ... insisted that even though my husband had abandoned the home and settled with another woman, I had to come and look after my children who were by then left in the home on their own. I would have left him long ago but I remained because of my children.

Kansiime's husband subjected her to regular physical abuse and once attempted to set her house on fire. He married other wives and then completely abandoned her. When asked whether she had ever thought of leaving her marriage, she said: 'Never. I could not think of abandoning my children.'

In the case of *Elizabeth Obaro*,[7] who killed her husband, the accused testified that the deceased was in the habit of beating her, but she had not left him because of her children. Similarly, the first question Karugaba's father always asked her whenever she took refuge in his house, refuge from intense marital conflict, was what kind of heart she had which enabled her to completely abandon her children.

Motherhood therefore leaves women vulnerable to patriarchal power because society and individual men hold the women's children hostage in order to force women into obedience. A woman's duty to her children plays a critical role in her subordination. Society expects her to sacrifice her joy and freedom, to remain in a violent home for the sake of her children. Society requires that a woman's obligation to her children should always take precedence over her own independence and safety. According to Roberts (1993:114), society always presumes that: 'motherhood subsumes a woman's identity as an individual self.'

The economic trap: nothing other than marriage

Del[8] (1982:xviii) correctly pointed out that women are abused in many ways over and above physical violence. They are abused by their spouses as well as by the double standards of patriarchal society which prepare most women for nothing but marriage, and thereby make women economically dependent on their husbands — such is the situation of many Ugandan women.

For those who may ask how a woman can remain in an extremely abusive relationship, part of the answer was given by Thelma in Carlen (1983:9), who said: 'I had to find some way of keeping my roof over my head, but the law won't listen to that. They're not interested.' Agaba, Asiimwe, Asaba and some others would have easily given the same answer.

Even without being told by her relatives that she must remain married, Agaba realised that she was trapped by her socio-economic situation; she had to endure marriage in order to ensure that she and her children had a roof over their heads. Agaba is a perfect example of a woman whom society denied the possibility of being independent of men and thus her only source of survival was to till her husband's land. She had left her husband many times and the husband had always come for her at her mother's home, often paying fines to her family as a sign of remorse. Not long after bringing her back, the husband would assault her again.

> *Lillian:* But after so many times of apology and no reform you must have realised that he would never change; why did you not eventually quit?
>
> *Agaba:* I had nowhere to go to. My mother was alive and that is where I used to escape to but I had to survive. ... My father died when I was young and the land *automatically* became my brother's.[9] My mother had no say in the property so she could not give me a piece to cultivate. My brother needed all the land; could I then have lived together with my sister-in-law? Yet I was too old to re-marry ... (my emphasis).
>
> *Lillian:* Do you think that if you had been economically independent, if you had been able to earn your own money, you would have eventually left your man?
>
> *Agaba:* A married woman can never claim to have personal property. Even when you produce income, it still belongs to your husband.

Since she knew that marriage was the only way to survive, she could not contemplate living a single woman's life. Hence the statement that she could not leave her marriage because, among other reasons, she was too old to re-marry.

> *Lillian:* You told me that at one time you had wanted to report your husband to the police; what did you expect the police to do for you?
>
> *Agaba:* I wanted them to divide up the land between me and my husband. I wanted to be given a piece so that I could live on and till that piece in order to sustain my children and my self. I would then leave my husband on his own.[10]

When I asked Agaba whether she had ever contemplated leaving her marriage and getting employment, she emphatically answered in the negative. But before answering this question, she hesitated as if she could not envisage any kind of employment for a person like herself — a person who had never seen the inside of a classroom.

> *Lillian:* Where will you go to after you leave prison?
>
> *Agaba:* Back to my husband's house. Nobody will persecute me.

> My children used to check on me while at Mbarara prison but Luzira is too far. But I will go back.

Agaba realised that if she had to retain any access to land at all — the only source of survival for a woman like her — she had to stick with her husband. She did not see any alternatives to marriage. She accepted that her own brother had no duty to cater for her. She expected society to understand her clinging to her husband's land. Even after prison she planned to go back to till this very land. She realised that in her society a woman can only get access to land use rights as a wife. As a peasant woman, divorce was a threat to her survival. Stories such as Agaba's elucidate the fact that, in patriarchal societies, the inheritance system, among other things, turns women into property-less dependants.

In a different way, Asaba too was trapped in her marriage, and like Agaba, she looked at marriage as her source of survival.

> *Lillian:* Did you ever leave him due to his violence?
> *Asaba:* I never left him even once; I got used to his fights and realised I was too old to leave him. ... With this AIDS I could not afford to change men. ... Both my parents are dead. ... *He used to dress me, to feed me; what else could I look for?* ... At the time of the offence I was unemployed. When I met my husband, I was employed as a casual labourer by the Coffee Marketing Board but in the 70s I was laid off. ... My husband, however, continued working (my emphasis).

In Asiimwe's case, even after realising that she and her husband could no longer live together, she still insisted that they could only assist her if she lived on her husband's land. Asiimwe was told to leave her father's home where she had sought refuge and to return to her husband. The husband was supposed to give part of his land to her and retain the other part. Only if Asiimwe continued to live on that land would the village elders ensure that her husband financially helped her children. As soon as Asiimwe took up residence on her husband's land, he resumed his physical abuse of her. The experiences of women like Asiimwe are strikingly similar to those of women inmates of Cornton Vale Prison, of whom Carlen (1983) said:

> ... however coolly the women analysed their situation, they did not believe they could free themselves of their dependency upon men. They felt trapped, not by their own desire, but by their economic and social situation.

Legal barriers to divorce

Although the women's 'failure' to divorce is more a function of socio-cultural values attached to the institution of marriage and the women's economic dependency on that institution than the law per se, it is worth noting that: 'There is no law in Uganda that exemplifies the discriminatory character of our laws [more] than the law governing divorce' (Tamale 1993:173).

Whereas inability/unwillingness by the woman's parents to refund bride wealth may make it impossible for her to divorce under customary practice and law, the Divorce Act requires different, gender-based grounds for divorce. The Act does not recognise 'irretrievable breakdown of a marriage' as a ground for divorce and a person seeking dissolution of her/his marriage must prove the existence of specified circumstances.

Adultery by a wife is by itself adequate grounds for a court to grant the husband a divorce. But a wife cannot divorce an adulterous husband who has not, in addition to the adultery, either deserted her or been cruel to her, or committed bigamy or had an incestuous relationship. In treating the sexes differently and giving men more freedom, the legislators have been passive followers of trends in the Ugandan social order. The law thereby sanctions inequality between men and women.

Although the amendment of laws that legitimise discrimination against women would not on their own remove the social structures that relegate women to the position of second class citizens, it is important to formalise legal equality at the very least, and consequently to provide a legal platform from which women can challenge customs, traditions and practices that discriminate against them. The differentiation between requirements for wife- and husband-initiated divorce should, therefore, be abolished.

The need to be free

Women's inability to escape from conflict-ridden marriages is therefore a result of the stigma attached to divorce, the frightening prospect of leaving their children behind when they leave their husbands' homes, and the economic consequences of divorce. In their failed attempts to divorce abusive husbands, the women realised that they had no option but to remain married. But each of these women had become a prisoner of that option and the only way she could put an end to 'enforced' marriage — was to kill the husband. The situation of such women lends credence to Bardsley's (1987:34) contention that:

> For a woman, ... autonomy of action is still something for which she must fight. Female crime can be an expression of that struggle: a deep-rooted need to be free, sometimes articulated, sometimes not; ... the crime is an expression of herself — either tortured, defiant or just plain impoverished — which is inevitably caught up inside her action.

Some women's spousal homicides are therefore expressions of the need to be free; free from an informal hostile prison — marriage. In regard to such women, one might say that formal imprisonment was merely a change of warders. Prior to their imprisonment in government prisons, they had been prisoners of their womanhood.

Notes

1. Jones (1980:xviii). Jones related this contention to the fact that whereas murders committed by men in the United States had increased at an alarming rate during the 15 years prior to her publication, murders committed by women dramatically declined. Experts attributed the decline to the proliferation of shelters, services, and legal remedies for battered women.

2. See the Divorce Act, Chapter 215 of the Laws of Uganda, which relates to divorce in civil marriages. Customary divorce is recognised by the Customary Marriage Decree, Decree 16 of 1973. The Marriage and Divorce of Mohammedans Act, Chapter 213 of the Laws of Uganda, caters for the termination of Islamic marriages.

3. See *Muhinduka v Kabere,* Civil Suit No. 1 of 1971, Kabale (Unreported).

4. Church weddings are accorded a lot of respect in Ugandan society and even when no bride price has exchanged hands, the prestige of having been wed in church is a hindrance to divorces. The vows made on the wedding day are to the effect that only death would separate the husband and the wife, and these vows are interpreted by many as prohibition to divorce. And where a person married in church gets a divorce through the court, churches (even Anglican churches) do not in general recognise that person as unmarried and will not allow her or him to go through another church wedding.

5. Wedding rings are to many people synonymous with church marriages, since rings are not used in customary marriages.

6. A district is an administrative unit created by the Ministry of Local Government and the basis of geographical demarcation is largely based on ethnic composition.

7. H.C.C.S.C. No. 663/67.

8. In her introduction to Ginny NiCarthy's book, entitled *Getting Free: A Handbook for Women in Abusive Relationships.*

9. Since Ugandan society is basically patriarchal, property, including land, belongs under customary law to the husband, and on his death

it is usually passed on to his male relative. Where a person dies intestate, statutory law provides that his children — male and female — are entitled to an equal share in his property (Section 28 of the Succession Act), but since legal knowledge is largely a monopoly of the legal profession, the majority of people operate according to custom and in total disregard of legislation. Thus Agaba's statement that the land automatically passed on to her brother.

10. Agaba was talking about division of land for purposes of use, not ownership. She knew that she had no right to ownership but had a right to use the land as long as she was still married to her husband. The very act of occupying her husband's land rather than her father's land means that a woman is still a wife.

IV

Child Victims

'There is no more tragic type of homicide than that involving children' (Copeland, 1986:248).

The offender's child as the victim

Among the 91 court cases perused, 13 women (14 percent) were violent towards children and seven (eight percent) of these women had directed their violence against their own offspring. Among the 66 women interviewed in the various prisons, 16 women (25 percent) were violent against children and seven (11 percent) directed their violence against their own offspring. According to Bohannan (1960:253), 'in Africa women kill their children, usually in a state of emotional stress following breakup of the family or contravention of important norms.' With regard to American society, Duncan and Duncan (1978:173–4) said:

> The most common reason for killing [a child within the first 24 hours of birth] among married women is extramarital paternity, and the stigma of having an illegitimate child is the primary reason among unmarried women.

The circumstances of the relevant offenders I interviewed lend credence to both Bohannan's and the Duncans' opinions; the women seemed to have committed the offences under emotional stress, resulting from diverse social and/or economic causes. Furthermore, they were either single or married women who were experiencing intense marital problems. A reading of some of the court files in which women were violent against their own children also supports the same opinion.

Among the seven women who were violent towards their own children, five were unmarried mothers and three of these became impregnated by married men. Two of the unmarried mothers became pregnant while still attending school. The two women who had become pregnant within marriage had, at the time of the offences, been rejected by their husbands. They committed the crimes after the breakup of their marriages.

Of the seven women, three were charged with and convicted of infanticide.[1] Since each of these homicides occurred at the time of, or immediately after, delivery this in itself may be evidence of emotional stress. It should be noted that the offence of infanticide is evidence that the criminal law recognises that a woman may kill her child as a result of a disturbed mind caused by the effect of giving birth. Consequently, the woman's act which would otherwise have been murder is treated as the lesser offence of manslaughter.

The Ugandan law on infanticide, however, compares unfavourably with, for example, the Danish law[2] which recognises not only that a woman can kill her child as a result of an unbalanced mind (as does Uganda law) but also out of fear of disgrace, panic, etc., which in reality are often the feelings of many young unmarried mothers. Just as it has been said of the law in some Western societies (Morris 1987), Ugandan law too more readily regards mental instability or sickness as the cause of female homicide than it does socio-economic causes.

Twenty-four-year-old Mwesigye was an unmarried woman who became pregnant when she was working as a copy typist in the traditional civil service. The man responsible for the pregnancy was married. During his relationship with Mwesigye, he had attempted to ensure that his wife did not learn of his extramarital affair. He emphatically informed Mwesigye that he had no interest in having children outside marriage.

When Mwesigye realised that her lover would not take responsibility for the pregnancy, she tried to secure an abortion, but changed her mind, out of fear that she might die in the process. However, after she delivered the child, she killed it She was charged with and convicted of infanticide. A far as the law was concerned, her crime was a result of a disturbed mind arising from child delivery. She spent one month on remand and was, on conviction, given a five-year prison sentence.

Mwesigye underwent emotional stress arising from an unwanted pregnancy. During our conversation, she constantly interjected her answers thus: 'I will never have anything to do with men again; men are impossible.' She may have killed the child due to a disturbed mind but it is also highly probable that Mwesigye's crime was premeditated. She certainly realised the consequences of bringing into the world an unwanted child — a child whose father was unlikely to acknowledge him. As a mother of a 'fatherless' child, Mwesigye would been regarded by society as a loose woman, a prostitute. Her child too would have suffered emotional burdens in a patrilineal culture, where paternity is crucial to one's sense of identity. Furthermore, it would also have exposed Mwesigye to lack of financial support for the child.

Tibamanya too was charged and convicted of infanticide. Tibamanya was partially deaf and never went to school. At the time of the offence she was not living with her husband, the man responsible for her pregnancy. When she was a few months pregnant, her husband had (for reasons unknown to Tibamanya), sent her away from his home. Tibamanya had no alternative but to go and live with her only brother and his wife. According to Tibamanya, her sister-in-law had never liked her. When the time for delivery came, the two women were the only persons present in the house. Tibamanya's sister-in-law refused to take her (Tibamanya) to the hospital. She even refused to help in delivering the baby. Tibamanya delivered it on her own. The circumstances under which she delivered the baby were bound to bring about deep emotional stress. Tibamanya spent one year on remand and was sentenced to five years in prison.

Kinengyere was on remand on a charge of having killed her 11-month-old baby. Kinengyere became pregnant while she was a senior secondary student. When the school authorities found out that she was pregnant, they asked her father to collect his daughter. In response the father told his daughter not to go to his home since he no longer had interest in her — she had just wasted his money.[3]

The man responsible for the pregnancy was already married and had denied paternity. When Kinengyere informed him of her condition, his reaction was: 'Am I the only man who used you?'

Kinengyere's mother died when she was young and the only close relative was her maternal grandmother. On leaving school, Kinengyere went to stay with the old woman. She had the child at the age of 18 years.

When the child was 11 months old it fell sick and Kinengyere's grandmother insisted that the child be taken to its father. Unfortunately, the father of the child refused to have Kinengyere and their child in his house claiming that it was a taboo among his clan to harbour a girl who got pregnant outside marriage. But the old woman also insisted that she could not accept the sick child.[4]

In all probability Kinengyere's decision to kill the child was prompted by her realisation that as long as she had the baby with her, she would have no place of abode. The attitude of her relatives was clear enough. To them a child out of wedlock was a disgrace. Moreover, in a patrilineal society, the denial of paternity by the child's father must have greatly burdened its mother.

In H.C.C.S.C. No. 44/75, the accused was indicted for the attempted murder of her child. According to the court records, the accused, a 20-year-old unmarried woman, gave birth to a child whose father denied responsibility. At the time of pregnancy and delivery of the child, the accused was living in Lira town with her parents. Soon after delivering the child, her father banished her and her child to the countryside.[5] On that day, when the accused was left alone with the child, she threw him in a pit latrine. The baby was later rescued by villagers. The prosecuting attorney correctly observed:

> The accused was embarrassed by the child — a bastard — and her own parents were not happy with her because of the child. They were not prepared to maintain the child. In desperation she decided to bring the child's life to an end.

In mitigation, the defence counsel submitted that 'her parents' attitude, especially on the material day, made her lose all sense of proportion. The child's father was of no assistance.'

In H.C.C.S.C. No. 61/73, the accused was a young unmarried woman aged 18 years who was working as a barmaid. She had neither a mother nor a father. When she gave birth, the father of the child disappeared, leaving her without any material or emotional support. Soon her endurance snapped and she threw her two-year-old son in a pit latrine. She was indicted for attempted murder.

The circumstances of the women who had children out of wedlock lend credence to Mushanga's (1976:81) contention that, in Uganda, one of the reasons for infanticide and abortion is the realisation that they would not get assistance from the men who made them pregnant or from male relatives. Another reason is that such single women, by engaging in premarital sex, contravened social important norms.

The heavy punishment for infanticide, liability to life imprisonment, makes one wonder whether the law has gone far enough to recognise the non-culpability of those women who kill as a result of a disturbed mind. A look at several other offences punishable with life imprisonment reveals that infanticide has been lumped together with offences involving moral blame.[6] Furthermore, pronouncements given by some Ugandan courts clearly indicate that judicial officers have little insight into the circumstances under which infanticide is committed.

In H.C.C.S.C. No. 44/75 cited above, the two attorneys may have understood the anguish which the young woman was going through at the time she committed the offence, but not the judge. Although he acknowledged that the accused must have 'acted in desperation because of the atmosphere that surrounded her and her child', Justice Manyindo also said:

> The accused, being the very mother of this very young child, should have been the last person to want to remove him from the face of the earth. *In my view, her parents' attitude was quite proper in that no parent worth his name would like to have a daughter of loose character, bearing children out of wedlock* (my emphasis).

Consequently, the judge gave the accused a sentence of 18 months imprisonment: she had spent ten months on remand.

Justice Manyindo's attitude is representative of the hypocrisy of the wider patriarchal society and its attendant laws: a society which punishes a girl for engaging in pre-marital sex (by regarding her as loose, a disgrace; by chasing her out of school without hope of ever resuming her education; by chasing her away from home), while keeping a blind eye to her partner, sometimes a married and much older man. This double standard is evident in many areas of the law dealing with sexuality. For example, it is not a crime for a married man to have sexual intercourse with an unmarried woman but it is criminal adultery for a married woman to have sexual intercourse with any man who is not her husband, irrespective of the marital status of that other man.[7]

And under divorce law, a husband can divorce his wife for adultery but a wife cannot divorce her adulterous husband unless he has in addition to the adultery, also either been cruel, or has deserted her or been involved in an incestuous relationship. Furthermore, if a divorce has arisen out of the wife's adultery, the Divorce Act gives a judge discretion to deny such a wife any property she may be entitled to a divorce.[8] The rule does not apply to a man whose adultery has led to a divorce.

In H.C.C.S.C. No. 61/73 above, the defence counsel brought to the attention of the court the circumstances under which the accused had committed the crime and prayed to the court for leniency because 'a deterrent sentence would ruin her life.' The court gave a very lenient sentence to the accused, a non-custodial sentence. She was bound over in her own recognisance in the sum of 1,000 shillings for a period of 12 months to be of good behaviour and to keep the peace. But the question is: Is the lenient sentence evidence of the judge's appreciation of the circumstances under which the accused committed the crime, or is it solely in sympathy of the victim child? Explaining the reason for the sentence, Justice Kantinti said:

> The accused is a girl of 18 years. She has been on remand for nearly a year. She has neither father nor mother and her child is being cared for by her grandmother who is an old woman. I feel that sending her to prison for a long term will not do her any good and will greatly affect her child.

But perhaps it is Justice Mungoma's very recent pronouncements in *Namyalo Dativa*[9] that more clearly indicate that judicial officers only give lip service to the assumption that a woman who commits infanticide does so in circumstances which are beyond her control. Namyalo was charged with, and convicted of, infanticide. She was about 18 years of age and became pregnant outside marriage. She had never gone to school. Asked how she knew that she was pregnant, she answered:

> I did not know that I was pregnant but I felt a thing moving in my stomach and I told my grandmother about it. When she examined me she told me that I was seven and a half months pregnant. I was really scared....

Even when the baby came, Namyalo was not aware that it was time for delivery. She mistook labour pains for a need to pass urine. The prosecution's case was recorded as follows:

> Accused felt she wanted to go for a short call. Chose to go to an unused and old latrine. Delivered a baby girl. When she heard the footsteps of her grandmother, who was looking for her, she threw the child into the pit latrine.

It is likely that Namyalo's action was, to say the least, a result of panic. In sentencing her, one of the reasons why His Worship Mungoma gave a 'lenient' sentence was that, at the time of the crime, 'she was not in possession of her mental faculties' — a re-statement of the law on infanticide. He also correctly observed that 'the problem of infanticide, usually cases of unwanted pregnancies, requires a multi-sectorial approach, as it is more of a social problem than an ordinary crime'. He nevertheless went on to say: 'But infants should be protected' and gave the accused a custodial sentence — 18 months' imprisonment. If her actions were clearly beyond her control, how could her imprisonment be justified? If a person's action is a result of the fact that she is not in possession of her mental faculties, deterrence cannot be a sound principle on which to base a sentence.

It is also evident from Section 9(1) the Penal Code that Ugandan Criminal Law presupposes exercise of free will.[10] One who cannot exercise a voluntary choice is, therefore, not an appropriate subject of criminal punishment. Two of the women I interviewed were charged with attempting to kill their children and two other women were charged with having murdered their children, aged above 12 months. The circumstances under which these women committed the offences were similar to the women who were charged with infanticide, an indication that although the situations are treated differently in law, it is likely that they occur for sociologically very similar reasons.

Kampikaho was on remand for drowning her three children in a well. Her story is the life of a woman who had, for almost 15 years, been subjected to extreme physical and emotional abuse by her husband. She described her experience in the following words:

> ... that man has made me see hell; ... the suffering in my house is unbelievable. ... I do not know why I am still alive. He was so violent, I even wonder why I am not dead, it is only God who knows.

Kampikaho said she had several scars on her body — evidence of her husband's violence against her. She showed me a scar behind the ear and another deeper scar on her leg which she said was from an axe attack by her husband.

A few months after she had been married, she became pregnant. But when she was eight months pregnant, her husband beat her resulting in a miscarriage. Although his violence had steadily increased, she had, subsequently, given birth twice more. On the fourth pregnancy, however, he beat her so much that she delivered prematurely. One of the twins was stillborn. The birth of the twins brought a new dimension to the couple's already violent relationship. Kampikaho's husband began accusing her of infidelity on the basis that twins were unheard of in his family. He alleged that the twins must have been a result of prostitution; adultery.

After the twins, Kampikaho became pregnant once again and had a baby but when the child was one year and six months, her husband beat her and the child. The child had a split head and almost died. This time he alleged that the father of the child was Kampikaho's own brother — an accusation of incest.

On the day of the alleged murder, Kampikaho's husband sent her away from 'his' home and ordered her to take her children to their father — her brother. It was then that Kampikaho drowned her children in the well. The psychological torture indeed took varied forms, for she also said: 'He would find me cooking and pour the food away, he would pierce my cooking pots, *he really defeated me'* (emphasis original). Kampikaho also deeply believed that her husband had evil, supernatural powers, and that he used them against her. She said:

> And every so often he used to say to me, 'You do not know what I am sitting on, you do not know what is in my house; you will see.' Maybe the death of my children was what he was hoping for; it was this that he was ever alluding to. He also used to practice witchcraft against me. It is because of witchcraft that my legs are so swollen. I still have problems with my legs.

Kampikaho's legs were swollen and looked unhealthy.

It was not only Kampikaho who believed that her husband practised witchcraft, her belief was shared by the village residents. She recalled that some years back, when there was drought in the area, the villagers accused her husband of having stopped rainfall and ordered him to end the drought. When he refused, the family were banned from collecting water from the village well. Presumably it was partly because of the belief that he had supernatural powers that village authorities were extremely cautious with him.

When Kampikaho's husband assaulted her and one of their children, she reported the matter to the RC executive. But when they came to talk to him, he threatened to spear the officials who attempted to handle the problem. No action was taken against him — neither for the assault which had split the child's head nor for threatening violence against the RC authorities.

> *Lillian:* Did he have other wives?
> *Kampikaho:* He never had any other wife but had several prostitutes.

Unlike most of the women abusers I encountered during my research, Kampikaho's husband was 'whether drunk or sober, never a peaceful man'. The wider society which should have come to Kampikaho's rescue failed her. Society seemed so ready to tolerate her husband's whims.

Asked whether she had ever left her husband, Kampikaho said that she had left him numerous times. Her relatives were willing to return his bride price but he had always insisted that he was still interested in his wife and would not take the property. Kampikaho's family always gave in to her husband's wishes; if and when he wanted his bride price, they would give it to him; if and when he wanted his wife, they would hand her over to him. On her part, Kampikaho's duty was to submit to her husband's wishes. She was expected to live with her husband for as long as he demanded it. Indeed, she stayed with him until he chased her and her children out of his home. It was then that she killed the children.

When I interviewed Kampikaho, she was on remand awaiting trial. However, I got the summary of the evidence pertaining to her case, which was in the High Court registry. Not surprisingly, there were a lot of similarities between the contents of the summary and Kampikaho's story regarding her relationship with her husband. The prosecution stated the motive of the offence thus:

> The accused was prompted to drown the children because of domestic harassment and maltreatment meted out to her and the children by her husband. That her husband had denied her access to food by preventing her from getting bananas from the plantation to feed herself and family.

It is worth noting that Kampikaho's story is very similar to the stories of women whose experiences of extreme marital disharmony led to homicidal acts against husbands. This time, however, the children of the abused woman were the eventual victims.

Kagoya, aged 18 years, was a convict of attempted murder and the victim was her 11-month-old baby. She admitted throwing the child in a pit with the intention of killing it. She said she had done so out of anger because 'I was suffering a lot with the child; the child's father refused to give me any financial help. I had no soap, no clothes, nothing for my child.'

Kagoya's parents were both dead and she was living with an uncle whom she felt was already doing enough by looking after her and her two younger siblings. She could not expect him to cater for her child. Although the child's father had accepted paternity, he never came to see Kagoya and the child in hospital at the time of birth. He was a newly married man and did not want his wife ever to learn of his extramarital affair with Kagoya. He never even gave the child a clan name as is the custom among the Basoga of eastern Uganda. The child was nearly a year old when the offence took place, but its father had seen it only twice despite the fact that he lived near the home of Kagoya's uncle. Moreover, on both occasions, Kagoya had to sneak into the home of her lover's brother in order to facilitate the meeting between father and child.

Kagoya's lover may have accepted paternity but he denied her the emotional support she needed as an unmarried mother. Among the Basoga, a name is the strongest 'identity card' because it indicates clan membership. The name is given to the child by its father's family and refusal or neglect to name a child is tantamount to denial of paternity. With neither emotional nor financial support from the child's father, Kagoya resorted to destroying the child.

The story of Adong was similar to the others. At 21 years of age, she attempted to kill her two-and-a-half-year-old son. She admitted (to me) throwing her child in a pit latrine. When I asked her what she had intended to happen to the child she said: 'I wanted him to die in the pit latrine. My family had rejected him, his father's people had rejected him, no one was willing to have me with the baby. I had no where to take him.'

Adong became pregnant at about 18 years of age while attending a senior secondary school. The father of her child was a fellow student at the same school. After she had the child, her father took her back to school saying that she was too young to get married. Two and a half years later, Adong's father died. Her stepbrothers, who were already convinced that their father should never spend money on a girl who had become pregnant, told Adong's mother

— the youngest of four of their father's widows — that they were willing to look after her (their stepmother) on condition that Adong took her child to its father. If Adong could not part with her child then she should go and get married. If Adong's mother failed to get rid of her grandson, her stepsons would not cater for her needs.

When Adong sought assistance from her lover's father, the old man rejected both the baby and its mother. He said that his son had neither the means of looking after the child nor was he ready to marry, before completing his education. When Adong approached her lover, he replied that he was sympathetic but helpless in the face of his 'cruel' parents. It was then that Adong decided to get rid of the child, since nobody was willing to help.

The average sentence given to women convicted of infanticide or attempted murder of their own children under the age of one year was three years. The longest sentence was five years and this was also the most frequent sentence for convictions of infanticide. The longest period in custody was six years, by Tibamanya, who stayed a year on remand and was sentenced to five years' imprisonment. The average period in custody, including remand, was three years and seven months.

A look at the relevant custodial periods regarding women convicted of other homicide-related offences indicates that courts deal rather harshly with infanticide offenders. The average custodial sentence for women for the various violence-related crimes was two years and eight months. On the other hand, the average sentence for women imprisoned for infanticide was three years and ten months. The most frequent sentence for homicide-related offences in general was the same with the most frequent sentence for infanticide — five years. These revelations clearly show that judicial officers merely gave lip-service to the law's supposed acknowledgement that, in cases of infanticide, the women's homicidal acts were beyond the actors' control.

Ugandan law has attempted to lessen the financial burden of an unmarried mother by making it obligatory for the father of the child to contribute to its maintenance. Under the Affiliation Act[11] such a woman may apply to court for a declaration that the man responsible for her pregnancy is the putative (reputed) father of the child (S.3). Before the court makes the declaration, the woman must produce evidence to the effect that the man in question is the (probable) father of the child, and the woman's evidence must be corroborated in some material particular by other evidence (S.5). The court may then, if it sees fit, order the putative father of the child to pay money for the maintenance and education of the child and for expenses incidental to its birth to the mother. Neglect or refusal by the putative father to respect the court's order may lead to civil and punitive court remedies.[12]

In practice, however, the law in question does not offer a viable solution to women's financial problems, for a number of reasons. First, the woman's application must be made either when she is pregnant or within 12 months from the birth of the child; or thereafter, only upon proof that the alleged father ever paid money for the child's maintenance within the first 12 months of its birth.[13] In many cases, women are financially able to maintain children within the first year of birth and the burden only becomes unbearable later when the child's needs expand. By that time, however, they have lost the right to go to court unless the man in question has ever maintained the child as already mentioned. Secondly, the maximum amount of money which the court has jurisdiction to award — one hundred shillings a month until the child is 16 years of age or a lump sum not exceeding fifteen thousand shillings[14] — is not worth the antagonism which is likely to result from what the man is likely to consider a hand over to authority and a betrayal of the relationship. Another factor which makes recourse to the law untenable is ignorance of its existence by the women who need it most — the uneducated and financially weak.

Other child victims

Court records indicated six cases in which a victim of homicide was not the child of the woman offender. And nine of the women in prison directed violence against children other than their own.

Patrilineality and violence against children
Since Ugandan society is patrilineal, children 'belong' to their fathers and when a woman leaves her husband's home, whether

voluntarily or otherwise, the man has, under custom, almost an automatic right to the custody of the couple's children. Even when a man is involved in an extramarital relationship and fathers a child as a result, under custom, he not only has custody rights over that child but he is expected to exercise those rights and to remove the child from its mother so that the child can be brought up in its father's home. Ugandan society hardly differentiates between the rights of an illegitimate and a legitimate child; every child has a right to live in his/her father's home. Similarly, the Ugandan law of succession distributes the property of a man who dies intestate in equal proportions between his legitimate and illegitimate children.[15]

However, it is important to realise that the underlying concept of child 'ownership', or children being 'paternal property', is in itself a form of child abuse. It ignores the very crucial welfare principle which demands that, in determining any issues concerning a child, child custody being an example, the best interests of that child must be the guiding principle. 'Ownership of children' treats the 'owner's' interest as paramount.

Ugandan society gives the woman the role of wife, homemaker and child-minder, but she has no decisive say in the home she makes and the children she minds need not be her own offspring. What is of essence is that the children belong to her husband. It is the man as head of the family who decides which of his children will live in his home; he is the ultimate authority and the wife need not be consulted. This is evidence of the hierarchy and power relations within the Ugandan family. What is given to the wife is the responsibility to physically look after her husband's children whether born to her or to other women and whether born before or after her marriage to their father. Sometimes, children born to women other than the wife are subjected to various forms of abuse, sometimes culminating in permanent deformity and even death.[16] Six of the interviewed women were violent against stepchildren, one was violent against a stepbrother and one was violent against the child of her husband's sister who was living with the offender and her husband. Court records accessed revealed four cases in which the victims of women's violence were stepchildren of the offenders.

Kayita was accused of strangling her husband's six-year-old son. Relating part of her story, she said:

> My husband had an on-and-off extramarital affair with a certain woman and sired a child. After some time my husband decided to bring the child to live with us; the child was by then six years old.
> *Lillian:* Did your husband ask you whether you would be willing to look after the child before bringing him into the home?
> *Kayita:* No, he just told me he was going to bring his child and that I should look after him. I agreed.
> *Lillian:* Had you, before this, knowledge that he had a child outside marriage?
> *Kayita:* I was aware of the child and even knew his mother because she lives with her parents near my home.

Although she denied responsibility for the child's death, Kayita admitted that her marital relationship was not smooth.

> *Lillian:* Did you have any marital problems?
> *Kayita:* That woman was my problem. We used to fight over her and my husband would send me away and then bring her into the house. After quarrelling with the woman, he would send her away and bring me back. This happened twice in our marriage.

In light of the fact that Kayita blamed 'that woman' for her unhappy marriage, it would not be surprising if Kayita, in fact, killed the child.

It may be that Ugandan society assumes that women are psychologically and socially prepared to care for any child, that women have an instinctive ability and interest in caring for any child. This assumption is stretched to such an extent that even when a woman is believed to have either killed the child of a co-wife or attempted to kill her co-wife, the children of the offender are, on her arrest, handed over to the offended co-wife to take care of. Thus, although Natukunda was in prison for conspiring to kill her husband's other woman (an offence she admitted to me and in court), her children were left in the care of the would-be victim when Natukunda was put in prison. Asked why the children were not taken over by her own relatives, Natukunda said: 'Their father can never agree to such an arrangement.' She did not even find it a source of worry or anxiety.

Nalwanga too was in prison for attempting to kill her co-wife, an offence she admitted both in court and to me. Nevertheless, her children were handed over to that very woman whom Nalwanga tried to kill. Although the children stayed in their father's home, it was the wife who catered for their physical needs. Nalwanga expressed regret that her sisters were too poor to look after her children. Besides, they all had very young children of their own to look after. It was a source of great concern to her that her children, especially the youngest, had to be looked after by 'that woman!' But her husband found it only 'proper' to entrust those children to his other wife.

The children of Kayita, who was in prison for allegedly killing her husband's six-year-old son were, since her imprisonment, in the hands of the mother of the deceased child. As soon as Kayita was arrested, her husband brought 'that woman' into the house. At the time of Kayita's arrest, one of her children was aged three years and the other was still breastfeeding.

Nabisinde was indicted for the murder of her husband's 17-year-old son and for the attempted murder of another of her husband's son aged 14 years. After Nabisinde's arrest, her husband brought the mother of the 14-year-old boy into the house. Asked where her children were, Nabisinde repeatedly said: 'My children are in the hands of that woman; she will kill them.' She broke down and cried.

The children were aged six and three years respectively at the time of Nabisinde's arrest. According to Nabisinde, her husband had been married and divorced thrice before he married her. One of the earlier wives became the woman of the house following Nabisinde's arrest. Although Nabisinde had been on good terms with the other two women, she had, throughout her marriage, faced hostility from the very woman who took over the house.

Corporal punishment and child homicide

It is worth noting that some deaths which involved children occurred in the process of those children being subjected to 'disciplinary measures'. According to Gil (1970:vii) 'violence against children ... may be endemic in our society because of a child-rearing philosophy which sanctions and even encourages *the use of physical force in disciplining children*' (my emphasis).

After the facts had been presented in court to Katungwabusha (a woman who killed her stepdaughter) she answered: 'The facts are correct but I did not intend to kill her. I beat her because she had refused to bring the cows to the kraal.' In asking for a deterrent sentence, the state attorney said:

> She committed a very serious crime. The victim was aged only ten years old. The punishment inflicted upon the deceased was out of proportion. Children are vulnerable members of our society and should be protected. A deterrent sentence should be imposed.

In response the defence counsel retorted:

> She found her new husband with four children whom she had been looking after well before this incident. Accused is repentant ...[and] had no intention of killing the deceased. She only wanted to discipline her. I agree that children need protection. This was an unfortunate isolated incident.

In sentencing the accused, the judge observed:

> ... On the other hand this court views with serious concern step parents who treat their stepchildren with heavy hands under the pretext of discipline. Disciplinary measures should never be out of proportion so as to result in death. I agree with Mr Wamasebu [the state attorney] that this court has a duty to protect children, who are so vulnerable, from brutal acts like that of the accused. Considering all the circumstances of this case and the fact that maximum sentence for this sort of offence is life imprisonment, I feel a sentence of five years' imprisonment will serve the interests of justice.

Nakyanzi was accused together with her husband for the death of their 12-year-old nephew. She said that her husband beat the child in the night and the child was found dead the following morning. The beating had been administered purely to discipline the child. Nakyanzi said that since it was an unintended death, the mother of the child had even pleaded to the police to let the culprits free. As Gil (1970:vii) observed in the American context:

> *The dynamics of child abuse [are] thus found to be deeply rooted in the fabric of our culture.* Consequently, the widespread notion that this destructive phenomenon was primarily a symptom of individual psycho-pathology appeared to be too narrow an interpretation of the wide spectrum of child abuse (my emphasis).

In Katungwabusha's case, the court said that society must view with serious concern parents who treat their stepchildren with heavy hands under the pretext of discipline. However, in agreement with Gil, I contend that the solution does not solely lie in meting heavy punishment to the culprits. The problem does not lie with individuals. It lies with society's notion about the status of children on the one hand, and the role and status of women on the other.

Instead of declaring, as the court did, that disciplinary measures should never be out of proportion, we must:

> ... attack this violence at its source by changing our prevailing child-rearing philosophy and practice. We must reject the use of physical force in disciplining children, ... the deep-seated traditions which shape prevailing childrearing practices, and which need to be overcome if fundamental changes are to be widely accepted (Gil 1970:vii).

Traditionally, parents regard corporal punishment as a legitimate way of disciplining children. However, in a fit of anger some of them may find it difficult to draw a line between acceptable levels of physical punishment and excessive violence that is tantamount to abuse. Therefore, an attempt to draw a line between acceptable and excessive physical punishment is a futile exercise. We should instead reject corporal punishment as a form of disciplining children, or any other person, for that matter.

Stepmothers as first suspects

Among the six women charged with killing their stepchildren, none admitted guilt to me. The cases against them were based on circumstantial evidence. The story of Nabisinde, who was indicted for poisoning her husband's 17-year-old son, is evidence of the contradiction in terms of what society expects of a stepmother. She is expected to nurture the children of her husband, but society doubts her good will towards hem. She narrated her story thus:

> I visited David at his school on a Sunday and took him some food. From the time I became his [father's] girlfriend, it is me who used to visit my husband's children at school. He had no time for that. On the Tuesday following my visit, at around 11 AM while I was at home with my children, the headmaster of the school came with the police. I knew him very well and so I welcomed him. I was immediately asked whether I had visited the school on Sunday and I said yes. After all I had even signed the visitors' book as was required by the school regulations. The headmaster immediately said *I am a stepmother and had, therefore, taken poisoned food to my husband's children.* I said, of course I am a stepmother, but after that I was immediately ordered to enter the police car. All I could hear being said repeatedly was the fact that I am a stepmother. At the police station all I could hear being repeatedly said was that I was a stepmother, that I was a killer (original emphasis).

Mukandori, together with her husband, was arrested for the death of her husband's daughter. The allegation was that the two beat the child to death. Mukandori was aged 45 years at the time of the offence. She was a mother of five children and also used to look after her husband's four children, the victim included. At the time of the offence, the mother of the other children, who had been a junior wife to Mukandori, had left the home. Mukandori and her husband were cattle-keepers. Neither had attended formal school.

Later on, the case against the husband was dropped but Mukandori was convicted of manslaughter. The court records indicated that, in the opinion of the state attorney, the evidence revealed by a perusal of the case papers supported the charge of murder against Mukandori but was insufficient to warrant a case against her husband.

Mukandori's version of the story was, however, different. She said that on the fatal day, her husband beat his daughter for failure to tend the cattle properly. When the child died both husband and wife were arrested by the village officials and taken to the police station. Mukandori said:

> On the way to the police station, I heard one of the village officials say to my husband, 'When you go to the police you tell them that it is your wife who beat up the child; *after all, she is a stepmother to the victim; who would not believe it?*' At the police, my husband said that I had beaten the child to death for having eaten food without permission (my emphasis).

Whereas society expects women to look after their husbands' children, at the same time it perpetuates the myth of the cruel stepmother.

Conclusion

My analysis of women's violence against their own children revealed that women tend to be violent while under emotional stress resulting from diverse social and/or economic causes. Society's attitude towards a divorced woman such as Tibamanya is that she, not her husband, has failed in marriage. Society's attitude towards a girl who becomes pregnant out of wedlock is that she is a loose girl. Both kinds of women are regarded as a disgrace to their families. When, under such pressure, a woman gives birth to an unwanted child, she may decide to end its life.

Just like the women whom the law treated as having committed infanticide, the other categories of women whose violence was directed towards their own offspring acted under intense emotional stress arising out of unstable family conditions. The close similarity between the circumstances under which the women who were charged with infanticide committed the offences, and those who were charged with other homicide offences against their own offspring, raises one important question: Is the predominant cause of child-killing *puerperal mental disturbance* as assumed by Section 206 of the Uganda Penal Code; or is it socio-economic forces, such as an attempt to save the honour and reputation of an unmarried girl in a society that stigmatises pre-marital pregnancies; or is it the realisation, especially by unmarried mothers, of their financial inability to cater for the child's needs?

It may be that the law is more ready to portray women as ill than it is to expose the stifling social conditions and oppressive constraints of traditional female roles that contribute to the women's criminal acts. As Roberts (1994:11) said in another context, Ugandan society is more willing to cure women's diseases than to change women's social circumstances.

Women's violence against children other than their own offspring is a result of a patriarchal culture which gives the male the final say in family matters including the welfare of children. It is a result of societal practices which forcefully limit a woman's range of options and assign her the role of a child minder. Society renders woman powerless and forces her to resort to violence against children. For as Straus et al (1980:242) maintain about the American family, even in Uganda:

> The family is the outstanding example of a social institution which assigns jobs and responsibilities based on a person's sex ... rather than interest, competence, or ability. As long as we expect ... women to care for children because they are women, we are going to have potential conflict and violence in homes....

Child homicides are probably expositions of the fallacy that women have 'natural' mothering instincts and roles.

Notes

1. Section 206 of the U.P.C.: Where a woman by any wilful act of omission causes the death of her child being a child under the age

of twelve months, but at the time of the act or omission the balance of her mind was disturbed by the reason of birth to the child or by reason of the child, then, ... she shall offence be dealt with and punished as if she had been guilty of the offence of manslaughter of the child.

2. Section 238(1) of the Danish Criminal Code.

3. An even deeper insight can be read from the father's disappointment. Among the Bakiga (the ethnic group to which Kinengyere belonged), an educated girl fetches more bride price than her uneducated counterpart. Therefore taking a girl to school does not only improve her chances of good employment but also ensures her male relatives high bride price.

4. The grandmother's rejection of the sick child was probably for two reasons. One is that medical treatment is very expensive and it is unlikely that the old woman could afford the bills. Another reason is that among most Ugandan societies it is almost taboo to bury an unrelated person at the ancestral grounds of the his/her mother's family. Where this rule must be broken a lot of purification rituals are performed at the risk of the misfortune befalling the family which has buried a person who does not belong to the clan. The ceremonies involve spending money which the old woman most likely did not have.

5. This sometimes is done by urban parents as punishment to a child who is a disgrace to them; such are girls who become pregnant while at school. For anyone who has been brought up in the city, life in the village is great hardship. It is also done by parents because they do not want their associates to learn of what they consider a shame to the family — a daughter's pre-marital pregnancy.

6. E.g., robbery C/S 272 and 273 of the U.P.C.; attempted robbery C/S 274 of the U.P.C.

7. Section 150A(1) of the U.P.C.: Any man who has sexual intercourse with any married woman not being his wife commits adultery. Section 150A(2) of the U.P.C.: Any married woman who has sexual intercourse with any man not being her husband commits adultery.

8. Section 27.

9. M.M.A. 665/93.

10. Section 9(1) of the U.P.C.: Subject to the express provisions of this Code relating to negligent acts and omissions, a person is not criminally responsible for an act or omission which occurs independently of the exercise of his will....

11. Chapter 217 of the Laws of Uganda.

12. S.5(2): The court may order that the money due be recovered by distress and sale of the putative father's goods and chattels. Court may also order that the man be detained until the money due has been recovered from the said sale. And under S.5(3): If no sufficient distress can be had, then the court may commit the putative father to prison for a term not exceeding three months unless he pays the maintenance money and reasonable charges attending the distress.

13. S.3 of the Act.

14. S.5.

15. Sections 3 and 28(1)(a)(iv) of the Succession Act. Non-discrimination of children on the basis of circumstances of birth is in itself a positive attribute of Ugandan society but it may not be fair to the wife and her children. In marriage the spouses' financial affairs become so inextricably entangled that it is hardly possible to distinguish property belonging to either party. In most cases the property is registered in the man's name. On his death therefore it will be treated as his property to be divided equally among his children — those belonging to the wife and those he may have had with other women. Illegitimate children of unmarried mothers may thus be in a better position, getting part of their 'father's' property and all their mother's property.

16. The presence of stepchildren in a home has been recognised as a risk factor for spousal conflict and violence in America, albeit in a different context. Wilson and Daly (1992:199) reported that:

> ... children live with stepfather and natural mother much more than the reverse. Stepparents are much more often hostile and assaultive toward their wards than are natural parents (e.g., Daly and Wilson 1992; Flinn 1988; Wilson and Daly 1987).

V

Polygamy and Women's Violence

'[I]t is a known fact that every social phenomenon, good or bad, is the outcome of functioning of society. Social values, traditions, and rituals do contribute in shaping that phenomenon' (Tariq 1981:1).

What peculiar characteristics of the Ugandan family structure tend to contribute to women's familial violence?

The Woman I Share With My Husband

> I won't deny
> I am a bit jealous
> Lying is no good
> We all suffer
> From a touch of jealousy
> Jealousy seizes us
> And makes us feverish.
> (Okot p'Bitek, a Ugandan poet)

During my perusal of court records, I came across 13 cases in which the victims were co-wives ('the husbands' other women') and four cases in which the victims were children of such women (stepchildren). Among the 66 women I interviewed in prison 17 (26 percent) were violent within polygamous unions. Nine of the women directed their violence towards their husband's other women, six were violent towards stepchildren, one was violent towards a stepmother and one was violent toward a stepbrother.[1]

Sometimes husbands were also killed, because they had married other women, leading to the deterioration of the relationship with the first wives. In at least four cases of husband killing, court records indicated that marital problems between the victims and their wives had stemmed from the husbands having married other women. In one such case (H.C.C.S.C. No. 56/77), the judge justified a lenient sentence against the accused on the ground that: 'She was clearly very much provoked by her husband, who had transferred his affections to another woman.'

In yet another case (H.C.C.S.C. No. 62/69), the judge explained why he had found the accused guilty of manslaughter rather than murder in the following words: 'I have stretched the law and the evidence to the utmost in her favour; ... the fact that her husband had other wives must have added to the normal difficulties of married life....'

Similarly, in my interviews with women who killed husbands, it was often revealed that one of the sources of conflict was the husbands' involvement with other women. Such were the stories of Asiimwe, Byarugaba, Agaba and others.

Most societies in Uganda are potentially polygamous and Uganda marriage-law recognises polygamous unions as valid marriages.[2] It should be noted that the practice is not new to Ugandan or African society. According to Maillu (1988:1):

> Africa has practised polygamy as far back as the records can take us. ... It is and has always been a way of life in Africa. ... Since the arrival of the Whiteman in Africa, ... he has been doing his best to abolish polygamy. ... Yet the tradition has continued to survive.

Statistics to indicate the number of polygamists in Ugandan society are difficult to obtain, but I will borrow Maillu's argument that, since the worldwide ratio of women to men is 51:49, polygamy is usually practised by only a small percentage of the population of any given country, Uganda inclusive. This is because:

> There is only a small surplus of women who are available to married men as second, third, fourth or whatever number of wives. Nature does not produce as many women as would make it possible for every man or nearly every man in Africa to be a polygamist (Maillu 1988:2).

The ratio of polygamists in any society is even smaller than the surplus of women to men because some men marry more than two wives, reducing even further the possibility of other men taking on even a second wife. Maillu (1988:41) also said that even in traditional Africa not every man had more than one wife and that this is borne out by genealogical records.

The prevalence of polygamy in Uganda varies from one ethnic group or region to the other. Whereas Ntozi and Kabera (1991) reported it was 27 percent in Ankole, Curley (1973) put it at 33 percent in Lango, and Schopper (1991) said it was 33 percent in Madi. Kaijuka et al (1989) reported that, nationally, formal polygamy is lowest among the youth in western Uganda and he attributed this to Christianity. It is highest in the east; Kaijuka claimed that this was due to the concentration of Muslims in that part of the country.

Does polygamy precipitate women into familial violence? According to Mushanga (1974:110,111):

> Of all situations, relations, and interactive processes that bring about conflict and hatred among human beings, sexual jealousy seems to stand out as one of the most leading factors. Sexual jealousy results from the human desire to dominate and monopolise and also to enjoy uninterrupted sexual relationship with one's sexual partner. ... Jealousy, the attitude of envy towards a person who shows tendencies of affection towards one's lover, is a fence that surrounds sexual partners. Any attempt to make an opening in the fence calls for immediate and spontaneous reaction which is directed toward the intruder. The reaction ... which takes the form of aggression, may be directed toward either the individual who is making the affectionate gestures, or the one to whom such gestures are made. Thus, in what Americans call the love triangle, one of the three who make up the triangle may direct his aggression either to one or both. ... Some of these situations lead to violent encounters and end up in aggravated assaults and often in homicides.

Of love triangles (though not polygamy) in Ceylon, Straus and Straus (1953:463) reported that an important motive for homicide is unfaithfulness, and that 'in these cases, killing the mate or the rival is the traditionally acceptable solution, or, alternatively, one can commit suicide.'

Rivalry between co-wives is as old as polygamy, a fact evidenced by the meanings of the different words for co-wife in the different vernaculars of Uganda's societies. For example, in Luo a co-wife is referred to as *nyieko,* while in Lusoga she is *oweiwali.* In both languages the words mean jealousy of an intense kind. In my interviews with members of polygamous marriages, most women admitted having quarrelled with their co-wives. In fact, they said that quarrels between co-wives are inevitable. Many compared the situation of co-wives to that of a man carrying empty containers (gourds) in a basket; he 'cannot realistically expect them not to knock against each other' — *Agali awalala tigalema kukonagana.*

The question, therefore, is: has such rivalry always culminated in violence in general or homicides in particular? Asked whether co-wives of the past ever killed each other or each other's children, several elders in Bugono village answered: 'Yes, through witchcraft.' Many of them, however, had never heard of a woman using a weapon such as a knife against a co-wife. I was continually told that the level/degree of conflict between co-wives today is much higher than it was before. Many of the elders said they had never in the past heard of homicides arising out of co-wifeship. What is the cause of this change? In his study of homicides in western Uganda, Mushanga (1974:87) observed:

> A polygamous marriage has its own problems and creates situations in which strain and dispute can easily start. Disputes erupt between co-wives, between sons and their stepmothers, between wives as a group against husband and so on.

According to him, five percent of the victims in his study were slain in polygamous family patterns.

My interview with Namukasa, who allegedly threw acid in the face of her co-wife, also revealed what society expects of the polygamous relationship. Denying involvement in the offence, she said:

> I do not know who assaulted my co-wife but ... my being accused is because I am her co-wife. That is co-wifeship; even when a co-wife suffers malaria, fingers are pointed at you; you are the obvious cause of her ailment....[3]

In yet another case in which a woman was charged with setting the house of a co-wife on fire and thereby killing her co-wife's child, the accused (Mugisa) said to me:

> I had no previous quarrels with my co-wife; I am even the one who prepared the festivities for her marriage ceremony to my husband. That child I am alleged to have killed was born in my house, why would I want him dead? ... I was not anywhere near the house when it caught fire but as soon as my co-wife's relatives arrived on the scene with her, they said to her: *'Do not be silly, of course it is your co-wife who has done this to you.'* My co-wife said: 'I did not see her do it,' but later she was convinced into believing it and, in fact, she made a statement at the police to the effect that I, together with my two daughters, had set her house on fire (my emphasis).

The same negative assumptions about co-wifeship were brought up in my conversation with Nabwami, who was on remand for allegedly killing her grandmother. Denying the offence, Nabwami said:

> I am the second wife to my husband, and whereas I have no child, my co-wife has children. ... How could I have killed my own grandmother and yet I had a co-wife? If I could accept a co-wife, how could I have killed my grandmother? How could I kill my grandmother when I never touched my stepchildren; these are the people one would most likely not want to share anything with; these are the people whom one would not want her things to be given to. I used to work very hard and had even bought iron sheets. I was about to have my house roofed with iron sheets. My husband had never stayed in a house roofed with iron sheets before but I

had managed to acquire iron sheets. I had planted coffee trees and was hoping to get money from the crop. The first people I could have resented to have a share in my success would be my stepchildren and my co-wife, not my own blood and flesh. My husband had given each of us equal land to till and on harvest, the food would be shared equally between us (the wives), yet I had no children. My husband would sell the produce and the money would buy us clothes, including the children. He would even use the money to take my stepchildren to school. If I was willing to have my sweat spent on stepchildren, how could I hate the small task of cooking for my old woman?

Patrilocality and violence between co-wives

In his analysis of polygamy in Kenya, Maillu (1988:78) contended that one of the cornerstones of successful polygamy is the provision of at least separate houses, but preferably separate homes for each wife, and that such was the normal arrangement in traditional polygamy as practised in nearly every ethnic group. But he also pointed out that:

> The modern polygamy is fast developing a new brand of polygamists who ... are treating their wives more or less like domestic animals destined to live in a common shed. ... A man who thinks that all he needs is a big house with many bedrooms for his wives *is committing a terrible social evil* of not registering the fact that the union of a man and woman is a very personal one and psychologically it demands to be consummated privately. ... Although they share one man for a husband, *that man should realise that the two women are not married to each other.* ... He can force them to live in one house as the case with some modern uncultured polygamist, *but he cannot force them to like each other.* When he forces them *to live in one place ... they, in turn, spend most of their energy consciously and unconsciously trying to fight against each other* (my emphasis).

After his study of the patterns of homicides and suicides in Bunyoro, and in particular reference to a case in which a woman killed one of her co-wives, Beattie (1960:141) commented that 'it would be strange if in the close social confines of a polygynous African homestead ample pretexts for friction did not exist.'

The situation in which Komugisa killed her co-wife illustrates the tension faced by co-wives living under one roof or in one homestead. After seven years in marriage, her husband got another wife. But before bringing the wife into the home, he told Komugisa to visit her parents. She stayed at her parents' place without hearing from her husband. After six months her husband came to collect her and also informed her that he had married another woman.

> *Lillian:* Were you living in the same house with your co-wife?
> *Komugisa:* At first we were, but there was so much tension that later on, in order to get peace, my husband told me to leave the main house and to stay in the kitchen. The *mugole* (bride) stayed in the main house.

About her experience with a co-wife in the same homestead, Komugisa stressed:

> If this woman had never been brought into the home, I would never have gone through all this, would never have ended up here. Once you are together with another woman you are likely to conflict, fight, etc.

Since conflict in polygamous unions is inevitable, Komugisa preferred a husband getting a mere girlfriend or mistress to his getting another wife. About the fatal incident, Komugisa said:

> I was sitting outside my house (the kitchen) when my co-wife passed by me, entered my bedroom and removed my blanket from my bed. I asked her why she had taken my blanket but she did not answer me. Instead she started abusing me. A fight erupted when she hit me with a stick. I was annoyed and so I picked a hoe and struck her once. She died immediately.

Karugaba, who killed her husband, also found the idea of living next door to a co-wife intolerable. She said:

How can I go to sleep knowing that my husband is lying with another woman just next door. Just knowing that one's husband has another woman makes one crazy enough without having to see her every day.

Threats to women's socio-economic status: Natukunda's story

The stories of some women's violent reactions indicate that provocation or threats are not limited to physical violence. Some women have killed persons who did not pose physical threats but were threats to the offenders' socio-economic status, threats to their status as wives: the only meaningful status that society has prepared such women for. Such is the case of Natukunda, who reacted violently in order to destroy the economic threat posed by another woman. Natukunda's story is the story of a woman who regarded marriage as an economic unit.

What Carlen and Worrall (1987:9,11) said of British law can be said of Ugandan culture. It creates social situations in which women may be driven to violent behaviour. It puts women in an inferior socio-economic status and forces some of them to resort to crime as a means of fighting legitimatised inequality and oppression.

Natukunda was convicted of conspiracy to murder; the intended victim was another woman: a girlfriend of her husband whom the husband intended to marry. The 'other woman' was already expecting his child. At the time of the offence, Natukunda was a 30-year-old mother of two children.

> *Lillian:* How did you meet your husband?
> *Natukunda:* We had a love affair and I became pregnant. I was scared of my parents since I was still at school (in Senior 4). So I ran away from home and joined my husband. After some time my husband and his family went and told my parents that I was with them. My husband then paid bride price. I was 16 years old; he was 25.

Lillian: Can you explain the trouble which brought you into prison?

Natukunda: After we had stayed several years in marriage, we moved to Kampala. My husband got premises and both of us were involved in trade. After some time, I started commuting between Kampala and Nairobi to get things for sale. We succeeded in our business and my husband bought a lorry. The lorry was used to ferry matooke from Mbarara to Kampala. ... After some time, my husband suggested that we go back and settle in Mbarara. He also said that the trade we were involved in was no longer paying because of high taxes. That moreover it was a strain for me to continue commuting between Nairobi and Kampala. He said that he had, therefore, decided to use the available money to buy a taxi. ... We went back to Mbarara but after some time my husband changed and stopped telling me how he was using the proceeds from the vehicles. Although we had acquired two shops in Mbarara, he told me to stop working in the shops and to sit at home. Whenever I made any inquiries about our business, he would ask me whether I was not a woman. 'A woman should not ask me how I am spending money,' he would say.

After some time, he informed me that he was going to marry another woman and take her to church. He wanted to bring the woman in the same house with me but I refused. By this time I had two sons and had been married for 14 years. He refused to tell me who that woman was but I eventually learnt who it was. ... It was a school girl he had made pregnant. I knew the family and the family knew me as my husband's wife. My husband wanted to bring his second wife to the house but I refused. He then started mistreating me. He stopped buying anything in the house and would, whenever I asked for things, say: 'Who are you not to take sugarless tea or salt-less food?' It was obvious he wanted me to leave the home; he did everything to make it impossible for me to stay.

For about two months I was not speaking a word to him. I would prepare and serve food for him but without a word. I thought of committing suicide but later changed my mind. My mother lived near so I went and talked to her. I told her I would kill my husband in his sleep but she advised me to leave the man and go back to her. Eventually my husband said I should at least give him some space, should leave the home for a while so that he could bring his new wife. I left for my sister's place in Kampala and two weeks after that my husband brought the girl into the house.

My husband came to Kampala and told me that he would give me 500,000/= (Uganda shillings) but that I should not go back to his home for he already had another wife. That I was to stay in Kampala. He informed me that he had already formally introduced himself to the girl's family and preparations for a church wedding had commenced. That the money he was offering me would help me set up some business. ... I was mad; I had worked for years, had been married for 14 years, and together we had made wealth; of this wealth he was offering me a mere 500,000/= shillings. I rejected the money.

My husband informed me that he was just being of help; after all, 'his' wealth belonged to his children, not to me. He added that, moreover, he had a budget of eight million shillings for the wedding and could not afford to give me any more money. ... I informed him that if I found the woman in my home I would kill her. I also informed my sister that if I went back to Mbarara I would certainly kill somebody. My husband left for Mbarara but the following day I followed him to Mbarara. I found that the girl had been taken back to her parents. I met my husband and insisted that at least I be given a car but he just called his friends and derided me. He called me a thief. I suggested that at least he leave me in my home (i.e., the house we had been living in), but he refused. The house would be the venue for his wedding and he would not part with it, he said. I asked that at least I be given the house which was being built in town but he refused. I said to him that if indeed the fixed assets belonged to our children as he had told me before, then they should be registered in the children's names. He agreed that the two shops in Mbarara were for our two children. I asked for five million shillings to enable me set up some business so that I could look after myself but he refused.

Later on I decided that in order not to lead my children to lose everything offered to them, I would accept the offer of the two shops for them. ... I then suggested that we go to a lawyer to have it in writing and he agreed. At the lawyer's, my husband said the shops would become the property of the two sons on their father's death. Yet I had wanted to use the shops to generate money even if it meant me having to cater for the children's school fees, etc. My husband refused: he would be the one to use the shops to get money; after all, the children were his, he said. I insisted that I deserved something as an individual.

The lawyer agreed with me but my husband decided to give me only one million Uganda shillings. I decided to accept the money but made up my mind to kill the woman. ... Before all this I had, on learning about his love affair, approached the father of the girl and told him to stop his daughter from interfering in my marriage. That was before the girl's pregnancy and the father had said he would see what he could do about it. But when the girl became pregnant, it was the girl's family who insisted that my husband had to marry their daughter and in church, otherwise my husband would be taken to court for impregnating a school girl....

For a second time I decided to discuss the issue with the girl's father. I went and hired the father's taxi, pretending that I wanted to be taken somewhere; the father was the driver. He had agreed and when we reached a lonely place I had thought of knifing him but realised that this would only postpone the wedding but not put an end to it, since my rival would still be alive. And if I ended up in prison for killing her father I would not be able to fight my enemy, I had reasoned to myself. I had a knife with me that time. I changed my mind and instead decided to talk to him about his daughter. The father just said: 'If you have failed in your marriage let my daughter try her luck.' This really annoyed me. Moreover, I had heard rumours that the girl was bragging that she would enjoy free things, things she had not worked for, by marrying my husband. 'After all, I am pregnant; what can Natukunda do?' my rival had said.

Lillian: How could he have agreed to take you in his car?
Natukunda: I think he thought I did not care that much about my husband's getting another wife. After all, in court this very man said that a man has a right to get as many wives as he could financially afford.

Natukunda continued to say:

At the lawyer's place my husband had given me only 500,000 shillings and said the rest would be given to me after his wedding. I went and hired two army men to go and kill the girl. I was to pay them after the act. They agreed to work before payment because they knew my story; they were sympathetic to my plight since they were boys from my village. The two men attempted to get into the girl's home. One night, just like a visitor would, they knocked at her father's place where she was and the door was opened for them. But before they had entered the mother realised that they were with guns and before they shot her daughter, the mother raised an alarm. The two had managed to escape. After this I decided that I would do it myself. I decided to go with a *panga* (machete) to the girl's place in broad daylight. I told a cousin, a 19-year-old boy to escort me to go and fight my rival. He did not however know that I had a *panga*. There were however several people in the home of my rival and I was apprehended before I could complete my mission. On being arrested, a machete was found on me. We were arrested by the RC and taken to the police. My cousin is also now serving a prison sentence.

Lillian: If your husband had not been threatened with court action, do you think he would have ever thought of bringing the said girl as a second wife?

Natukunda: Well, I believe he had long ago decided to get a second wife. He had first had an affair with my stepsister, my father's daughter, and had even had the nerve to tell me that she was beautiful, that he was in love with her and was going to marry her. You see, men from Ankole have no respect for women. I had put my foot down and said no. After that he informed me that his decision to get another wife still stood and I was wasting my time. After I had resisted his plans, some of his relatives derided him that apparently he was being ruled by a woman. Some told him that they were ready to contribute to the bride price, but of course some were not in for the idea.

Natukunda's admission that her husband had made up his mind to get a second wife, long before his relationship with the girl Natukunda attempted to kill, is testimony to the futility of her violence. What needed to be eliminated was the existing unjust social order and not the individual. But since she had no means to change that order she directed her violence toward the only target she could clearly identify.

The man's decision to take his second wife to church must have added to Natukunda's sense of betrayal. As already mentioned,

Ugandan society accords a higher status (social, though, not legal) to church weddings than to customary or other civil marriages.[4]

> *Lillian:* What do you think is the best forum for solving marital problems: the police, the RC, relatives, friends, courts?
> *Natukunda:* The village RC is not useful due to the calibre of people on the executive. When the life you lead is better than the life most people live, how can you expect them to understand your problems? To such men you are a woman raising dust unnecessarily. Their belief is that once a man has money he has a right to get as many women as he wants.

Natukunda had dropped out of school before attaining any professional qualifications. She had put all her eggs in one basket — trade with her husband (her marriage was an economic unit). It was this future that her husband was determined to disrupt, just as the pregnancy had disrupted her education. In his act, he was supported by the immediate community in which they lived. For example, Natukunda's father, himself a polygamist, could not understand Natukunda's fight against polygamy. The father of Natukunda's rival bluntly told Natukunda that she had failed in her marriage and it was now the turn of another, and like the RCs, his view was that a man could have as many women as he desired as long as he could financially cater for them. The state prosecutor in Natukunda's case was right when he summed up his submission in these words: '[It was] a case of extreme emotion, ... *loss of hope and despair*' (my emphasis).

This was, however, a case — perhaps one of the very few cases — in which several members of the criminal justice system seemed to appreciate the position of a woman in a patriarchal society. The premise of the defence lawyer's appeal to the court for leniency towards Natukunda correctly described her dilemma. The defence lawyer informed the court that Natukunda had, while at school been impregnated by her then-boyfriend, later-turned-husband. As a result, she had to drop out of school. For 14 years she had worked hard to build up the property which her partner was now handing over to another woman. The circumstances had made Natukunda feel she had been treated like a porter by her partner. In addition, she had been denied custody of her children. The lawyer also drew the attention of the court to the fact that, in Ugandan society, it was unlikely that any other man would want to marry a woman who had previously been married — for 14 years. The lawyer submitted that under such circumstances Natukunda's reaction, though criminal, called for sympathy.

In passing the sentence, the magistrate acknowledged the seriousness of Natukunda's predicament. He gave the reason for the court's 'leniency' thus:

> ... she is a woman to sympathise with. [Her husband] seems to me to be a beast with no human consideration. He is ungrateful and I dare say utterly stupid. [Natukunda], after 14 years of ... faithful service found herself just thrown to the wind — second-hand, no prospect for marriage. This is Africa: where male chauvinism does not accept second-hand thrown-away women. ... She was motivated by anguish, the sense of loss....

However, it is hardly surprising that despite 14 years of 'faithful service', Natukunda walked out with hardly anything; after all, wives are unpaid family workers. Reading the magistrate's pronouncements one cannot also but ask: What is the place of emotional violence? — the kind of violence that Natukunda had been subjected to?

The magistrate's comments are also evidence of society's view of the role and place of a woman. In his opinion, Natukunda's predicament arose from the fact that she would henceforth be unmarriageable. He was silent on the financial hardship she would suffer, but implicit in his comments was the idea that a woman's comfort is derived from marriage.

Natukunda's action was evidently economically motivated and she made a conscious decision to offend in order to ensure financial security for herself. Her case supports Totman's (1978) assertion that: '... female killers, rather than acting out of passion, make a deliberate and conscious decision to kill ... to resolve a personal dilemma.'

Natukunda's analysis of the differences between one's husband having an extramarital affair on the one hand and a co-wife on the other, again emphasises the fact of economic motivation.

> *Lillian:* If your husband's intention had been to keep the said girl as a girlfriend rather than as a wife, would you have reacted in the same way?
> *Natukunda:* In a way a girlfriend is less of a threat insofar as property issues are concerned. All she ever gets are food and clothes. In any case until one is a wife there is hope that the husband would drop such a girl. The problem, however, is with AIDS. When a man is running [with] a girlfriend, that girl has no security in the relationship and is likely to move around with other men in addition your husband. You are therefore at risk of getting AIDS.
> ... But on the other hand, once a man declares a woman as his wife then it means that the new woman too has expectations in relation to the property you have worked for. She feels she has a right to share in the property.

Natukunda then reflected on the role of the law:

> The only way in which men will be controlled in their bad habits is if the law says that when a man and woman divorce/separate, all the property must be shared equally, even if the property is as little as a needle. The law should also state that once a man lives with a girl for at least two years as his wife then she is regarded as his wife. It is only then that men will stop playing around with people's daughters. Many times a man rents a house for a girl and even controls her life, setting rules as to what she should and should not do, but when he is tired of her he just abandons her; nothing is done to him, yet all along he has wasted the girl's time. Many times a man starts living with a girl, even starts visiting her parents (even if he never goes through customary ceremonies); the parents start regarding him as their daughter's husband and then such a man one day just leaves the said girl. After all, what is there to show that they are married? The law should declare as it is in England (sic) that as long as one brings a woman into his house she is a wife. A woman who stays with a man must be treated as a wife for she is different from one who is taken to hotels and lodging houses just for sexual pleasure. A woman who

lives in the home is, unlike the prostitute, not paid for her services and yet she contributes to the man's wealth. Sometimes even women who have jobs suffer when their men get other wives. And you see, men never want women to have independent money. If a woman is making money, what the husband does is to stop buying anything in the home so that all the woman's money is spent. The man may use his income to build a house. He is free to give the house to another woman. That is why the law should declare that in marriage, property be jointly owned.
Lillian: Do you think the law has any role to play in solving marital problems?
Natukunda: The law in Uganda should copy the Rwanda case: that where a man marries another wife he is obliged to pay a tax — the amount being dependant on the value of his property at the time — which money is given to the first wife as personal property. The rule is based on the assumption that a man only gets another woman because he has a lot of money. Right now, men take women as their property. That is why they are proud to have hard-working women: just to exploit them and then get rid of them.

As Natukunda narrated how much she had contributed to the family wealth and how she attempted to make her husband give her a reasonable share of that property, it was clear, to use the words of Carlen (1983:42) in another context, that women justify their own extreme acts of violence on the ground that legitimate and effective protest was not open to them.

Natukunda's story also brings to light the inadequacies of the Uganda law insofar as fair distribution of property between husband and wife on divorce is concerned. Although there has been judicial acknowledgement of a woman's right to own and dispose of property, and although Uganda law does not differentiate a married from an unmarried woman, the marriage laws operating in the country are all silent about women's property rights within marriage. Laws on succession and divorce as well as on land do not recognise women's invaluable contributions to 'family property'.

The law governing divorce is the Divorce Act. But this does not apply to the dissolution of customary marriages. In the case of these marriages, divorce falls under customary law. Since divorce is the dissolution of a marriage, the relevant question is: What happens to family property in the event of divorce? Though the Act does not directly address this question, it provides that where a judicial separation has been decreed, the wife is to be treated as unmarried with respect to her property which she may have acquired after separation. She is therefore free to deal with that property as if she were unmarried. If she dies intestate during the subsistence of the separation, her husband would not be entitled to any portion of that property.

Whereas this provision protects property acquired by the wife after the separation, it does not ensure that on such separation, the wife is entitled to any part of the matrimonial property. Additionally, under Section 19, the Act purports to protect the wife's proprietary rights where a husband has deserted her. Under this provision, a wife in whose property the husband has acquired an interest by virtue of the marriage may, if deserted by him, apply for a court order to protect any property which she may have obtained or may obtain after the desertion. The order would protect her property against the husband and his creditors.

Again this provision only protects property which the woman obtained after the desertion. Would it not be fairer that such husbands lose rights acquired by virtue of the marriage, even in property which the wife acquired before the desertion, since the basis of that right has been put to an end by the husband? The apparent protection given to such a wife is made more of a mockery when the section gives the husband a right to apply to court for a discharge of the order where the desertion has ceased. Since the property belongs to a wife, it should be the wife to choose whether the order should be varied or discharged. It is even possible for a husband to return to the wife in order to use her property to settle his debts and then desert her again.

The law of divorce is not only inadequate in protecting the wife's property but it is also discriminatory against women. Under Section 27, where a woman's adultery has been the cause of the divorce or judicial separation and such a wife is entitled to any property, the court may order the whole or part of the property to go to the husband and/or the children. A man is not subjected to this punishment even when he is the guilty party. Should the law not separate questions of morality from proprietary rights? And why should the law treat men and women differently?

Although the Divorce Act does not make provision for the division of property on divorce, courts often divide such property between the two parties. Wide discretionary powers are given to courts by Section 17 of the Married Women's Property Act which empowers them to settle questions of title between a wife and husband. There are no specific rules on how property should be divided. Consequently, there is confusion and, sometimes, contradictory decisions as some cases reveal a marked difference of opinion amongst judges.

Although in cases where each party made direct contribution to the buying of property courts will generally order division of the sales of property in ratios representing the contributions, the position on indirect contributions is not certain. For example, where both spouses are working and they agree that the easiest way to buy a house is for the husband to save his earnings, while the wife pays the household bills or buys children's clothes, whose house should it be? Is it fair to declare that the house belongs to the husband because payment comes exclusively from his earnings? Is it not obvious that the acquisition was made possible only because the wife's contribution to the home 'freed' her husband's income?

Besides, what if the wife is not formally employed but gives unpaid help in the home as is the case in the majority of Ugandan homes? A wife's contribution in the home should, in all fairness, be given economic value. For it is now widely acknowledged that women's domestic roles make it possible for their family members to exchange their labour power for wages.

It is only if women's contribution is recognised that they will ever be said to have a beneficial interest in 'their husband's property.' Without such recognition women will more often than not become paupers on divorce. For as Isaacman and Stephen (1980:52) observe: 'It is not at all uncommon in cases of separation for a man to expel a wife from his home with nothing but the clothes she is wearing.'

Another form of injustice to a wife on divorce occurs where though she did not contribute to the purchasing of property, she made improvements on it. Whereas men traditionally own the land, wives usually till it and many even contribute towards building a house on that land. However, such efforts do not give them any interest in such land. The injustice of such laws was revealed in the case of *Edith Nakiyingi v Zadeke* (1973 H.C.B., 23). The parties had been married for 12 years during which time the wife tilled the husband's land. A house was also erected on that land and the wife contributed some iron sheets towards its construction. The husband terminated the marriage and ordered the wife to leave the house.

The Court of Appeal held that, although in law expending money on another person's property does not give one any interest in such property, the doctrine of equitable estoppel may apply if a wife has incurred expenditure on the property in the belief that she already has or will be given some proprietary interest in it. In the event of sale, the wife was to get 50 percent of the market price.

It was further held that it was not necessary to establish any express or implied agreement that the wife made a contribution to the family property with a view to acquiring an interest. In his evidence, the husband had conceded that his wife had, indeed, tilled the land and contributed to the house but that she had done so as a wife and not for the purpose of acquiring a beneficial interest in the property. Had the court not applied equity, the wife would have lost all that she had invested in her husband's home.

The court's decision may have gone a long way in protecting women's interests but this was due to the recognition of the wife's 'substantial' contribution. Courts demand substantial contribution before applying the equitable principle. The question however is: What is 'substantial' contribution? Does it only cover contributions such as iron sheets in the Nakiyingi case or does it extend to unpaid labour in the home? In most Ugandan societies, when a girl marries she is encouraged to believe that she 'belongs' to her husband, and when she develops his land, she does it in the belief that she has an interest in it. It is hard to imagine circumstances in which the husband would discourage such a belief.

Given the current position of Ugandan law, it is imperative that women are made aware that marriage does not automatically give them any rights in their husband's property. Nor does it rob them of a right to hold property in their own names. Marriage does not culminate in automatic co-ownership between husband and wife. For co-ownership to exist there must be an agreement to that effect. A woman can therefore be certain that she has beneficial interest in property only if it is registered in joint names. Even where the husband buys property for their common use, whether it is a house, furniture or a car, this cannot give the wife any proprietary interest per se. In case a wife seeks to establish a beneficial interest in the property registered in her husband's name, she can only do so by proving that he holds the property on trust for her use. In law, property ownership depends upon the purchaser's intention at the time it is bought. Yet spouses buying property rarely contemplate the termination of the marriage except by death. When the marriage breaks down, the courts are faced with a problem of establishing what the intention of the purchaser was at the time of purchase. In the absence of direct evidence, the court must infer the intention from the purchaser's conduct at the time. In reality, the courts impose their own opinions.

Divorce under customary law does not offer the woman any better treatment. Not only does she go away empty-handed but her parents must return the bride wealth to her former husband as if the work she did in his home was worth nothing. The marriage institution in Uganda must be re-examined in order to recognise women's invaluable contribution to family property. There should be legislation governing the division of property on separation or divorce just as there is legislation governing family provision on death. This should be accompanied by making women aware of their rights.

Choice of the victim: husband versus co-wife

Polygamy involves a man and at least two women. In discussing criminal homicide as a possible result of 'love triangles', Mushanga (1974:111) said that one of the three who make up the triangle may direct aggression either to one or both of the other participants. In the context of the present study, a wife whose husband shows interest in another woman may either assault her husband or her husband's other woman, or both parties. What informs the choice of the victim? According to Totman (1970:25):

> ... homicide (and violence as such) is assumed to have particular meaning in relation to the offender's situation and represents a distinctive kind of action resolution of a conflict or conflicts in a significant relationship.

Natukunda contemplated committing suicide, but she decided against it 'because I realised that if I died I would be the loser. My husband would just go ahead and marry his lover.' She at one time thought of killing her husband, but:

> ... the more I thought about my problems, the more I became determined to kill the woman. I realised that if I killed my husband, again I would be the loser. I would be a widow and yet that woman would go ahead and marry somebody else.

At yet another time she had thought of killing the father of her 'rival', but changed her mind because 'I would go to prison and thereby give room to the two love-birds to celebrate their wedding.' Natukunda eventually decided to kill her rival. Her choice of the victim was evidently rational.

Some other women also directed their violence towards 'the husband's other woman.' Both Odoi and Namukasa reported that their husbands had abdicated their responsibility to financially support their wives once they had got involved with the other women. Namukasa allegedly threw acid at the 'other woman' and

Odoi hit her husband's 'other woman' with a bottle and also bit off her nose. As mentioned earlier, when Komugisa's husband got another wife, one of the indignities Komugisa suffered was eviction from the house she had occupied with her husband for six years. The kitchen was henceforth to be her bedroom. When Komugisa's co-wife invaded the former's 'bedroom,' a quarrel erupted and Komugisa hit the woman with a hoe.

Nalwanga helped her husband to acquire a second wife, but once this happened, he often preferred the younger woman and neglected Nalwanga sexually. He also often bought necessities for the younger woman and none for Nalwanga. Nalwanga attacked her co-wife with a spear.

After four years of marriage, Namanda's husband got involved with another woman. That woman constantly boasted about her love relationship with Namanda's husband. The new woman would pass by Namanda's home and declare her status as a 'wife to Namanda's husband'.

He was already paying rent for the woman. Namanda used her sister and a friend to throw acid in the face of this provocative woman.

Perhaps these women, like Natukunda, realised that destruction of the men they loved or depended on would be futile. They considered the other women as the intruders whom the injured parties decided to get out of the way. Just like Natukunda's marital experience, all these women reported that their husbands had never physically assaulted them. These women presented pictures very different from the stories of all the women who admitted killing their husbands. The husbands of the latter group of women subjected them to intense physical abuse. It is probable that a husband's acquisition of another wife per se does not make him a likely victim of his wife's violence. Whether in a polygamous or monogamous marriage, a husband is only likely to become a victim of his wife's violence if he subjects her to regular physical abuse. This is well articulated in the words of Karugaba, who, when recalling the various types of abuse that she was subjected to by her husband, said she would have tolerated other kinds of abuse but not physical violence because 'touching one's body is tantamount to touching one's life.'

Predominance of junior wives as victims

All the nine women imprisoned for violence against co-wives were the first wives and their victims were the subsequent wives. A similar pattern emerged in the court records. Among the eleven cases, only two cases involved first wives as victims. In two cases, the court records did not reveal which of the two actors was the senior wife and in seven of the cases, the second wives were victims of the senior wives.

In the two cases where first wives were the victims of the violence of junior wives, the first wives greatly provoked their juniors. In H.C.C.S.C. No. 64/90, the deceased (senior wife) went to the accused's house carrying a knife. She picked up a quarrel with the accused and their husband. The husband left the two women in the house and went outside. As the abuses and quarrels continued, the accused tried to go away but the deceased blocked the way out. A scuffle developed. Out of fear that the deceased would use the knife against her, the accused picked a pestle and hit the deceased once on the head. The deceased fell down and died almost instantly. It was also testified that this was not the first time that the deceased had harassed the accused. Indeed, it was due to this continued harassment that the husband had hired a separate house for the accused. The defence counsel's submission was as follows:

> It was for fear that the deceased might use that knife on her that the accused picked a pestle and struck the deceased on the head. This is a borderline case of manslaughter and self-defence, which would justify the killing.

The other case in which a junior wife killed the senior wife is H.C.C.S.C. No. 131/74. The accused believed that the death of her five children was due to witchcraft. On the fateful day, both the accused and the victim had taken alcohol. The defence submitted that the deceased provoked the accused by threatening that the deceased would die by witchcraft like her children. To make matters worse, the deceased unwrapped what the accused believed to be evil charms. In the heat of passion, the accused killed the deceased with a *panga*.

In contrast, most assaults involving junior wives as victims were not the consequence of such direct provocation. Since it is the second (subsequent) wife who violates the first wife's monopoly over the husband and over marital privileges/rights, it is hardly surprising that most victims are the second wives.

Polygamy and societal change

Although polygamy is not a new phenomenon, it is likely to have different consequences in contemporary society due to economic and cultural changes.

Economic change
The hard economic conditions in the country mean that few men in Uganda can maintain more than one home and yet many modern women cannot accept living in the same homestead with their co-wives. Consequently, once a man starts running with another woman it is likely that the needs of his first wife and her children will no longer be a priority. Since most women are financially dependent on their husbands, it is no wonder that often, when a man develops interest in another woman, bitter rivalry develops between the two women and this may culminate in violence. To the first wife, the new woman is not just competing for sexual companionship but also for financial resources. The issue of polygamy is therefore not merely an ideological one.

Polygamy was originally linked to the traditional rural economy. Having several wives was both a sign of wealth (because of bride price) and a source of income for the man. Women were not only a direct source of labour but they were also producers of new labourers (the children). However, the economic base for polygamy in rural areas is disappearing and it has no place in urban areas. In light of such developments, having several wives is an economic burden rather than a source of income for the man. Hence, women in polygamous unions may experience real problems in terms of inadequate or lack of financial support.[5]

This problem of financial neglect in polygamous unions is clearly illustrated by the case of Namukasa, who was accused of assaulting her husband's lover with acid:

> Yes, I will call her my co-wife. ... My husband had more or less permanently moved to her house. But my husband was that woman's wife since the house belonged to the woman.[6] He no longer bought anything in the home, yet my only employment was as a housewife. I would often tell him: 'Your husband must be very tough, so tough that she cannot allow you to notice that your family here lacks all the basic necessities in life.' ... He had more or less abandoned me....

The story of Odoi, who hit her husband's girlfriend with a bottle and bit off the victim's nose as well, is no different. According to her:

> Before my husband's involvement with that girl, he used to give me enough money. After he had got this other girl, it became ever so difficult to get enough money from him. Whenever he gave me any money and I told him that it was inadequate for the home necessities, he would just rudely ask me to return what he had given me since 'I was so ungrateful,' he would say.

But even when a man keeps all his wives in the same homestead, the presence of a second wife may have negative economic implications for the first wife. Nalwanga was convicted of attempting to murder her co-wife, a second wife of her husband. I asked her what she had found as the most difficult aspect of marriage and she said it was quarrels between wives.

> *Lillian:* What usually is the source of such quarrels?
> *Nalwanga:* It is usually because men give different treatment to

the women. One wife may request for something [e.g., material] and her request is granted, and when the other wife requests for a similar thing, the husband denies her the request, saying he has no money. Then a quarrel inevitably erupts between the women.

In his study of criminal homicides in Uganda, Mushanga (1974:42) attributed the differences between the participation of women in homicides among the Banyankore, the Bakiga and the Batooro to different family patterns in these societies. His study revealed a higher rate of women homicide offenders in Kigezi (27.5 percent) than in Toro — where the rate was only 4.6 percent. In Ankole the rate was 13.9 percent. At the same time, he observed that in Kigezi, where female participation in homicide was the highest, there was also a higher rate of polygamy than in Toro. Ankole again fell in between with a higher polygamous rate than Toro but not as high as Kigezi. Mushanga then concluded (p.142):

> Polygamy as a type of marriage is or tends to be characterised by strain though not necessarily family instability. ... The husband in a polygamous family is a man in demand; he is also in a position in which he is most likely to violate the rules of the game and engender hostility from any one of his wives, in which case one of the wives may be infuriated and use violence. ... The conjugal unit is maintained not only by economic provisions but requires some personal and psychological attachment, and where these are wanting, criminogenic situations develop. The husband ... is expected to be fairly fair in the way he treats his wives; this he does by providing his wives equally; and by entertaining them equally. A man with, say four wives, may not entertain one wife twice at a time till he has gone around and start all over again. ... [I]n case he breaks the timetable, ... ill-feelings begin to develop between the co-wives.

In line with Mushanga's findings, Nalwanga could not accept her husband's partiality and inequity. She, therefore, reacted violently towards her co-wife. According to Kilbride and Kilbride (1990), although the ideal is cooperation among co-wives, more commonly, relations are strained and often competitive. Interviews with members of polygamous families and with the women in prison also collaborate Cutrufelli's (1983:54) observation that:

> Relations between co-wives are usually bad, no matter what the supporters of the customary polygamous family say. Reciprocal accusations of witchcraft as well as practices of magic intended for one another are commonplace....

Nalwanga's dissatisfaction with her marriage was not only because she was getting less than her fair share of material needs but also because her husband used to spend more time with her co-wife, and yet each was entitled to 'her days'. When I first asked her what had led to the assault on her co-wife, she replied that 'it was because of the man that we fought. He was cheating me on my days', which literally means that the husband was spending more nights with the second wife than with Nalwanga.

Nalwanga's experience lends credence to Maillu's observation that one of the negative effects of polygamy is the fact that, although the day will always remain 24 hours even to the polygamist, each wife expects full marital relations with the husband and this connotes time. This means that 'time, being the most precious commodity, [the husband] must share it with a high degree of fairness just like any other property ... if he has to maintain a sound marriage.'

Yet Nalwanga urged her husband to get another wife, which indicates, as Maillu (1988:59) states, that:

> Whereas some of the traditions are dying out, *there are still cases in which the first wife encourages the coming of the second wife.* For example, her husband may appear to spend most of his time with that woman out there where he also seems to spend most of his money; or if he goes out to sleep with all kinds of women and risks the first marriage with a sexual disease; or as in the case of some communities a child is fathered outside the marriage but is automatically brought to the marriage and has to be taken care of by the man's wife. In such situations, the wife may feel that it is much better for this man to marry a second wife (my emphasis).

It is however clear that, before one can assert that a particular first wife encouraged and therefore preferred polygamy to monogamy, her encouragement must be put in its proper context. In the examples given by Maillu, one notes that such wife's encouragement is a recognition of the fact that the husband has already proved unfaithful. The wife's action is, therefore, not really a choice between polygamy and monogamy but rather between polygamy and infidelity.

It is therefore hardly surprising that 'even when the first wife had participated in the decision to bring in a second one, that decision does not stipulate that friction between the two wives should never arise' (Maillu:127). After all, the first wife's choice of polygamy will have been a forced choice.

In my interview with Nalwanga I asked her why she had advised her husband to get another wife. She replied as follows:

> My husband had another house apart from the one we were living in. He would take different women to that house and spend nights with them. It had become a habit so I decided that it would be better that he gets a second wife, put her in that house so that the woman would help me with the family chores.

To Nalwanga it was only fair that the women on whom her husband was spending money should contribute to the family income.

Cultural change

Society's attitude towards polygamy has also changed. Western culture and Christian teaching have fostered new ideas about marriage and about the husband–wife relationship. Consequently, doubt has been cast on the hitherto acclaimed values and practices of polygamy. In the past, it was accepted and, indeed, expected that a man could marry more than one woman. Even the most jealous of women could not complain if her husband got another wife. If a woman left her husband just because of another woman, or even complained about her husband's intention to get another wife, such a woman would be publicly ridiculed even by her own mother. Consequently, any feelings of jealousy were at most expressed only verbally. In modern society, a woman's resistance against another woman would be met with sympathy from several quarters.

In traditional society, the process of acquiring subsequent wives often involved a husband consulting and getting the approval of his senior wife. Quite often the wife would then bring her young sisters or her brothers' daughters as brides for her husband. Since subsequent wives were often relatives of the senior wife and were often her own choice, it is reasonable to assume that chances of conflict were reduced. Mushanga (1974:88) reported that, among the Banyankore and Bakiga, most polygamists prefer to marry either sisters or girls who are related in one way or another. It is believed that although sisters may hate each other, they will not harm each other (e.g., with poison or witchcraft) as women who are not related may do.

Polygamy is now scorned and few women are willing to share a husband even with a sister. In my interview with Natukunda I asked her: 'If your husband had told you that he wanted to get another wife but gave you the duty to look for a wife for him, would you have considered doing it?' Her answer was: 'He could never ask me to do that because he knew I would never do it.'

As already discussed, the idea of a sister for a co-wife was not acceptable to Natukunda. I got a similar answer from Komugisa, a woman who had killed her husband's other wife. I asked her: If your husband had ever asked you to find him another wife, would you have complied? Komugisa's answer was an emphatic: 'No! There is no way I could have done that.' She said it as if she was surprised that anybody would expect any woman ever to find a wife for her husband.

> *Lillian:* Supposing he had expressed the wish to marry your sister or a niece, would that be more acceptable to you?
> *Komugisa:* No! Not even that. In fact, I would rather he marries a stranger. I would certainly never want to have a sister or anybody close as a co-wife. Such a person knows all about you. It would be so bad to conflict with such a close person.

For Komugisa, it was clear that co-wifeship inevitably meant conflict situations and rivalry.

> *Lillian:* Is it common for men to marry sisters in the community you come from?
> *Komugisa:* It is not common. A few do it but it is not common. Even the parents of the women are not likely to appreciate such an occurrence.

Komugisa was vehemently against polygamy. For her, sisters marrying the same man was even more unacceptable. When I asked her if there were circumstances in which a man should have more than one wife, she replied, 'No.' Karugaba too had strong feelings against polygamy, but unlike Komugisa, she acknowledged that under certain circumstances it may be inevitable.

> *Lillian:* If your husband tells you to look for a woman for him, would you do it?
> *Karugaba:* It should be him to look for a wife for himself, not me. It is impossible. I would never have agreed. Can one ever consciously invite hell into one's own life! (*Gwe oyinza okweletera olumbe nga olulaba!*)
> *Lillian:* Some women get wives for their husbands in order to be relieved of too much work, would you not consider that?
> *Karugaba:* Even if there was a lot of work, what are maids for?
> *Lillian:* But supposing you had no maid?
> *Karugaba:* Even then I would rather do all my work. ... Just hearing that your husband has another woman makes one go crazy, how then can I want her under the same roof with me?
> *Lillian:* If your husband had married another wife, would you have preferred it to his extramarital affairs?
> *Karugaba:* Well, if a man is really determined to get another wife you can do nothing to stop him. But he should keep her away from me; I should never be made to live under the same roof with her — seeing her every day — even knowing that he is sleeping with her next door. If he had ever dared bring another woman into the home, he would have gone hungry; I would not have prepared meals for him, and supposing the other wife also refuses, he would go hungry.

Karugaba later said: 'Talking about extramarital affairs, once a man has children with a woman that woman is no longer a girlfriend; she is a co-wife.'

Polygamy no longer has functional value for today's women. Even the possibility of having a say as to who should be their husbands' second wife, does not make the practice any more acceptable. In all my interviews with members of polygamous families, most women expressed the view that having a sister for a co-wife did not make polygamy any easier. Many of them were strongly against such an arrangement because they would thereby lose a friend in the sister who becomes a co-wife.

Interviews with both the men and women in polygamous families also revealed that in contemporary society, it is rare for a man to discuss with his wife plans to get an additional wife. The most that today's husband may do is to inform the wife about his decision and, even then, it is usually a few days before the arrival in the home of the new wife.

In his ardent support for African polygamy, Maillu (1988:112) argued that:

> The so-called jealousy among co-wives is largely a condition of the mind and depends very much upon the cultural background in which those women were brought up. A woman who grew up in a polygamous marriage would tend to appreciate polygamy more than the one who was brought up in a monogamous setting.

But it is worth noting that, in my prison sample, the women who resisted polygamy were born and brought up in polygamous families. Karugaba's father had several wives; so did her father-in-law. However, she expressed very negative feelings about sharing a man with another woman. She also believed that her father did not appreciate her complaints about her husband's infidelity because was also a polygamist. Natukunda's father had four wives. Nalwanga too had been brought up in a polygamous family. Similarly, she had also assisted her husband to get another wife. It was nevertheless this wife that Nalwanga assaulted with a spear.

It is worth commenting about the court's reaction when it heard that it was Nalwanga who got a second wife for her husband — a reaction which is clear evidence that a woman who fits in the conventional image of womanhood and femininity is likely to thereby earn herself leniency from judicial officers. Chief Magistrate Mungoma said:

> ... the offence [of attempted murder] carries a maximum sentence of life imprisonment. I have considered the fact that *the accused wanted a good family, she brought a young lady to her husband as she [the accused] is barren* ... (my emphasis).

He then went on to speak of 'leniency', and recommended 'two years'. Nalwanga had proved herself a woman who knew her subservient role in patriarchal society and her paramount duty to please her man. Having failed in her duty to bear children for her husband, she had relinquished the advantages of monogamy and got her husband another wife. Consequently, she was rewarded with leniency by a judicial officer belonging to that society.

What then is the functional value of polygamy to men? It is reasonable to presume that polygamy is practised in areas where the status of women is lowest. For as Eaton (1986:55) said:

> The divisions of class [and] gender, ... which characterise our society, are accomplished within the distinctive life patterns of families in different sections of society. ... Furthermore, there is a close connection between the form of the family and the socio-economic structure of society. ... The contemporary forms of family life, and the ideology supporting them, are important in the reproduction of the contemporary social structure. They also have serious implications for the position of women in society.

Mistresses

Society's change in attitude towards polygamy has resulted in some men informally and secretly taking on additional 'wives' while proclaiming monogamy. According to Maillu (1988:143), this situation is also prevalent elsewhere in Africa:

> ... among the elite Nigerian men, there is a definite upsurge in polygamy, even though there is still an attempt to maintain a *semblance of monogamy for public consumption* (my emphasis).

The secret nature of these relationships creates feelings of insecurity and humiliation in these women, since secrecy indicates non-recognition in a society which does not respect concubinage. The position of a mistress is certainly weaker than that of a second or third wife. Such a woman, therefore, often goes out of her way to inform the public, including her lover's wife, of the existence of the hidden relationship. Many times such a woman uses provocative ways of declaring her secret relationship to her lover's wife and this sometimes culminates in fights during which one of the women may lose her life.

Nalinya was convicted for throwing acid in the face of another woman. At the age of 16 years she had become pregnant and as a result had to leave school. She had subsequently married the man who had made her pregnant. After four years in marriage, Nalinya's husband got involved with another woman. The woman constantly sent messages to Nalinya about having a love relationship with Nalinya's husband. Nalinya asked her husband about the affair but he strongly denied the relationship. After some time, the 'other woman' to used pass by Nalinya's house on her way from work, and loudly boast about having a relationship with Nalinya's husband. She also sent a message to Nalinya to the effect that it was useless to fight for the man, since the trio — Nalinya, 'the other woman', and the husband — were all going to die. The other woman said she had a boyfriend who died of AIDS and there was no doubt that Nalinya and her husband must have been infected too. Although the man denied the affair, Nalinya was convinced that he was having an affair with the said woman. In answer to why she had assaulted the victim, Nalinya simply said: 'She provoked me into it, whenever she passed by my home she would hurl insults at me.'

Conclusion

Women's violence against each other is often a result of the socio-economic order that makes them dependent on men and marriage. In Uganda, the majority of women have no access to material resources necessary to provide for self-sufficiency and economic independence. Many of them are not engaged in paid employment and the majority of those who are employed outside the home are in manual, menial, low-paid jobs. For most women, the only financial security they can ever have is through marriage. Del (1982:xviii) had a point when he argued that economic dependence on men is one of the abuses patriarchal society subjects women to.

Assuming that women recognise the absolute necessity to hold on to men for financial reasons, any expression of interest by their husbands in other women invariably precipitates very bitter rivalry between the women concerned. Such rivalries may culminate in fights in which some of the women may lose their lives. But it is important to note that killing a 'rival' need not always be preceded by a fight, since:

> By definition, acts of aggression culminating in homicide involve an interaction between participants. ... A study of the nature of such interaction ... suggests that the role of the victim is not restricted to precipitation of the crime as set out in the now classic description given by Wolfgang, in which he applies it to cases involving the victim inducing his death through his own menacing actions. ... The victim can contribute in many different ways to the interaction preceding the aggressive behaviour; ... such involvement ... may involve little more than the mere presence of the victim in a given *situation* ... (Avison 1974: 228) (my emphasis).

A co-wife or mistress who becomes a victim of another woman's assault may be described as an *agent provocateux*. Totman (1978) observed that female killers, rather than acting out of passion, make a deliberate and conscious decision to kill, to resolve a personal dilemma. Accordingly, women's violence against co-wives is often economically motivated. Women's crimes are consciously committed in order to ensure financial security for self and children.

Society expects women to marry and raise families. It denies such women the possibility of being independent of men. In the eyes of patriarchal society, women have no value as individuals. As Totman (1978:16) said:

> Woman's success in (our) society is still largely measured in terms of her attractiveness to men. Marriage and the home are defined as the culturally approved goals, and success consists of a suitable, happy marriage and motherhood. This is to be *attained through a personal attachment with a man* ... from which relationship her status, her income, and *all the attendant symbols of her position depend* (my emphasis).

A divorced or unmarried woman occupies an awkward place in Ugandan society. Wives, therefore, jealously protect their marriages. On the other hand, mistresses go out of their way to show that they too are wives. Since a woman's social status depends so much on whether or not she is married, any threat to her marriage is likely to lead her into violent behaviour.

Socio-cultural practices such as polygamy are evidence of the hierarchy and power relations within the family. They represent male domination in a patriarchal society. Although the practice of polygamy has been with Africa as far back as the records can take us, fundamental economic and cultural changes have induced women to resist and challenge this male domination and oppression. In resisting the practice and its concrete implications, some women resort to violent crime.

Fiala and LaFree (1988:432) acknowledged that the disruption of institutionalised patterns of social behaviour without adequate replacement of new patterns of social organisation often results in deviance. In his introduction to Mushanga's *Criminal Homicide in Uganda* (1974:2), Marshall said also that in 'the developing countries criminal homicide can be interpreted in terms of culture conflict resulting from social change....'

Similarly, in his *Murder and Homicide in Pakistan,* Mahfooz (1989:1) linked deviance to rapidly changing societies. He pointed out that 'a changing society ... faces a struggle between the "old" and the "new". Sometimes there is confusion ... which contributes, to some extent, to deviant behavior.'

What is the significance of changing patterns in traditional behaviour (polygamy) for women and violent crime? Ugandan society is still in the process of merging the traditional and the modern, the old and the new. Therefore, people cannot claim to live in isolation from each other. As Clifford (1974:15) noted:

> ... the transition from traditional to modern urban living has been accomplished with ... speed: the cultural contrasts have often been carried over into the towns. ... Most families, *however sophisticated and intellectually advanced, in the towns of Africa still have one foot in the rural tribal villages of their ancestors* (my emphasis).

This may perhaps lead to confusion and deviance.

Notes

1. I however must mention that I expected a lot more violence within polygamy than was revealed by my study. I started off on the assumption that a larger portion of women's victims would be their husbands' 'other women'. This was partly because of the consistent coverage in the press of violent encounters between women arising from 'rivalry' over men. Ugandan press also gives wide coverage to reports of 'the cruel stepmother', The results of my research instead corroborated Mushanga's observation after his study of criminal homicides in western Uganda: 'One surprising thing is that one would expect a higher rate of criminal homicide involving co-wives and yet this was lacking even in areas where there is a high rate of polygamy' (1974: 87,164).

2. The Marriage and Divorce of Mohammendans Act, Chapter 213 of the Laws of Uganda; The Customary Marriage (Registration) Decree, Decree 16 of 1973. Although legal polygamy does not exist in Western society, it is pertinent to reflect on Taylor's (1986:1694)

comment quoted by O'Donovan (1991:226), that while [English criminal law] 'sympathised with the jealous rage of men, it assumed that wives did not experience similar rage'. In 1946, 274 years after a court announced the defence of provocation, an English court finally stated that wives who killed their husbands or their husbands' lovers could also avail themselves of the defence. (Taylor was referring to *Holmes v D.P.P.* [1946] 2 All E.R. 124.)

3. She referred to malaria because it is a common ailment and everybody knows that it is a result of mosquitoes — very common insects.

4. Because of the higher status accorded to church weddings, it is not uncommon for a couple to under go a customary marriage ceremony and then, years later, go through a church wedding. In law such a couple is deemed to have got married at the earlier date but to the public, a 'man's decision' to wed his wife in church is evidence of a more serious commitment than if he only (sic) undergoes a customary or civil but not religious marriage. Consequently, church weddings are accompanied by a lot of pomp and heavy spending.

5. The wives of a polygamous man have equal status in the eyes of the law. For example, when he dies intestate all the women are entitled to an equal share in the husband's estate irrespective of the period spent in marriage by each wife.

6. In traditional Ugandan society it is the duty of a man to provide housing for his family. Where a family stays in a house provided by the wife, the husband of such a woman is often derided as the wife.

VI

Reactions to Victim Precipitation

'[M]ost acts of violence grow out of an interaction situation in which the act comes to be defined as requiring violence and in which the victim plays a part in precipitating the resulting action.'[1]

The term 'victim precipitation' refers to incidents in which a victim of violence was the first to use or threaten the use of violence or a deadly weapon against the offender. In other words, the reaction of the offender was a result of *provocation* from the victim.[2] Victim precipitation is a broad concept, encompassing (legal) provocation, and it is for this reason that in defining the former concept, the latter term often appears in the definition. For example, Gobert (1977:514) said '*victim precipitation* refers to some overt, identifiable conduct or omission on the part of the victim which *provokes* an individual to commit a crime' (my emphases).

Referring to Gobert's definition as one of the most succinct definitions, Wolfgang (1993:167) acknowledged that the term *victim precipitation* does not exist in judicial decisions or in statutory law, whereas *provocation* is legally accepted. However, after noting the dearth of dialogue between legal scholarship and behavioural science scholarship, he implicitly treated the terms as synonymous.[3]

Legal provocation is narrower than the sociological definition of provocation in that the legal meaning refers to the commission of the offence in the *heat of passion* arising from *loss of self-control*. The offended person must have lost control as a direct result of an unlawful act committed by the victim. To successfully plead provocation the offender must have reacted immediately after the provocation, without having had time to cool from the passion caused by that provocation.[4] But for the purpose of this study the definition of victim precipitation includes incidents in which the woman's violence was a reaction to past regular violence by the victim; i.e., reaction to accumulated violence.

In light of the wider and inclusive nature of the above definition, it is not necessary to distinguish between successive incidents since the definition covers precipitation of the specific violent act as well as retaliation for some earlier but repeated violence by the ultimate victim. In line with Loftin's (1986:551) concept of *reciprocal assaultive violence*, it includes not only incidents in which the victim is the first to strike a blow, but also incidents in which the victim has a history of violence (against the offender). This is in recognition of the fact that in the majority of homicides, serious violent attacks and similar violent confrontations 'have occurred between the same participants numerous times in the past, and the history of these events is a partner, albeit a silent partner in the current incident' (Block 1993:189).

Victim precipitation also covers the legal defence of self-defence. But self-defence, as will be discussed in detail later, is narrower than victim precipitation partly because the law only recognises an act, as done in self-defence, if it was done in reaction to an imminent attack. Consequently, when a person is threatened with future injury and she/he reacts violently against the person posing the threat, she/he cannot plead self-defence. My definition of victim precipitation covers incidents in which the woman's violence was a reaction to threats of *future* injury, in anticipation of threatened harm which is nevertheless *highly probable*. If a person has ever threatened, and in fact carried out a threat, against another person, any subsequent threat by that person is likely to be considered as highly probable to happen, although the time of occurrence is unpredictable. When the threatened person therefore reacts violently to a threat of future injury, this should be considered a result of victim precipitation.

Despite the difference between the sociological and the legal meanings of provocation, it is imperative to note that both recognise the fact that a person's commission of a crime is sometimes a result of the actions of the victim of that crime.

My definition of victim precipitation is a modification of that of Wolfgang's in *Patterns in Criminal Homicide* (1958), where he focused on the victim-offender relationship in homicides. Wolfgang's definition is, in line with the law, limited to incidents in which the offender's violence was a reaction to imminent danger. He (1958:252) excluded 'mutual quarrels' from his definition of victim-precipitated violence, but I consider this to be part of the definition as long as it was the victim who invariably precipitated the fight.

Wolfgang (1993:180) said that the rate of victim-precipitated crime in American society was unclear and so was the question whether there were more or fewer victim-precipitated crimes than unprovoked ones. The present research findings on women-homicide offenders in Uganda revealed that Ugandan women frequently kill as a result of victim precipitation.

The battered woman

The extensive literature on Western industrialised societies indicates that a large percentage of women who kill husbands are, prior to the homicide, victims of their husbands' abuse for long periods of time.[5] In Western society, the characteristics typically exhibited by a woman who has systematically been subjected to repeated physical and psychological abuse by her mate are collectively and commonly referred to as the *battered woman syndrome*.[6]

As indicated in Chapter II, many of the husband killers I interviewed could easily fit the definition of battered women. Besides, various perused files also give evidence that the women killers in question often were battered women.

Sofia Auma[7] confessed in court that she had poisoned her husband because he used to beat her a lot. Similarly, *Tereza Namboze*[8] said: 'It is true ... I killed my husband. ... *He used to beat me* before the incident ...' (my emphasis).

In *Elizabeth Nyacho*,[9] the accused alleged that her deceased husband had threatened to kill her and even picked a *panga*. The court accepted that 'the deceased was a drunk and quarrelsome person. ... *This was not an isolated case* of a sudden attack upon the accused. ... The evidence of neighbours as well as of the accused ... showed that these two invariably resorted to mutual violence in their frequent quarrels' (my emphasis).

In *Elizabeth Obaro*,[10] the accused gave evidence that her deceased husband was in the habit of beating her. In *Faisi Apio*[11] the court gave a lenient sentence because 'the accused was more sinned against than sinning. She was provoked into this deed by the *persistent* provocation of her drunken husband' (my emphasis).

Cipparone (1987:431) said of battered women:

> Several characteristics are common among women who have been subjected to repeated physical and psychological abuse by their mates. These traits relate to the state of mind of battered women and the typical ways in which such women react to various situations. ... [A battered woman] often believes that no one, including even herself, will be able to resolve her predicament. This feeling of helplessness stems from, among other things, society's reluctance to involve itself in marital affairs. ... The process of victimisation experienced by a battered woman may be perpetuated to the point of psychological paralysis: *even where options of escape exist, the woman may be unable to act or even perceive the existence of such options* (my emphasis).

Discussing battered women in American society, Ewing (1987:3) quoted the testimony of a psychiatrist who gave evidence in a murder charge against a battered woman:

> [T]he abused wife undergoes a personality change as abuse increases. She becomes frightened and unable to project her thinking into the future. She lives her life from one beating to the next and her thoughts relate solely to her efforts to avoid the next beating. The wife is usually hopeful that, if she pleases the husband, the abuse will stop. ... *[T]he wife eventually feels that she cannot escape her tormentor and that she will be tracked down if she attempts to flee the situation.* ... She feels that no one would believe her if she told them about the abuse and, thus she keeps it to herself (my emphasis).

In the case of *State v Kelly*,[12] the New Jersey Supreme Court recognised the fact that a battered woman did not have the choice to leave her husband. The court rightly said that:

> ... one of the common characteristics of a battered wife is her inability to leave despite such constant beatings; her 'learned helplessness'; her lack of anywhere to go; her feeling that if she tried to leave, she would be subjected to even more merciless treatment; her belief in the omnipotence of her battering husband; and sometimes her hope that her husband will change his ways.

The picture of a battered woman portrayed by the above authorities is not far from the personal stories of the Ugandan battered woman such as Karugaba, Asiimwe, Agaba, Byarugaba and others. But whereas in Uganda, relatives and friends readily interfere in marital conflicts, it is largely for purposes of reminding women of their duty to remain married. Such people are reluctant to accept that a particular marriage has irretrievably broken down. Many close associates continue to advise her to try harder to make her marriage work rather than sever her marital relationship. Society's negative attitude towards a divorced woman compounds her problems and creates in her a feeling that her worth in society is contingent on marriage.

As already mentioned, the economic and cultural set-up in Ugandan society also forces women to stick to unhealthy relationships. Most women are financially dependent on their husbands and this makes it unrealistic to expect them to readily leave their marriages. The customary laws which give men custody rights over their children also force women to remain in violent relationships, for fear of leaving their often very young children without a mother's daily care and often at the mercy of another woman.

Law enforcement agencies like the police are usually reluctant to treat assaults by husbands against their wives as criminal. Thus Agaba said of arrests of her husband by the RC:

> They would take him away for a little while but he would never even reach the police station. The only time he was ever taken

right to the police station and was imprisoned is when, having failed to beat me, he speared the neighbour's cows out of anger.

In other words, the destruction of a neighbour's animals was considered serious enough to warrant custody, but not the many wounds Agaba suffered at her husband's hands.

Legal recognition of victim precipitation

If the Ugandan woman homicide offender is first and foremost an abused woman, does the law recognise her dual status as victim and offender? To what extent does the law acknowledge proof of victim precipitation as relevant in determining an assaulter's responsibility for violent crime? When should the criminal justice system entertain an obligation to give effect to the precipitator's conduct?

Ugandan criminal law recognises the fact that victim precipitation may be a factor in a homicide and justifies killings in circumstances where the killer's fatal attack on the victim was the only reasonable way in which the killer could have avoided being killed or maimed by the victim. Under such circumstances, the killer is declared not guilty on grounds of self-defence.[13] The law also treats with some leniency a killer whose fatal blow was a reasonable reaction to the victim's provocative behaviour towards the killer, by reducing the homicide from murder to manslaughter.[14]

Some Western feminists have however revealed the near-total inapplicability of similar legal defences to battered women who kill their battering husbands in Western society. They insist that this inapplicability is due to the narrow and inherently discriminatory prerequisites attached to concepts like 'reasonableness', which are crucial to a successful use of the defences. The criticism was echoed by Naffin (1987:3) when she wrote that:

> Law's 'reasonable man' ... represents the male point of view. That is to say, the mythical man of law is intended to be ungendered, an objective standard of human conduct, and yet the characters are invariably men. And, of course, they are deemed to be

> 'reasonable men'. In [the law's] search for a perfectly impartial standard of reasonable human behaviour, [courts] have retained in their mind's eye an image of a man, not a woman.

Writing on American society, Jones (1980:310) also said that:

> The problem for ... most battered women, is that at every step of the legal process the prevailing standard of justice is male. The acts of men and women are subject to a different set of legal expectations and standards.

The failure of the law to present an ungendered standard of a violent but reasonable reaction stems from society's stereotyped view of women: passive and nonviolent. Thus, Mushanga (1974:40) distinguished what is expected of men, on the one hand, and of women, on the other, among the Banyankore and Bakiga of western Uganda, in these words:

> Although a man is expected to get on well with fellow men, to be kind, to respect his elders, to control his anger, ... it is [also] expected of a man to be tough, not to be submissive and ... [that he] be able to defend his family, status and rights. In response to these expectations, a man will define a situation as requiring the use of violence when a situation arises. Women, on the other hand, are expected to be humble, meek, and not to raise disputes with men.

These expectations are also prevalent among other societies in Uganda.

In a case where a woman had killed her husband, Justice Youds of the Uganda High Court said: 'It is not normally in the nature of women to kill.'[15] In the eyes of the male-dominated society, it is only an unreasonable woman who can ever react violently, so women's attempts to plead self-defence and provocation are often frustrated. These defences are consequently the prerogative of men, men who, in spite of being reasonable, can *understandably* act violently.

The net result is that the court's perception of a homicide event in a situation where the actor is a woman is likely to conflict with, and be alien to, the actor's perception. The law fails to balance the multiple perceptions represented by various groups: male prosecutors and male judges on the one hand, and the woman killer on the other.

The working-class woman (the uneducated woman) is said to face extra barriers by virtue of her class (just as does the working-class male). In the words of Worrall (1990:155), such women are 'doubly muted in their relationships with middle-class professional men [judges and lawyers] — by class and by gender'.

As already discussed in Chapter I, only nine (14 percent) of the 66 women I interviewed went beyond the first seven years of formal education, and 52 percent of the group had never attended formal school at all.

Arguably, the Ugandan woman is not only disadvantaged as a woman but also as a Ugandan. For as Seidman (1966:xi) said:

> Nowhere in the world is the tension in law between the 'is' and the 'ought' sharper than it is in Africa. ... Wherever the act involved might seem strange or barbaric to readers who are unaware of the social and economic milieu in which the accused lived, [one should] ... place the act in its proper societal matrix.

In specific reference to homicide, Tanner (1970:61) correctly commented that:

> The dyadic aspects of homicide are particularly significant in the Ugandan situation, because there is a clear difference between the customary accepted factors precipitating non-culpable homicide and those which the western law orientated in the courts of the country.

Similarly, Mushanga (1974:136,137) has said:

> There is nothing as confusing as to have foreign norms and ideals dominate the legal system of people. ... If there is anything that

our people have failed to understand, it is the British law regarding homicide.

To what extent do Ugandan courts accommodate the accused women's perceptions of homicide events as perceptions of reasonable, rational human beings? In what specific ways is the uneducated woman disadvantaged by the criminal justice system? How far is the legal interpretation of self-defence in Uganda different from its popular meaning?

As long as the court's and the actor's perception of the same event differ, then the very important concept of guilt will also have different meanings for the different groups. The women will, as Worrall (1990:80) reported, see their action as self-preservation (if not self-defence), and thus justify their acts of violence. As long as the actors see their actions as justified, the law will lose its claim as an expression of justice.

Of the 91 High Court cases perused, only four women[16] (four percent) were acquitted on grounds of self-defence; their violence was considered reasonable in the circumstances. In addition, 39 women were judged to have killed on provocation.

The doctrine of self-defence and the concept of 'reasonableness'

According to Section 17(a) of the Uganda Penal Code, criminal responsibility for the use of force in the defence of person and property is based on the principles of English law.[17] Consequently, the law regarding self-defence is basically judge made/case law.[18]

The doctrine of self-defence permits the use of reasonable force against another person when one reasonably believes that person is threatening her/him with imminent and unlawful bodily harm and that such force is necessary to prevent the threatened harm. A person is privileged to use deadly force against another only in the reasonable belief that the other is threatening him/her with imminent death or serious body injury and that the deadly force is necessary to avert the infliction of such harm. What do courts consider to be serious enough injury to warrant a fatal attack?

The case of *Margaret Kazigati*[19] clearly elucidates the narrow and inherently discriminatory prerequisites attached to concepts like serious injury and reasonable force. The facts of the case were that the accused and her friend sold *enguli* (a local brew) in the accused's house. The deceased and another man had a drink in the house of the accused. The accused asked them to leave but the men wanted to drink more. The accused then went to her bedroom to sleep. The light was switched off and she closed the door. Some time later she felt someone holding her by the throat. She tried to free herself. The accused struggled with the stranger in the course of which she got a knife and stabbed him. After the deceased had been injured he revealed he was her brother-in-law. The accused stopped but the deceased had been fatally injured and he died later.

In his judgement, His Lordship Justice Ssekandi said:

> This appears to be a borderline case. On the facts, the accused could have been entitled to self-defence. ... It may very well be that she went far to use a knife on a person whose designs in advancing towards her were very clear. The intruder quite obviously was not a robber or killer. It appears he was seeking to assault the accused sexually. The use of a knife would have been the last resort but not an immediate alternative. In any case the accused was trying to protect her womanhood and ... the case is really borderline....

Had the attacker been interested in physical property, the judge would have considered the use of a knife by the woman an immediate alternative: reasonable force, and the homicide would have been justifiable. The judge's differentiation between robbery and rape, however, is not sustainable. The law scales the gravity of offences by referring to the less serious offences as misdemeanours and to the more serious offences as felonies.[20] Both robbery and rape are felonies. Another method of scaling is through prescription of punishments. When Kazigati's case was decided in 1975, persons convicted of robbery and persons convicted of rape were liable to life imprisonment.[21] Since the law scales the two offences as equally serious, the force allowed to persons threatened with either offence should be equal.

His Lordship conceded that the woman was trying to protect her womanhood but considered the use of a knife in such circumstances an extreme reaction: unreasonable force for purposes of warding off a sexual assault. The decision lends credence to the contention that, as it is now, it is clear that 'Law's "reasonable man" ... represents the male point of view' (Naffin 1987:3).

From the case, it appears that for a woman to kill a man who is attempting to assault her sexually merely makes it a borderline rather than a case of self-defence. One's physical property is considered more important than one's womanhood. What Jones (1980:310–1) said about homicides in American society is also true of Uganda:

> Standards of justifiable homicide have been based on male models and expectations. Familiar images of self-defence are a soldier, a man protecting his home, family, or the chastity of his wife, or a man fighting off an assailant. Society, through its prosecutors, juries, and judges, *has more readily excused a man for killing his wife's lover than a woman for killing a rapist* (my emphasis).

A man who kills his adulterous wife or her lover will have a murder charge against him reduced to manslaughter. As Jones (1980:311) said:

> The man's act, while not always legally condoned, is viewed sympathetically. He is not forgiven [and thus acquitted], but his motivation is understood by those sitting in judgement upon his act since his conduct conforms to the expectation that a real man would fight to death to protect his pride and property.

Why should a man's anger be tolerated on the basis that he is protecting the chastity of a woman who is not interested in that 'chastity', when that very woman would not be justified in being angry enough to kill a man invading her body? The anger of a woman towards a man who wants to rape her should be greater than a husband's anger towards his wife's adultery, and she should be acquitted of that particular offence.

Since rape is a felony, it should follow that if a person kills another in order to protect herself from imminent rape, she will have done so in the process of defending herself from serious injury and should be acquitted on grounds of self-defence. Justice Ssekandi did not perceive the injury to be serious enough to warrant self-defence. That is why he considered the force that was used to have been unreasonable. Yet as Schneider and Jordan (1978:8) contended, 'rape is inherently a violent crime [and should be] treated with the same seriousness as other violent crimes [e.g., homicide and robbery].'

Rape is a violation of a woman's body. The law should allow a woman to protect herself, even with deadly force, whether or not the rapist is armed. Most women are smaller in size than men and are usually untrained in physical combat. To deny such a woman the use of a weapon in order to ward off the imminent assault is to deny her effective self-protection.

In such a case, the crucial question should have been: what would a reasonable woman do in the face of a rape? After all, Ugandan law assumes that it is only women who can be raped.[22] In reference to an insult (which could presumably only humiliate a woman), the English Court of Appeal in 1978[23] similarly expressed the view that the sex of the accused could be taken into account in assessing what might reasonably cause loss of self-control. In the words of Lord Diplock:

> If words of grievous insult were addressed to a woman, words perhaps reflecting on her chastity or way of life, a consideration of the way in which she reacted would have to take account of how other women being reasonable women would or might in like circumstances have reacted.

The Ugandan decision compares very unfavourably with a similar recent case that came before the High Court in Swaziland — *Rex v Nana Jabu Lukhele*.[24] The accused who worked as a gardener left work with a friend and went to a drinking place. When the two left the drinking place, they were joined by the deceased. The deceased stood in front of the accused and told her that he wanted to have sexual intercourse with her. She resisted but he continued to harass her. In the process she fell or he pushed her down and pressed her on the ground. The accused's face was, as a result, bruised. The accused got up and ran away. The deceased went after her, caught up with her and blocked her way, insisting that he wanted to have sexual intercourse with her by force. The accused produced a knife and stabbed him. In his judgement, His Lordship Thwala said:

> He wanted to have sexual intercourse with her by force. Then the accused at a later stage produced a knife and stabbed him. Was she not acting in self-defence? Rape is like any other property or life. To be raped you have to protect/defend yourself. ... There was a reasonable explanation as to how the knife came to be in her possession. The knife was in her dust-coat pocket. It is a tool of her employment. She cuts vegetables with the knife at the garden. ... I do not think that her action exceeded the legal bounds of self-defence. I find that her actions were justifiable in the circumstances. I come to the conclusion that she acted in self-defence; I therefore acquit her.

Likewise, in 1975 a woman prisoner, who stabbed an unarmed male guard because he threatened to rape her, was acquitted on the plea of self-defence by an American court[25] 'despite the arguable absence of equal force' (Rosen 1986:35).

The East African Court of Appeal acknowledged the significance of culture, on the one hand, and class, on the other, in determining whether an offender's action was reasonable in any particular circumstances. For example, in *Rex v Hussein s/o Mohamed*,[26] the court held that:

> The standard of the reasonable man is the reasonable man *within the cultural background of* the accused ... where ... the wrongful act or insult is of such a nature as would be likely to deprive *an ordinary person of the class to which the accused belongs* of the power of self-control, there is provocation within the meaning of the statute... (my emphasis).

Even in *Yovan v Uganda*,[27] the East African Court of Appeal, sitting at Kampala, held that provocation must be judged by the standard of an ordinary person of the community to which the accused belongs and that what might be a deadly insult to a member of one community might be a mere triviality to members of another community.

As shown in *Director of Public Prosecutions v Camplin*,[28] there is also evidence that English courts are willing to recognise attributes like the age of the offender in determining the reasonableness of an act. In that case, a 15-year-old boy killed a man. His only defence before the House of Lords was provocation. Contrary to the summing up of the defence lawyer, Lord Diplock took pains to instruct the jury that they must consider whether:

> ... the provocation was sufficient to make a reasonable man in like circumstances act as the defendant did. Not a reasonable boy as [counsel for the defendant] would have it; ... it is an objective test — a reasonable man.

The jury found Camplin guilty of murder. On appeal, the Court of Appeal, Criminal Division, allowed the appeal and substituted a conviction for manslaughter on the ground that Lord Diplock's instructions were a misdirection. The court held that 'the proper direction to the jury is to invite the jury to consider whether the provocation was enough to have made a reasonable person *of the same age as the appellant* in the same circumstances do as he did (my emphasis). The applicable test, therefore, was what a reasonable boy, 15 years of age, would have done in the circumstances.

Although the cases discussed above dealt with the defence of provocation and not with self-defence, it is worth noting that cases applicable to one defence are also applicable to the other insofar as the court interpretation of the concept of reasonableness is concerned. Section 188 of the Penal Code, which, in defining provocation, refers to 'the ordinary person' as the measure of acceptability of an act, does not use the term 'reasonableness'. Yet courts in Uganda and elsewhere have consistently used the term 'reasonable' man in determining the issue of provocation in cases such as *Rex v Hussein and DPP v Camplin* above.

Since courts acknowledge the significance of culture, class and age, gender, too, must be considered in determining the reasonableness of an action. It is only then that the law will have incorporated women's experiences and perspectives into existing concepts of criminal law: concepts which so far represent, fundamentally, the male point of view. Courts have already accepted other variables; therefore, the acceptance of gender will not be tantamount to a call for a separate defence for women.

Accumulated violence

Where a woman kills her assaulter during an acute battering incident, she is likely to be acquitted of any offence on the ground that she killed in self-defence. But where a woman who has endured years of brutality and has been subjected to systematic violence by her husband or cohabitant, one day reacts by killing her assaulter, not in the fury of a violent assault but in the aftermath of a row, such a woman is unlikely to succeed on a plea of self-defence. This is because of the requirement of imminent danger attached to the plea of self-defence. Since the danger has already occurred, (i.e., she has already been injured), she cannot successfully plead self-defence. This is evident in several of the cases studied in the course of the research for this book.

In *Terezina Karawali*,[29] the accused killed her husband, who had on the fateful day 'beaten, strangled, kicked and boxed' her for two hours. As a result of his assault, Terezina's body, mouth, elbows, etc. were full of bruises. She lost the ability to hear properly and her clothes were torn. Terezina hit her husband with the stick which he had used against her. The fact that she had been severely beaten was corroborated by the police officer who saw her and recorded a statement from her, three days after the assault.

Terezina was charged with and convicted of manslaughter. She could not be acquitted on grounds of self-defence because, as Justice Russell stated:

> It [was] apparent ... that she could have escaped had she so wished and that when she struck the deceased with the stick she was not doing so purely by way of self-defence but also in retaliation for the severe and illegal beating which she had received at the hands of her husband. ... The accused caused the death by an unlawful act....

In *Tereza Nakayima*,[30] Justice Youds ruled out the plea of self-defence because her act was in reaction to completed acts of assaults against her. Tereza killed her husband after he had wounded her on the forehead, cut her left index finger and bruised her middle finger. It was also reported that there was a history of persecution of the accused by the deceased. Tereza was convicted of manslaughter.

In sentencing the offender, Justice Youds said, 'I am sure you must have been very much provoked and persecuted by your husband before you resorted to the desperate ... act of ... cutting him to death....'

Despite the fact that her act was recognised as desperate and a result of much persecution, the same court referred to it as a 'dreadful' and 'wicked' act, and

> Justice [was] done by ... [Tereza's] imprisonment, ... since the law must be observed and wives cannot be allowed to go and kill their husbands *even when persecuted by them*, without receiving punishment (my emphasis).

The judge's emphasis of the gender of the accused was also unfortunate. The statement that wives cannot be allowed to kill their husbands carried gender-biased connotations. The role of the law is to prevent unlawful killings irrespective of the relationship between the potential perpetrator and the victim. A deterrent sentence is meant as a warning to every potential offender, irrespective of gender. Furthermore, women need not always be wives.[31]

Unlike Ewing (1987:96), who appreciated the situation of American women who kill their batterers, His Lordship Youds did not realise that when the criminal justice system punishes women like Tereza, it ignores the fact that 'these women are doubly victimised; once by the men who have battered them and again by a system of criminal justice which holds them to an unrealistic standard of accountability.' The definition of the concept of imminence is too narrow and/or the importance attached to it is unnecessarily strict in the context of women's violence.

Threats of future injury

Many times violent husbands threaten wives with future injury if the wife tries to leave the relationship. If a woman kills her husband in anticipation of harm, however sure she is of its certainty, the plea of self-defence will not succeed. Future threats are not recognised by the law as sufficient reason for a woman to hurt the one who has threatened to injure her. Such is not considered to be imminent danger.

But if a person has ever threatened and in fact carried out a future threat, should this not be a defence, since the threat — though unpredictable — is certain to happen at some time or the other? The terror and anxiety the threatened woman goes through in anticipation of the torture should offer her justification for her assault against her tormentor. But the present law of self-defence does not apply to fear that danger will become imminent. Certainty in law does not mean imminence.

Consequently, in the case of *Tereza Nakayima* above, the fact that the deceased, who had a history of persecuting his wife, had threatened to kill her did not absolve her of criminal responsibility for killing him.

The law allows deadly force only if there is no safe avenue of retreat available to the person who resorts to that force to repel an attack. A woman who kills in fear or contemplation of future injury will find it difficult to convince the court that deadly force was the only avenue for avoiding the injury. The question would be: why did the woman not just flee from the anticipated attack, or why did she not report the threat to the police or at least seek help from neighbours? Yet from stories of women like Karugaba, Kampikaho, Agaba and others, it is clear that the belief that a battered woman can leave her batterer is a myth. The neighbours she flees to will urge her to go back to her husband. The law authorities she reports to will not treat a threat from a husband as criminal. The husband will demand or at least persuade the woman to come back. The question: 'why did you not leave?' fails to recognise the socio-economic, cultural and other constraints that keep women in violent homes.

Many battered women fail to successfully plead self-defence because of the prerequisite that a person is allowed to use deadly force against an attacker only if there is no available safe avenue of retreat. Several psychologists[32] have contended that the process of victimisation leads to psychological paralysis so that even where options of escape exist, the battered woman may fail to use them. Evidence that a woman homicide offender was suffering from such paralysis (the *battered woman syndrome*) has been accepted by some American courts, sometimes leading to acquittals, sometimes to the reduction of the charges, and sometimes to leniency in sentencing.[33]

One of the criticisms against the acceptance of the woman's psychological paralysis as a defence may be that the woman was not suffering from the paralysis when the abuse started. At one stage she was capable of leaving the relationship and her continued stay, at least at the beginning, was voluntary and tantamount to consent to abuse. Such an argument however ignores the fact that a woman's decision to leave or to stay in a marriage cannot be understood in isolation of the wider socio-economic and cultural context within which she operates. As Rosen (1986:4) said, such a woman 'is a victim of her social reality, responding to circumstances in accordance with the values of femininity and life-long marriage to which she was acculturated'. I contend that evidence of a history of previous retreat which has not worked should be treated as relevant to the question of the reasonableness of the woman's homicidal act.

The importance attached to the concept of imminence is unnecessarily great. In a 1977 American case, *People v Garcia*,[34] the Superior Court of Monterey County, California, acquitted, on self-defence, a woman who killed a man who had threatened her with further injury in the future. According to the facts of the said case, Garcia was physically and sexually assaulted by two male acquaintances. Before leaving the scene, the men threatened to return and rape her again. She took her gun and went to search for her assailants. Several hours later she found one of the men on a street and shot him. The court permitted the jury to consider the accused's ethnic background, her rape, and the men's threat to repeat their attack, when determining whether she reasonably believed that the use of deadly force was necessary to avoid an imminent threat of serious bodily harm.

Just as the court in Garcia's case allowed the previous rape to be considered, Ugandan courts should accept, as relevant to the question of reasonableness, previous assaults of the victim against the accused. The woman's experience of previous assaults makes her fear of threats of future injury well-founded and reasonable. The accused's act should be considered in light of all the information that was known to her at the time of the killing. Where, as in the case of battered women, the victim's prior conduct with the accused has been violent, this will inevitably influence the accused's perception of the danger posed by the victim at the time of the homicide.

In my prison interviews I asked 'husband killers' whether they had, during trial, presented their stories of persecution to the court. They consistently answered that:

> ... the court was not interested in history; ... I was told to stick to what happened during the assault; ... my lawyer told me to stick to the homicide incident....

It is hypocritical of the law to determine reasonableness on the basis of one overt act when, in fact, the victim and the accused had a history together.

How much force may be used in self-defence?

Elizabeth Obaro[35] did not succeed on a plea of self-defence when indicted for the murder of her husband. Although her act was in response to the husband's attack on her, the court ruled that her action exceeded the limits allowed by the law. She was judged to have used force far in excess of what was considered reasonable for purposes of warding off an attack.

The facts were that the accused and the deceased had a bitter quarrel after the deceased had unjustly accused his wife of adultery. He refused to have supper with her and also prevented her from sleeping in their bed. They quarrelled almost the whole night and the deceased kicked the accused three times. He then took up an axe but before he could cut her, she seized it from him and inflicted several injuries on him. The accused, too, had some injuries.

In delivering judgement, Justice Dickson said:

> The accused might have been provoked and unjustly accused by her husband, but should not have taken the law into her hands. Moreover, she had not delivered one blow but several blows and with a lethal weapon, a dangerous weapon. *Even if it was a matter of self-defence, your retaliation would have exceeded whatever force might have been given you, ... [inflicting] several cut wounds.* ... By doing that, it clearly shows that you in a way meant to kill your husband, ... to do him grievous harm ... (my emphasis).

In other words, the force used will only be accepted as reasonable if it was the minimum amount necessary to avert/prevent the imminent danger.

The judge's implicit disapproval of the fact that the accused 'in a way meant to kill' her husband is in my opinion, a misdirection of the law of self-defence. Intention to kill does not per se rob an accused of the defence as long as her action was necessary to prevent/avert imminent death or serious bodily injury. Even proof that the woman's retaliation was partly out of anger should not rob her of the defence of self-defence, for I concur with Schneider and Jordan (1978:20) that:

Many people, including many lawyers, think that if a woman's response is even partially motivated by anger at the victim, the defence of self-defence is precluded. However, in cases involving rape, sexual assault or wife assault, rage is a perfectly legitimate response, and a self-defence should not automatically be ruled out.

The decision in Obaro's case differs significantly from *Regina v Tamale Grushie*,[36] a Ghana case in which the Court of Appeal held that:

> ... the question that has to be decided was whether the act done was in necessary self-defence, and not whether it went further than was necessary in self-defence. Homicide is justifiable *as soon as* the act is found to be in necessary self-defence (my emphasis).

Obaro's case is also inconsistent with the case of *Manzi v R*.[37] In the Manzi case, the East African Court of Appeal held that, once there is a finding that an accused was entitled to use lethal force, what he did after he had used it could not affect his liability on the charge of murder. Where an accused inflicted a number of blows against the deceased, and it is proved that he acted in self-defence, the onus of proving that the fatal blow was struck after the deceased had been incapacitated by an earlier and less fatal blow lies on the prosecution.

On the other hand, the judgement in *Bituresi Kakurungu*[38] is consistent with the just-mentioned Tamale and Manzi cases. In the Kakurungu case, the Uganda High Court held that:

> The accused ... struck the fatal blow. I find that she did so in self-defence. ... I do not disregard that several blows were struck but finding as I do that the accused was entitled to use lethal force what blows she struck thereafter could not affect her liability on the charge of murder. ... [I hold her to be] acquitted of murder and of any other lesser offence.

The views expressed in Kakurungu, Manzi and Tamale should represent the correct standard of accountability. Once a person is 'forced' to use lethal force to ward off an attack, it would be unrealistic of the law to expect her to think so clearly as to notice that she has delivered enough blows to incapacitate her attacker and to immediately gain self-control and thereby resist from any further blow against her attacker.

However, it is likely that Obaro's case is the correct (though not the desirable) interpretation of the law, in light of Section 218 of the Uganda Penal Code, which provides that a person is criminally responsible for the use of excessive force.[39] Cases have established that in light of Section 218, a person is guilty of manslaughter if he/she uses excessive force in defence of person or property. Perhaps justice would be better served if Ugandan law adopted the position in the Danish Criminal Code which under Section 13(2) provides that 'any person who exceeds the limits of lawful self-defence shall not be liable to punishment if his act could reasonably be attributed to the fear or excitement produced by the attack.'

The use of weapons

Most women interviewed in prison used fatal weapons in their assaults (as indicated in Table 7) and so did most women appearing in the court records. This is true of both the women whose assaults were against men as well as those against fellow women. This pattern may be because 'it is possible that a would-be homicide case may be an assault one if a less lethal weapon is used instead. This is especially true of homicide cases which are perpetrated by females' (Mushanga 1974: 55).

The women who killed children in the process of 'disciplining' them used no weapons. This is consistent with Mushanga's (1974:66) contention that:

> ... the use of physical brute force is not very popular. It is not humanly easy for a person to [kill another without a weapon and] without any help. But when this happens, it means that the victim was in one way or another at a greater disadvantage. Either he was quite young or quite old in comparison with his slayer; ... the

person who dies as a result of a kicking (or choking, etc.) is either already in poor physical health or is too young or too old when compared to his slayer.

The records indicate that six of the 91 court cases involved no weapons. In 18 cases the records did not indicate whether or not

Table 7: Weapons used: court and prison records

Weapon	No. among court records	No. of women inmates
Stick	13	4
Panga	8	5
Axe	6	1
Unidentified sharp instrument	5	0
Pit	4	3
Knife	4	5
Gun	3	0
Poison	3	6
Hoe	3	5
Water (Drowning)	2	2
Pestle	2	0
Spear	2	1
Rope	2	1
Hot water (Scalding)	2	0
Fire	2	3
Bucket	1	0
Acid	0	3
Stone	0	1
Bottle	0	1
Iron bar	0	2
Other	0	2
Total	**62**	**45**

any weapons were used but, among these 18 cases, two cases recorded strangulation as the method used and two showed that the victims had been beaten to death. In three cases, the homicides resulted from mob justice. In one case, the accused allegedly hired other people to carry out the homicide, and she had no direct involvement in the act of homicide. The nature of weapons used in the remaining 62 cases is indicated in the table.

Note that a wide range of weapons were used. Nevertheless, the majority of weapons (32 out of 62, or 52 percent) were either farming or household implements. If the stick is added to the number, the percentage is even higher: 73 percent. In reference to a 'stick', one should note that the said term includes any piece of wood irrespective of size (and marked in the court records either as stick, or piece of wood, or log, etc.). Lumping of sticks and other pieces of wood together is necessitated by the lack of clear definitions for the terms, a fact also noted by Mushanga (1974).

The pattern which emerged from the prison study was similar to the court-records cases. I could not get information regarding the weapons used in 14 cases. This is because the women concerned not only denied having assaulted the victims but also denied any knowledge about the weapons used. The common reaction in regard to the question of weapons was: 'I was arrested on the allegation that I killed the victim. After the arrest I was not even given a chance to look at the victim's body. I have no idea who or what could have killed him.'

In seven cases no weapons were used. Three women beat their victims to death; in two cases, women bit their victims; and in another two, the victims were pushed and fatally injured in the resulting fall. In two infanticide cases, the women insisted that they had stillbirths, but these were erroneously recorded as 'infanticide'. In other infanticide cases where weapons were involved, 24 out of 45 were household and farm implements.

The predominance of farming implements among the weapons is hardly surprising. Most of the women homicide-offenders I interviewed were peasant farmers at the time of arrest. As Bohannan observed, 'killers commit homicides with whatever weapon may be handy. The implication is that the weapons used are no more than a reflection of patterns of cultural activity in the society concerned' (1960:247). This shows that the more frequently a weapon is held by a particular segment in society, the more it will figure in violent homicides perpetrated by members of that group, and vice versa.

Mushanga (1974,1976) also stated that people will use whatever weapon is available to cause death. Interestingly enough, as Mushanga (1976:73) discovered more than two decades ago, it appears that in Uganda today, 'the use of firearms has not yet become a social problem as it is in other parts of the world.' This may seem odd given the fact that firearms were generally available during that period. In any case, it should be noted that peasant women would not have had access to firearms anyway.

Carlen (1983:44) threw light on women's use of weapons against violent husbands when she said that 'when the crunch comes, when women can stand no more, they have to use a weapon and something more effective than the traditional and much parodied rolling-pin.' Carlen's Clare, a woman who had suffered beatings and kickings from two husbands and subsequently attempted to murder the first, and succeeded in killing the second, said (Ibid: 44):

> You've got to use a weapon. *It's only a weapon that's going to stop a man*, because if you just hit him with something like a rolling-pin you're going to get an awful kicking (my emphasis).

For the women who used weapons against their attackers it can be contended that 'only a weapon could stop their men.' They used weapons because they found themselves in situations in which they believed that violence was the only way of getting out of danger. For many women, it is virtually impossible to overcome a violent man without the use of a weapon.

But does the law of self-defence recognise the need to use a fatal weapon? In cases where the court is of the view that only lethal force could keep off the original assailant (the subsequent victim), the use of a lethal weapon will not rob an accused of the defence of self-defence. Thus in *Bituresi Kakurungu* (above), the accused was acquitted of murder and even of any minor cognate offence despite the fact that she had inflicted several blows on her husband using a *panga*. His Lordship Justice Mead said:

> I believe the sworn statement of the accused ... that the deceased fought with her, and had threatened to leave the children parentless that night. I find that the accused, gaining possession of the *panga*, ran from the house; ... the deceased was chasing her. She was stopped by the pit; the pit is only 20 yards from the house. In that distance I find that the danger apprehended by the accused to her life at the hands of the deceased was still imminent. The accused believed that if the deceased succeeded in arresting the *panga* from her he would kill her. The accused turned and struck the fatal blow. I find that she did so in self-defence of her own life.

The use of a weapon may, however, bias courts against an accused, since according to Jones (1980:300), 'when one man attacks another with his fists, the court assumes that they are more or less evenly matched and generally does not allow the man attacked to counter with a weapon.' In the court's eyes, therefore, using a weapon may indicate that the accused intended to kill rather than protect her life from the assaulter. Thus, in *Elizabeth Obaro*, her use of a lethal, dangerous weapon weighed against her plea of self-defence. In *Kazigati's* case (above), the judge pronounced that use of a weapon against an assaulter whose intentions were to rape the accused exceeded reasonable force. Such courts' pronouncements have failed:

> [t]o acknowledge that a 110-pound woman might need a weapon against her 255-pound husband. ... To a small woman untrained in physical combat, a man's fists and feet appear to be deadly weapons, and in fact they are: many women killed by their husbands are not shot or stabbed but simply beaten and kicked to death. The woman who counters her husband's fists with a gun may *in fact* be doing no more than meeting deadly force with deadly force (Jones, 1980:330) (emphasis original).

Most courts have also failed to appreciate Schneider and Jordan's contention (1978:5) that:

> ... due to a variety of societally-based factors, a woman may reasonably perceive ... lethal danger in a situation in which a man might not. This perception will justify for her, as it would for a man who perceives such danger, recourse to deadly force.

Some American courts, however, have acknowledged that women's social history and relatively smaller sizes may necessitate them to use weapons against unarmed assailants. For example, in *State v Wanrow*,[40] the Washington Supreme court reversed Wanrow's second-degree murder conviction on the basis that the use of the 'reasonable man' objective standard of self-defence violated Wanrow's right to equal protection of the law because it did not adequately include a woman's perspective. Nor did it reflect women's social reality.

Wanrow shot an intoxicated, unarmed man whom she knew had a reputation for violence when he approached her in a threatening manner. At the time, Wanrow, who was five-foot-four-inches tall, had a broken leg and was using a crutch. The court held that:

> The impression that a 5'4" woman with a cast on her leg and using a crutch must, under the law, somehow repel an assault by a 6'2" intoxicated man without employing weapons in her defense ... constitutes a misstatement of the law. ... [Women have] the right to have their conduct judged in the light of the individual handicaps which are the product of sex discrimination [such as denial of training in physical combat, socialisation into belief that display of physical aggression is unfeminine and therefore undesirable, etc.] To fail to do so is to deny the right of the individual woman involved to trial by the same rules which are applicable to male defendants.

The court also ruled (as in the Garcia case above) that it was improper to preclude consideration of the circumstances prior to the occasion of the killing, such as the accused's knowledge of the deceased's reputation for violence.

The arguments in relation to the use of weapons are again not only relevant when an accused pleads self-defence but are equally important in any discussion of the issue of legal provocation (to be discussed later). For example, Viscount Simon of the English Court of Appeal summarised the relevant propositions of the law in *Mancini v DPP*[41] and, among other things, said:

> In deciding the question whether [legal provocation can be pleaded], regard must be had to the nature of the act by which the offender causes death; ... the mode of resentment, as instanced by the weapon used, must bear a reasonable proportion to the provocation.

In *Rex v Lesbini*[42] the same court had previously said that:

> ... in applying the test, it is of particular importance to take into account the instrument with which the homicide was effected, for to resort, in the heat of passion induced, by a simple blow, is a very different thing from making use of a deadly instrument like a concealed dagger. In short, the mode of resentment must bear a reasonable relationship to the provocation if the offence is to be reduced to manslaughter.

East African courts have for a long time followed the same principle and in a 1942 case,[43] the East African Court of Appeal held that 'where a deadly weapon is used the provocation must be great indeed to reduce the offence to that of manslaughter.' I reviewed the relevant court records in order to find out if there is a relationship between the nature of weapon used and the sentences awarded to an offender.

The longest period of imprisonment among the court record cases was six years, given in two cases. In both cases, the women's assaults involved the use of weapons. In 331/71, the woman killed a man using an axe. She was convicted under Section 182(1) of the Penal Code. Having spent ten months on remand she was sentenced to an additional six years in custody. The longest possible period spent in custody was 'more than eight years'. This was case 19/90 in which a woman killed another woman, a neighbour, with an axe. She was convicted under S.187 the Uganda Penal Code. Having spent 'more than six years' on remand, she was sentenced to a two-year prison term.

The most lenient sentences were the non-custodial sentences. In 598/69, a woman who killed her brother-in-law using a stick was convicted under S.187 of the Penal Code and was given a suspended prison sentence of 12 months. Having spent eight months on remand, she spent the shortest period in custody among the relevant cases. In 116/75, a woman who used a knife to kill her brother-in-law was convicted under S.187 of the Penal Code. She was then cautioned by the court. In 295/69, a woman killed her husband with a hoe. She was convicted under S.187 and was bound over in the sum of 3,000 Uganda shillings (not cash), to keep the peace and be of good behaviour for 12 months.

In 61/73, a woman threw her child in a pit, and on a conviction of attempted murder, she was bound over in her own recognisance in the sum of 1,000 Uganda shillings, for 12 months to be of good behaviour and to keep the peace.

In four cases, women were sentenced to imprisonment 'until the rising of the court'. In one such case, a woman had 'slashed' her female employer and was convicted under S.187 the Penal Code. In another case, 558/68, a woman used a stick to kill her co-wife and was convicted under S.187. In 79/90, another woman killed her adult stepson with a *panga* and was convicted under S.187. In the fourth case, a woman pushed a man, who hit his head against a wall and died. She was convicted under S.187. In the two cases where the accused persons used no weapons, the sentences were relatively lenient — one day in case 12/90 and six months in case 651/70.

As already mentioned, only 20 of the 66 interviewed women were convicts. Among them the longest prison sentence was eight years, given to Karugaba, who killed her husband with a *panga* and was convicted under S.187. Karugaba's total calculated period in custody was also the longest since she spent six years on remand. The shortest sentence of imprisonment was five months, given to

Nalukwago, who used an iron stick in her assault and was convicted under S.228 of the Penal Code (covering assaults causing actual bodily harm). Nalukwago was never remanded. Among the homicide cases, the shortest prison sentence was one year and three months, given to Kuri for having killed her (female) cousin with a stone.

Although the data is difficult to interpret, there is a tendency by the courts to pass lenient sentences where offenders used no weapons in the assaults (e.g., where an offender fatally pushes her victim). Courts also tend to be lenient where the offender uses a non-lethal weapon such as a stick. Nonetheless, where the victims of homicide are children, courts tend to pass relatively harsh sentences even if no weapons have been used.

An offender who uses a fatal weapon such as an axe, knife or hoe is likely to get a harsh sentence. However, this is subject to the circumstances of the homicide. In cases where the victims were the first to attempt to use (or in fact use) fatal weapons against their subsequent slayers, and the latter used the same weapons in the homicide incidents, courts passed lenient sentences. These are cases in which the offenders' acts could easily be interpreted as self-defence homicides but the offenders pleaded guilty to manslaughter.

Provocation as a defence[44]

Among the 91 perused files pertaining to women prosecuted between 1967 and 1992 for homicide and related offences, 54 (59 percent) ended in convictions of manslaughter. Under the Uganda Penal Code, manslaughter can be committed either in accordance with Section 182(1), or Section 187, or Section 188B(1). None of the 54 cases involved women who killed in pursuance of suicide pacts, Section 188B(1).[45] Twenty of the 54 women (37 percent) were guilty under Section 182 (discussed in detail later). But the large majority (63 percent) of women who were convicted of manslaughter fell under Section 187.[46] In these cases we can assume that the courts accepted that the offender's reaction was reasonable in the face of the provocative act in question.

Under Section 187, if a person in the heat of passion unlawfully kills another, as a consequence of being provoked by that other person, such killing is treated as 'manslaughter only'. Section 188 defines provocation, inter alia, as a wrongful act or insult which is likely to deprive an ordinary person of the power of self-control and to induce him to commit the kind of assault which he committed upon the victim: the person who had provoked him.[47]

As noted earlier, although the section refers to an 'ordinary' person, the interpretation attached to the phrase by the courts is identical to that attached to 'reasonableness' in self-defence in several cases already discussed in this book. Just as it is with self-defence, an unreasonable degree of retaliation to provocation will exclude the defence. It has been held that the 'ordinary person', whose standard of behaviour is taken as the test of justifiableness of the accused's reaction, must be considered to be an ordinary person of the same community as the accused himself.[48]

In reference to the phrase 'heat of passion' used in Section 187 the Uganda Penal Code, the East African Court of Appeal, in the case of *Yovan v Uganda* (above) held, that 'the heat of passion required refers not only to a state of anger but to any emotional state caused by the provocation and which is such as to deprive an ordinary person of self-control.' In the judgement of the court read by Justice Duffus, it was said:

> [I]t has been suggested in some of the previous cases that the heat of passion refers only to a state of anger. We think that this might be too narrow an interpretation; the intention of the section is to denote an emotional state which has been caused by the act of the person assaulted and is such as to deprive an ordinary person of self-control. ... In certain circumstances it would be difficult to say if an appellant acts partially in desperation or in sudden fear or whether he acts wholly in anger. The main element is the sudden reaction which causes such an overpowering emotion as to deprive the appellant of self-control

It is also worth noting that in *Doto s/o Mtaki v Regina*,[49] the East African Court of Appeal held that:

> ... it is not the law in East Africa that, for the defence of provocation to succeed, it must appear that the accused was so provoked as to be incapable of forming an intent to kill or cause dangerous harm.
> ... There is no reference in the definition to the question of the capacity or otherwise of the accused to form an intent.

Since close to two-thirds of the cases analysed in this study ended in convictions under Section 187, it is possible to contend that, in Uganda, most women's violence is a result of provocation.

Provocation and accumulated violence

Does proof of persecution by the victim reduce the accused's responsibility for her crime? For one to successfully plead provocation, she must have assaulted the victim in the heat of passion resulting from the victim's wrongful and provocative act. She must have acted before she had time to cool down from the emotion caused by the victim's wrongful act. Consequently, the history of violence by the victim against the offender cannot of itself be taken as having provoked the offender. 'Accumulated' violence cannot reduce an accused's legal responsibility for her crime.

A perusal of cases in which women were convicted of manslaughter only on the basis that they acted under provocation, shows that Ugandan courts have accepted provocation in cases which do not fit within the restrictive definition of the Penal Code. This tendency may, as O'Donovan (1991:224) suggested in another context, be evidence of divergent opinions between the courts and the legislature. In Uganda, the courts' liberal interpretation of the law is even more crucial because of the more limited categories of homicide: either manslaughter or murder. Rejecting the defence leads to a conviction of murder, an offence carrying a mandatory death sentence.

In *Sofia Auma* (above), the husband used to severely beat his wife whenever she refused to give him money for gambling. On the day before the homicide, she was beaten as usual. She reported the matter to the village authorities. Since it was a Sunday, the case could not be heard and she was told that her complaint would be handled the next day. On Monday, the husband again demanded money for gambling and when the wife refused, he beat her once again. That day, the accused served her husband poisoned food and he died.

This was certainly a premeditated act but the court did not only give a loose interpretation to 'provocation' but also gave her a relatively lenient sentence: two months imprisonment. One of the factors submitted by the defence counsel in mitigation was that the accused and the deceased had a very unhappy marriage frequented by assaults on the accused by the deceased. In passing sentence, the court admittedly took into account submissions of counsel.

The court's leniency in Auma's case differs from what transpired in *Tembo v the King*,[50] a case whose facts were similar. In Tembo the accused killed her husband by poisoning his beer. The husband had subjected her to physical and other abuse throughout their nine-year marriage. On the day in question, he beat her severely with a hoe handle. She was convicted of murder. The court said that:

> Under any circumstances, the act was not done in the heat of passion caused by sudden provocation. *It is open to doubt whether the defence of sudden provocation is ever likely to succeed* in reducing the crime of murder to manslaughter *in cases of killing by administration* of poison with proved intent to kill (my emphases).

Witchcraft as both motive and defence

Several court cases show that witchcraft is a belief deeply embedded in Ugandan society and sometimes it is because of belief in witchcraft that homicides occur. In 11 of the cases perused during the course of research for this book, the accused women killed persons they believed to have been practising witchcraft. Five of the cases involved polygamous marriages; women killed co-wives suspected of witchcraft. In one of the cases, the accused killed her mother-in-law, whose witchcraft was supposedly responsible for the accused's infertility. In another case the accused killed a neighbour whose witchcraft was blamed for the death of the children of the accused.

Similarly, Nabowa, who was on remand for killing her stepmother, justified the homicide to me thus:

> She [the stepmother] had cursed me to suffer throughout my life. As a result my three attempts at marriage were all frustrated. On the day of the crime I went to contact the deceased in order that she revokes the curse on me, but she was rude and told me that if I insisted on the curse issue, I was going to suffer even more. I grabbed a hoe and struck her....

A few months after my interview with her, she was convicted of manslaughter although she had been indicted for murder. Nabowa had been on remand for two years and three months. She was given a six-year prison sentence.

Common sayings in the vernacular languages are evidence of society's belief in witchcraft. In Lusoga, for example, it is said that if a person dies and nobody is singled out as the witch/wizard, the deceased cannot fit in the grave or her/his soul cannot rest in peace — *aziraku mulogo tasuga magombe*. In Rukiga it is said that there is no person who dies without being bewitched — *tiharhio mufu otarogwa*. Both sayings portray the belief that all misfortune is caused by witchcraft. And La Fontaine (1960:96) said that in the past, and to a less extent by the time of his research, among the Bagisu of eastern Uganda, all deaths were considered murder, in that responsibility for each death was laid at someone's door and accusations and counter-accusations of witchcraft and sorcery were rampant.

Ugandan courts have taken judicial notice of this belief and, under certain circumstances, accused persons who kill persons they believed to be practising witchcraft have been convicted of manslaughter rather than murder. For example, in *Kenjeru w/o Karindori*,[51] the deceased and the accused were co-wives. The deceased entered the accused's bedroom and removed the latter's blanket and spread it on her own bed. The accused tried to retrieve her blanket but the deceased resisted those attempts. The accused got a hoe and pursued the deceased and cut her across the skull once. The victim died immediately.

The defence counsel for the accused argued that the fatal attack was provoked by the belief that the victim intended to bewitch the accused and her child. The defence counsel said that 'the accused ... [was] sorry about what happened, but ... the deceased's action had angered her, it was a threat of bewitchment, and the accused had decided to finish off the deceased before she could harm her.'

In mitigation the defence counsel also said that the deceased had previously threatened to kill the accused by 'all means'. Accordingly, when the deceased took a blanket from the bed of the accused, the latter thought it was going to be used in witchcraft. The defence counsel further prayed to court that the fact that Kenjeru had lost four children earlier on should be taken into consideration. She believed that those deaths had been a result of witchcraft. Her only surviving child was sick at the time of the assault and the fear that the deceased's aim was to finish off that child as well, was understandable.

The defence counsel contended that the belief in witchcraft is deeply embedded in Ugandan society and that the accused's belief was, in the circumstances, not far-fetched. Although Kenjeru was indicted for murder, the court accepted the submissions by the defence counsel and convicted her of manslaughter. Having been on remand for two years, she was sentenced to five years in prison.

Courts, however, emphasise that it is not a belief in witchcraft per se that constitutes a circumstance of mitigation for killing a person believed to be a witch or a wizard. The belief must be accompanied by an immediate provocative act by the 'witch' or 'wizard'.

In H.C.C.S.C. No. 123/76 the court revealed in great detail circumstances under which witchcraft can constitute provocation:

> [I]f the facts proved to establish that the victim was performing in the actual presence of the accused some act which the accused did genuinely believe, and which an ordinary person of the community to which the accused belongs would genuinely believe,

> to be an act of witchcraft against him or another person under his immediate care (which act would be a criminal offence under the Criminal Law (Witchcraft) Ordinance of Uganda, ... he might be angered to such an extent as to be deprived of the power of self-control and induced to assault the person doing the act of witchcraft. And if this be the case, a defence of grave and sudden provocation is open to him. It must always be a question of fact as to whether he is in all the circumstances of the particular case acting in the heat of passion caused by grave and sudden provocation.

However, the court also noted that if an accused kills another person in revenge for supposedly for causing a fatal bewitchment of a relative in the past, this would not be a legal provocation. The killing must have been a result of an immediate act by the victim in the presence of the accused. As other provocations, witchcraft must be immediate to be provocative.

It is not only the courts that have taken notice of the significance of witchcraft in Ugandan society. In 1957 the legislature passed a statute specifically dealing with the subject — the Witchcraft Act.[52] The Act makes it an offence to practice witchcraft or to hold oneself out as a witch, to hire or procure another person to practice witchcraft, or to consult with such practitioner 'for evil purposes.'[53] It is also an offence to impute, except to a person in authority, the use of witchcraft to another person, if harm thereby results to him.[54] The most serious crime in the Act is that of threatening a person with death by witchcraft or other supernatural means. The offence is punishable with life imprisonment. The Act allows evidence to be brought in court to show the reputation of a person as a witch, and to show that by common repute 'any substance, means, process or ceremony ... administered, used or performed ... is commonly administered, used or performed in the practice of witchcraft' (Section 8).

In view of the legislature's recognition of witchcraft as anti-social behaviour, it is perhaps not surprising that judges appreciate the likelihood that anybody who perceives herself to be in danger of its consequences would be partially justified to react violently.

The courts' recognition of witchcraft as possible provocative behaviour is also in line with the definition of the section of the Penal Code that requires an act to be unlawful before it can be recognised as legally provocative.[55]

Provocation and sentencing

Provocation is not only a partial defence to a charge of murder, which, if proved, reduces the offence to the less serious offence of manslaughter, but it is also a mitigating factor in other violent crimes in the sense that it may reduce the severity of punishment to be meted to an offender.[56] In Uganda, courts are given wide discretionary powers in determining the gravity of a sentence to be awarded to a convicted person. For the majority of offences (manslaughter inclusive), the Penal Code prescribes maximum sentences and it is up to the judicial officer to use his/her discretion to determine the exact punishment to be given within the prescribed limits. As noted earlier, the maximum punishment for manslaughter is imprisonment for life.

Justice Odoki (1990:152) had a point when he said that 'a person who commits a crime when he has lost his self-control deserves leniency because of the reduced moral blameworthiness.' Odoki's view is also supported by Wolfgang (1993:180) in the following words:

> The defendant in victim-precipitated crimes should probably be viewed as less morally blameworthy, less culpable than his premeditating or unprovoked counterpart. The offender of an offence that would not have occurred without victim precipitation is probably less dangerous than the unprovoked offender; he responds to limited kinds of circumstances and may be deserving of some societal sympathy.

Do the cases which have been cited in this book indicate that Ugandan courts subscribe to Odoki's view? In some cases, there is evidence that where the accused woman's unlawful act was in retaliation for the victim's provocation, she received a relatively short sentence in recognition of the great provocation that caused her to act violently.

In *Terezina Karawali* (above), the accused killed her husband, and on a conviction of manslaughter, she was given a probation order. The facts, based on a statement made to the police by the accused and accepted by the prosecution were as follows:

> I do not know how he died; I left him still alive on 13.2.70 at about 15 hours. He had been beating me. He started beating me at about 13 hours until 15 hours. He beat me, strangled me, kicked me, boxed me until all my body was full of bruises which you can see now. I cannot hear properly, my mouth is bruised, all my elbows are bruised. All my clothes were torn. I, because he had beaten me so much, took the stick with which he was beating me and I beat him only once. I do not know where I beat him. I beat him once and ran away....

As discussed earlier, the court concluded that the circumstances of the case showed that her act was not in self-defence since she could have escaped without striking back. The court, however, accepted that when Terezina struck the deceased it was in retaliation for the severe and illegal beating which she had received at his hands. While the court realised that the accused had taken the law into her own hands and had, contrary to the law's prohibition, avenged her injuries, it subjected her to a probation order. A probation order not only relieves the offender of imprisonment and its consequent disadvantages, but it also relieves her of a criminal record.

This does not mean that in all cases where a person kills under provocation, she will get a lenient sentence. Five of the women convicted under Section 187 were given non-custodial sentences. Among the women who were given prison sentences, the shortest sentence was 'imprisonment until the rising of the court'. The longest prison sentence for a conviction under Section 187 was five years given in three cases (215/91, 237/75 and 23/83). It is worth noting that all the three cases involved women who had spent long periods on remand. The average term of imprisonment was two years and four months. The most frequent prison sentences were one day's imprisonment and three years.

Among the cases where information on both the period of remand and sentence is known (25 cases), the longest custody period possible to be served was in H.C.C.S.C. No.19 of 1990: 'more than eight years'. In this case, the judge said that the accused had spent 'more than six years' on remand. He gave her a sentence of two years' imprisonment. The shortest time spent in custody was in case No. 744/69, where an accused spent two months on remand and was, on conviction, given a non-custodial sentence: bound over for two years to be of good behaviour in the sum of 200 Uganda shillings. From the studied cases, therefore, there is no clear pattern regarding the extent to which proof of provocation earns a woman a lenient sentence.

Accumulated violence and sentencing

Proof that the accused had been a victim of her victim's persecution before the homicide event sometimes affects the court's view of what amounts to an appropriate sentence for the convicted person. *Faisi Apio* (above) is a case in which the victim's persecution of the accused led to a lenient sentence. Since the accused had in the words of the court 'been [more] sinned against than sinning', she was bound over for two years to be of good behaviour in the nominal sum of 200 Uganda shillings, not cash.

It cannot, however, be stated with certainty that in all cases where there is a history of persecution by the deceased against the accused, courts will pronounce a lenient sentence. In *Tereza Nakayima* (above), the judge, after noting the evidence of persecution (history of violence) against the accused by her husband, still declared that her action could not go unpunished. The judge declared that justice would be done by meting a prison sentence of 12 months — to a persecuted woman who had been on remand for 17 months!

Verdicts under Section 182 of the Uganda Penal Code

As already mentioned, 20 women were convicted under Section 182, which makes it manslaughter if a person by an unlawful act or omission inadvertently causes the death of another.[57] Since there is no proof of malice aforethought,[58] courts cannot return a verdict of murder.[59] The assaults which led to the deaths are unlawful and must be punished but the intention accompanying the said acts is not malice aforethought.

Verdicts under this section are usual in circumstances where the homicide is carried out through 'mob justice'. For example, in *Monika Nagadya and Others* (above), Justice Ssekandi said of three offenders (one of them a woman who had attacked and killed a villagemate on allegations that he was a wizard, and had prevented rain and caused drought in the area):

> ... the intention of the accused ... in beating the victim ... was not to kill. ... [The] intention was to punish the deceased and force him to show them the articles of witchcraft. ... It is my view that in cases of witchcraft there is generally lacking the intention to kill necessary to constitute murder (see *Uganda v Gabriel Ojoba* H.C.C.S.C. No. 260/75).

Another example is *Tereza Ngamita and Others* (above), in which seven persons, three of them women, were accused of murder but convicted of manslaughter. Believing that one of their relatives had bewitched a son of one of the accused persons, they beat him to death. They were convicted of manslaughter, because according to Justice Wambuzi:

> Court was doubtful whether any of the accused persons had any intention to kill the deceased. Also of doubt as to whether any of them knew that the beating would result in grievous harm. The deceased and others [three other women] were tortured so that they may confess that they were wizards.

Although these cases involved allegations of witchcraft against the victims, the courts returned verdicts under Section 182 and not under provocation. The courts handled the cases in ways similar to instances where a thief, or any other person considered anti-social, is killed by a mob. Verdicts under Section 182(1) are, however, not limited to cases of mob justice. In the recent case of *Violet Katungwabusha*,[60] a woman who killed her stepchild 'in the process of disciplining her' was charged with murder but convicted under Section 182(1).

I analysed court sentences to find out whether the courts treat women who kill without intention to do so and those who kill as a result of provocation differently. Among the cases on which information was complete (13 cases), the longest possible period in custody was six years and ten months — case 331/71. This was also the case in which the harshest sentence was given: six years. The shortest calculated custody period was one year: 12/70 and 375/69. The most lenient sentence given was in case 12/70: one day's imprisonment. The average prison sentence was two years and 11 months. The most frequent prison sentences awarded were two years and five years.

Whereas the longest possible custody period was by a woman convicted under Section 187: eight years, the harshest sentence given was to a woman convicted under Section 182(1): six years. For convictions under Section 182, none of the women received a non-custodial sentence. The average term of imprisonment under Section 187 was seven months shorter than the average term under Section 182. The most frequent sentences under Section 187 were shorter than the most frequent sentences under Section 182. On the whole, therefore, it might appear that offenders convicted under Section 187 tended to get off slightly better than those convicted under Section 182.

Conclusion

This study has thrown some light on the way the criminal justice system deals with women who have committed violent crimes. There is no doubt that, in theory, Ugandan law recognises the fact that: 'the murdered is not unaccountable for his own murder; ... Yea, the guilty is often times the victim of the injured[61] as evidenced by the 'availability' of self-defence and provocation as legal justifications for homicide.'

But it remains doubtful whether this recognition is fully reflected in the way the courts deal with women who appear before them. Several of the court pronouncements and decisions indicate that the guardians of justice have little insight into what a woman considers a serious threat to her life as well as the extent to which certain actions provoke a reasonable woman into violence. The Penal Code establishes self-defence and provocation as defences available to all persons irrespective of sex. Besides, there are hardly any rules within the criminal justice system that clearly differentiate between female and male offenders. However, what Sampa et al (1994:1) wrote about the Zambian court system is also applicable to the Ugandan criminal justice system. According to them:

> Discrimination on the basis of gender comes in different forms such as cumbersome court procedures, content and effect of the law, and the *manner in which these laws are interpreted* (my emphasis).

The narrow interpretation of the law cannot adequately take into account women's perceptions arising from their social reality. This is because homicide defences are based on male behavioural practices.

The system and the law have different effects on women, especially arising from discretionary powers given to the officers of law. As Jones (1980:311) observed about American law:

> The body of law, made by men, for men, and amassed down through history on their behalf, codifies masculine bias and systematically discriminates against women by ignoring the woman's point of view. Today the law is largely enforced, interpreted, and administered by men; so it still works in the interests of men as a group. Women, schooled like men to good citizenship, accept the law's male bias as objective justice; women lawyers, judges, and jurors, taught the same rules, usually uphold the same male standard. And whether that male standard constitutes conscious sex discrimination or the innocent side effect of a shared male point of view, the result for women is the same: they are deprived at every step of equal protection under the law. ... Often that male bias shows up at one stage or another of the legal process in the exercise of 'discretion.' That built-in flexibility which allows a judge or a prosecutor or a police officer to use 'better judgement' is essential, experts agree, to a legal system that tries to deal fairly with individual cases. But since discretion usually is exercised *by* men (or by women trained to the male standard), it is usually exercised *for* men, for the male standard. Judicial discretion, repeatedly exercised to protect the same male interests, becomes a mask for the law's underlying systematic discrimination against women ... (emphases original).

The question is: How should the law deal with victims of perpetual violence if and when they turn violent towards their oppressors? And more specifically: Do women who turn against their abusers deserve a special kind of forgiveness? In many cases, women's acts of violence are acts of self-preservation and society should recognise this. Some activists for battered women such as Walker (1984) have argued for changing the criteria of self-defence, while Ewing (1987) has called for creating new components of self-defence such as psychological self-defence.

Ugandan courts should look at developments in other common law jurisdictions[62] and reformulate the defences of self-defence and provocation. There is need for a law whose interpretation of imminency and proportionality of force takes into account women's social reality. And in recognition of the fact that in Uganda a large majority of women kill abusive husbands, the law should be amended to reflect an increased awareness of domestic violence. In the words of O'Donovan (1991:235), 'the events immediately prior to the killing should be de-emphasized.'[63]

Apart from a broader interpretation of imminency and proportionality, there is also a need to broaden our understanding of what constitutes the 'self'. Current homicide law is based on the belief in the sanctity of human life. One of the consequences of this is the law of self-defence, which justifies a person's killing of another when the latter threatens the subsequent killer with death or serious bodily injury. But the aggressor's right to life is also protected, and one is only justified in killing the aggressor if there is no non-fatal alternative for avoiding the threatened harm. The law's current perception of what constitutes 'self' or life is, however, too narrow — since it protects a person only against physical injury. Thus, as Ewing (1987:62) said:

> As commonly understood *outside the law,* 'self' encompasses not only the physical aspects of being, but also those psychological functions, attributes, processes, and dimensions of experience that give meaning and value to physical existence (my emphasis).

In other words, the notion of 'self' encompasses the psychological as well as the physical. There is, therefore, no reason why a person who retaliates against psychological injury should be less deserving of legal recognition and compassion than one whose reaction is against physical harm.

Ewing proposed that when a person is faced with the threat of impairment of her/his psychological functioning, which impairment would significantly limit the meaning and value of her/his physical existence, and s/he, in retaliation against this threat, kills the 'assaulter', the homicide should be justified as psychological self-defence. This is in light of the fact that physical existence devoid of psychological existence is worthless.

Giving battered women as an example, Ewing contended that the cumulative violence they suffer at the hands of their abusers induces in them a 'disintegration anxiety', a fear of the breakup of the self — as equally destructive and frightening as physical death.

Thus 'the battered woman who kills in psychological self-defence has, in effect, sacrificed the life of another ... to preserve her psychological integrity' (Ewing 1987:80).

In asserting the notion of psychological death or grave psychological injury experienced by battered women due to persistent abuse, Ewing was inspired by studies of criminal victimisation which have established that, for most people, being the victim of a violent crime has serious psychological consequences.

Acceptance of psychological self-defence would justify killings by those women who have been subjected to prolonged abuse, but whose acts of homicide take place outside acute battering incidents and/or are not in reaction to an imminent threat of danger to serious bodily harm. It would cover many of the cases where, as seen in the foregoing discussion, Ugandan courts have erroneously returned verdicts of manslaughter on the basis of provocation when the facts did not fit within the restrictive definition of the Penal Code — acting while under loss of self-control caused by sudden provocation. It would also cover cases where the killers' acts of homicide were premeditated but the judges, due to sympathy with the women's extreme suffering at the hands of their husbands, entered verdicts of manslaughter rather than murder. Ewing's (1987:96) recognition of the advantage of this doctrine in the American law is also pertinent to Uganda:

> [I]t would provide jurors with a *legitimate legal basis* for acquitting battered-women homicide defendants who, by virtue of their psychological plight, do not deserve to be convicted or punished but would not be acquitted under current self-defense law. ... Under the proposed doctrine, the legal fate of these women would be determined by *an honest application of the law* rather than the unpredictable willingness of some jurors [judges] to *ignore the law* (emphases mine).

As already mentioned, under Ugandan law, if somebody performs in the presence of another, an act commonly reputed to be witchcraft and the latter in this belief kills the performer, the homicide will not be murder. Similarly, if one finds his/her spouse committing adultery and kills either the spouse or the spouse's lover, such homicide would not be murder. At the same time, if a person kills another as a result of loss of self control brought about by an insult offered by the victim to the killer, whether the insult is by word or gesture, such homicide may, depending on the surrounding circumstances, be held not to constitute murder. Also, if a person kills in defence of her/his property the homicide may, depending on the surrounding circumstances, not constitute a murder. In all such killings, the actors are reacting to psychological rather than physical injury. Yet the law is sympathetic to their plight. Accepting that psychological injury arising from persistent physical abuse is serious enough to cause an act of homicide would therefore not be too fundamental a change in policy.

Another important question that demands serious thought has been raised by scholars such as Gobert (1977:546) and Wolfgang (1993:180). This is whether and to what extent the victim as precipitator should be held liable or in any way accountable for his/her actions since this 'would constitute legal recognition of the moral obligation of every person not to encourage crime needlessly' and underscore 'society's interest to deter precipitative conduct'. This becomes even more important when it is realised that many victims of homicide have prior to their deaths had histories of violence against members of society, sometimes against persons other than their slayers. Criminal law should treat 'innocent' victims and those victims who have somehow contributed to their own injury differently. This would be analogous to the concept of contributory negligence in the law of torts.[64]

Notes

1. C. Marshal in the Introduction to *Criminal Homicide in Uganda* by Mushanga (1974).

2. The term *provocation* in this sentence is used in the sociological rather than in the legal sense.

3. See Wolfgang's comment reproduced later in this chapter, under the section on 'Provocation and sentencing'.

4. Court interpretation of Sections 187 and 188 of the U.P.C., which create the defence of provocation, will be discussed later.

5. See for example Schneider and Jordan (1978); Jones (1980); Browne (1987); Cipparone (1987); Ewing (1987).

6. It was Denver psychologist Lenore Walker (1984) who first used the term *battered woman syndrome* to explain the behaviour of abuse victims.

7. H.C.C.S.C. No. 77/91.

8. H.C.C.S.C. No. 5/90.

9. H.C.C.S.C. No. 49/82.

10. H.C.C.S.C. No. 663/67.

11. H.C.C.S.C. No. 744/69.

12. (1984) 478 A. 2d 364. Cited in Ewing (1987:53).

13. Section 17 of the U.P.C.

14. Sections 187 and 188 of the U.P.C.

15. *Uganda v Tereza Nakayima* H.C.C.S.C. No. 378/71.

16. *Bituresi Kakurungu,* H.C.C.S.C. No. 674/67 whose victim was her husband; *Silivia Barushwa,* H.C.C.S.C. No. 7/76, who killed her co-wife; *Joyce Nyakiriti,* H.C.C.S.C. No. 120/68, whose relationship with the victim was not indicted on the court record; *Jane Hanagwa,* H.C.C.S.C. No. 30/76, who killed a co-wife.

17. Section 17 of the U.P.C.: Subject to any express provisions in this Code or any other law in force in Uganda, criminal responsibility ... for the use of force in the defence of person and property, shall be determined according to the principles of English law.

18. a) Compare with the Danish Criminal Code, which under Section 13(1) sets out in relative detail the circumstances under which the

defence of self-defence can succeed: 'Acts committed in self-defence are not punishable if they were necessary to resist or avert an unlawful attack that has begun or is imminent, provided that such acts do not manifestly exceed what is reasonable with the regard to the danger inherent in the attack, the aggressor and the importance of the interests endangered by the attack.'
b) 'Judge made/case law' refers to legal principles or rules that are formulated by courts as they interpret statutory law.

19. H.C.C.S.C. No. 116/75.

20. Section 4 of the U.P.C.

21. Note that in reaction to the AIDS pandemic, the maximum punishment for rape was in 1990 changed from life imprisonment to the death penalty. (Section 118 of the U.P.C.). Is this change likely to have any impact on judges' perception towards the seriousness of the offence and consequently towards the amount of force a woman may use to protect herself from an imminent rape?

22. Section 117 provides that a person who has unlawful carnal knowledge of a *woman or girl*, without her consent ... is guilty of the felony termed rape (my emphasis).

23. *Director of Public Prosecution v Camplin* [1978] 2 All E.R. 168.

24. Crim. T. 121/93: in the High Court of Swaziland, held at Mbabane, judgement delivered on 10 May 1994.

25. *State v Little*, 74 Criminal No. 4176 (Superior court, Beaufort County, NC, 1975). Cited in Rosen (1986:34).

26. 9 E.A.C.A. 52 as cited in Tanganyika (1942). The facts of the case were that the accused alleged that his father-in-law was planning to move to Nairobi and to take his daughter, the accused's wife, with him. Accused finally forbade his wife to go. She replied: 'Go away, *sala, budmash, Harami*' (terms of abuse which literally mean 'brother-in-law, vagabond, scoundrel'). She spat at him and said: 'I have seen many males like you and I shall see in the future. You are not the only man in the world; ... open the door for me, I want to go to my father just now. I do not want to live with you.' Accused lost his self-control, seized a dagger and stabbed his wife many times,

so that she died. The two assessors were of the opinion that if a wife utters those particular words to her husband, words so bad and with deep hidden meaning, the man would naturally lose the power to control himself.

27. [1970] E.A. 405.

28. Camplin (1978) 2 A E.R. 168.

29. H.C.C.S.C. No. 593/70.

30. H.C.C.S.C. No. 373/71.

31. One may argue that judges normally like to be concrete and that the judge could have made the exact statement in a case in which the offender is a husband who had killed a wife. But in a patriarchal society such as Uganda, judicial officers should abstain from making statements which may be challenged as being either gender biased or at least gender insensitive. To say the least, the judge's choice of words was unfortunate.

32. For example, Walker (1984); Ewing (1987); Cipparone (1987).

33. Ewing (1987:41–42) gave a report of such cases studied by Walker (1982) and Browne (1984). He also presented the results of 'his own' 100 battered-women homicide cases, and in some of these cases evidence that the woman was a battered woman was accepted in favour of the woman offender. Ewing was however quick to add that not all (in fact, relatively few) battered women who kill their batterers are acquitted of criminal charges.

34. Criminal No. 4259. Cited in Rosen (1986:35).

35. H.C.C.S.C. No. 663/67.

36. [1959] Ghana Law Reports 125.

37. [1964] E.A. 289.

38. H.C.C.S.C. No. 674/67.

39. Section 218: Any person authorised by law or by the consent of the person injured by him to use force is criminally responsible for any

excess, according to the nature and quality of the act which constitutes the excess.

40. 88 Wash. 2d 221, 559 P. 2d 548 (1977). Cited in Jones (1980:286).

41. [1942] A.C.

42. [1914] 3 K.B. 116.

43. [1942] E.A. 413.

44. In this section the term *provocation* is used in the legal sense.

45. The section provides that if a person kills another in pursuance of an agreement between the deceased and the offender that they kill each other or help each other commit suicide, such is manslaughter rather than murder.

46. Section 187 of the U.P.C.: When a person, who unlawfully kills another under circumstances which, but for the provisions of this section, would constitute murder, does the act which causes death in the heat of passion caused by sudden provocation as hereinafter defined, and before there is time for his passion to cool, he is guilty of manslaughter only.

47. Section 188 of the U.P.C.:
(1) The term 'provocation' means and includes, except as hereinafter stated, any wrongful act or insult of such a nature as to be likely—
(a) When done or offered to an ordinary person; or
(b) When done or offered in the presence of an ordinary person to another person —
    i) who is under his immediate care; or
    ii) to whom he stands in a conjugal, parental, filial or fraternal relation, or in the relation of master and servant, to deprive him of the power of self-control and to induce him to commit an assault of the kind which the person charged committed upon the person by whom the act or insult is done or offered.
(2) When such an act or insult is done or offered by one person —
(a) to another; or
(b) in the presence of another to a person —
    i) who is under the immediate care of that other; or

ii) to whom that other stands in any the former is said to give to that other provocation for an assault.

(3) A lawful act is not provocation to any person for an assault.

(4) An act which a person does in consequence of incitement given by another person in order to induce him to do the act and thereby to furnish an excuse for committing an assault is not provocation to that other person for an assault.

48. *R. v Fabiano Kinene and Others* (1941) 8 E.A.C.A. 96.

49. Criminal Appeal No. 192 of 1959. Judgement delivered by Forbes, V.-P. See also an earlier case *Chacha s/o Wamburu v Rex* (1953) 20 E.A.C.A. 339. In answer to the question whether intention to kill necessarily negatives the defence of provocation the Court of Appeal said that '... the mere existence of an intention to kill or inflict grievous harm ... would not of itself deprive an accused of provocation ...' Even in the case of *R. v Luseru Wandera* (1948) 15 E.A.C.A. 105, it was held that for provocation to succeed as a defence, the retaliation must be in the heat of passion, but the existence at such time of an intention to kill does not necessarily negative the defence of provocation.

50. [1944–46] Rhodesial Law Reports 123.

51. H.C.C.S.C. No. 215/91.

52. Chapter 108 of the Laws of Uganda.

53. As Morris and Read (1966:302) said: 'this qualification reflects the common distinction between the use of witchcraft for ill and the use of it for purposes of divination or the cure of ill health.'

54. The offence is justified since there is more than ample evidence that such imputation often puts the life of a person labelled a witch in danger; many such persons have been victims of mob justice. See for example *Monika Nagadya and Others* (H.C.C.S.C. No. 123/76) and *Tereza Ngamita and Others* (H.C.C.S.C. No. 729/69), discussed later in this chapter.

55. Section 188(3) of the U.P.C.: A lawful act is not provocation to any person for an assault.

56. Provocation is a mitigating factor in both homicides and non-homicide offences. As Wolfgang (1993:180) said: 'In non-homicide cases, provocation has been used mostly by the defence to mitigate the penalty. (Mitigation of penalty occurs, of course, in charge-reduction but is implied in homicide, while it is explicit in non-homicides.) Victim-precipitated offences of attempt to kill: ... aggravated assault, for example, could contain mixtures of reduced charges and mitigated sentences for the defendants.'

57. Section 182 of the U.P.C.: (1) Any person who, by an unlawful act or omission, causes the death of another person is guilty of the felony termed manslaughter.
(2) An unlawful omission is an omission amounting to culpable negligence to discharge a duty tending to the preservation of life or health, whether such omission is or is not accompanied by an intention to cause death or bodily harm.

58. Section 186 of the U.P.C. defines malice aforethought as either the deliberate intention to cause death, or a reckless attitude as to whether one's act or omission causes death.

59. See Section 183 of the U.P.C., which defines murder as unlawfully causing the death of another with malice aforethought.

60. H.C.C.S.C No. 25/93.

61. Kahli Gibran, quoted by Macdonald (1986:58) in *The Murderer and His Victim*.

62. This is not an assertion that Ugandan courts cannot get any inspiration from legal systems outside the common law, but is a recognition that it is easier to adopt concepts from similar jurisdictions.

63. In New South Wales, the Crimes (Homicide) Amendment Act of 1982 allows any past conduct of the deceased towards the defendant to be the basis of provocation. Cited in O'Donovan (1991:235).

64. According to this doctrine, negligence on the part of the injured party that combines with the negligence of another in causing injury, will diminish or even bar the recovery of damages for the injury.

VII

Consequences of Imprisonment

There is a popular (albeit erroneous) assumption in many quarters that prisoners, by the fact of imprisonment, lose all their constitutional rights. To many people, 'to talk of prisoners' rights is a contradiction' (James 1989:1033). As Hawkins (1985:2020) pointed out:

> The deprivation or denial of rights for prisoners is apparently generally accepted as a normal concomitant of penal measures imposed in response to criminal behaviour. What might be regarded as morally objectionable in a non-penal context seems to be regarded as unobjectionable when it is a feature of a penal method of practice. In fact, it is widely felt to be appropriate or deserved in the case of those judged guilty of criminal offences. Prisoners are seen as belonging to a group which has had its rights legitimately curtailed as a consequence of the commission of crimes.

Yet one of the aims (probably the most important aim) of punishment is rehabilitation/reformation of an offender. Under this theory, a prisoner should come out of prison a better person than when she or he went in. But if a person is to be reformed, for eventual return to free society, he or she must be treated humanely during incarceration.

The United Nations has, under the *Standard Minimum Rules for the Treatment of Prisoners* (1955),[1] set out what is generally accepted as good principle and practice in the treatment of prisoners and the management of institutions.[2] An appreciation of the principle enunciated in Rule 57 thereof would go a long way in changing the above-mentioned presumption. The rule says:

> Imprisonment and other measures which result in cutting off an offender from the outside world are afflictive by the very fact of

taking from the person the right of self-determination by depriving him of his liberty. Therefore the prison system shall not, except as incidental to justifiable segregation or the maintenance of discipline, aggravate the suffering inherent in such a situation.

Custodial institutions should, as much as possible, reflect what civilized society has accepted as appropriate. It is for this reason that in assessing the conditions of detention, one should constantly analyse the extent to which those conditions are in line with the recommended minimum standard set out in UN rules. In the proclamation of the rules, it was recognised that:

> In view of the variety of legal, social, economic and geographical conditions of the world, ... not all of the rules are capable of application in all places and at all times. *They should, however, serve to stimulate a constant endeavour to overcome practical difficulties in the way of their application, in the knowledge that they represent, as a whole, the minimum conditions which are acceptable as suitable* by the United Nations[3] (my emphasis).

In promulgating penal policy, therefore, the rules rather than the state of the country's economy should be the basis of our ultimate goal.

A person under lawful detention is entitled to proper accommodation and clothing, sufficient food and medical care. But, in light of Uganda's economic state, it might be impossible to provide persons in detention with most of life's basic needs at all times. Nevertheless, it is a fact that the judicial system has under-utilised punishments other than imprisonment and this fact has greatly contributed to overcrowding in prisons. It makes it even harder for the government to adequately cater for the needs of prisoners.

Uganda has only two fully-fledged prisons for women and, therefore, in most parts of the country, women are imprisoned within the wings of men's prisons. The facilities in those wings were designed for men and are hardly suitable for women inmates. Masaka women's wing provided the worst example of neglect extended to women in detention. The conditions of the female inmates are specifically difficult because their wing was created from what was originally the punishment cells for male inmates who broke prison regulations. Ventilation is poor and all the women complain that the premises are very cold. Most of the women had no blankets and generally the conditions were appalling. The women who had stayed in prison long enough knew that the present women's wing was originally a punishment wing, and this knowledge compounded their sense of injustice. In Masaka, government has definitely failed to provide healthy and suitable accommodation facilities for the women inmates as required by Rule 10.[4]

It is also worth noting that, in all the prisons I visited, the majority of women were being held on remand and only a very small number were convicts. Remand prisoners greatly swell up the number of detainees, and the slow pace of the criminal justice system is the greatest cause for overcrowding in prison.

Separating categories

Rules 8(b) and 85(1) of the *Standard Minimum Rules for the Treatment of Prisoners* provide that on remand, prisoners should be kept separately from convicted prisoners. In all the prisons I visited, both women awaiting trial and those serving sentences were held together in the same cells. Perhaps this was partly due to the fact that custodial institutions for women are very few in number. In fact, there is no single remand prison in the country for women prisoners. I also noted that in all these institutions, the system of dormitories is in use but remand prisoners are kept in the same dormitories with convicted prisoners. This may be due to the fact that, at any one time, there are always more women on remand than those serving prison sentences, in each and every prison. Consequently, it is not possible to separate the two categories of detainees even at the dormitory level.

Rule 8 further provides that the categorisation of prisoners should depend, inter alia, on the criminal record and legal reason for detention. In the dormitory system used in all the prisons, none separated first offenders from recidivists. There was also no separation according to the nature of the crime. Failure to separate categories of prisoners is a clear indication that policy makers and the prison system have failed to appreciate the role of prison in rehabilitating offenders.

Far away from home

Due to the limited number of women prisons, many women are locked up in institutions that are far away from home. Whereas a woman awaiting trial is usually kept in a prison nearest to her home, once she is convicted and sentenced to a long prison term, the practice is to transfer her to Luzira Women's Prison. In Luzira I met several women who had been transferred from Kabale (about 350 km from Kampala) and Mbarara (about 250 km from Kampala) on conviction. Many of the prisoners from poor families receive no visits from their relatives because the places of incarceration are too far from places of origin. This does not augur well for their eventual return and re-integration into society, especially for those persons who serve long prison sentences.

Another great disadvantage of the absence of contact from family members is that such women lack basic necessities of hygiene. Government has failed to provide prisoners with blankets, soap, sanitary towels, and other toiletries, and women have to rely on their families as much as possible. To a woman who receives no visitors, the conditions in prison are humiliating. One of the cases which specially drew my attention was a woman in Masaka who informed me that, on her arrest, she was putting on a very old dress which she used for farm work. She was not allowed to change into a better dress and, since her arrest and detention, she had received no visitors. In prison she had been allowed to put on a convict's uniform (the only type of uniform available), but when she appeared in court for mention of her case, she could not appear in a prisoner's uniform because she was not a convict.[5] Describing the humiliation she felt in putting on her threadbare dress, she said:

> I dread going to court because my breasts are uncovered. ... I find no humiliation in putting on a prisoner's uniform because. ... [T]hey say I am not a prisoner; ... what is the difference between me and a prisoner? I see no difference; ... but to appear in public with my body exposed is the greatest humiliation....

There are few things that shatter a woman's dignity as much as being unable to keep her body clean, especially during her menstrual periods. Insofar as material requests by the women are concerned, the most frequent and desperate demand was that of sanitary towels and knickers. In all the prisons the women complained about the lack of soap and cited visitors as the only source of the commodity.[6]

Children of women prisoners

In Uganda society, women are the primary caretakers of small children. As a result, the social costs created by a woman's imprisonment are immeasurable. In sentencing or detaining an expectant mother or a mother of an infant, it is very important that special consideration be given, as far as possible, to the welfare of the unborn child or infant. I came across several women detainees with infants in prison. Some of them had been detained while pregnant and had delivered in prison, while some had brought their babies with them on imprisonment.

Africans often boast of an excellent extended family system and one would have expected that a woman facing a prison term would have a relative ready to take responsibility for the child until the mother's release. The presence of infants in prison indicates that not all is well within our society. Why are these children in prison? One answer may be that for a breastfeeding child, prison may be the best alternative if the relatives of the child are too poor to afford breast milk substitutes for such a child. But this is only part of the answer to the problem. Some women would want their children taken away from prison but there is nobody to play that part.

Moreover, some of the women may have offended family members and thus have alienated themselves from their families, and therefore no one wants to have anything to do with a the child of such a woman. In some cases, the women have killed husbands and there is no father to look after the child. In other cases, women are single mothers and whatever the reason for their detention, there is nobody willing or capable of taking over responsibility for the child. Many of them would say: 'The only person willing was my mother but she is too old.' Others still would say: 'I sent a message to my relatives to come for the child; I have had no reply.'

The condition of infants in prison is pathetic considering the possible psychological and physical effects of incarceration. The possible trauma which these children are likely to face hit me hardest on one of my visits to Mbarara women's wing. I was interviewing one of the inmates and we were seated within the prison grounds, surrounded by a metal fence. Two toddlers belonging to the women prisoners were seated nearby with forlorn expressions on their faces. I then heard excited laughter coming from somewhere nearby. I looked up and saw several children — children of free citizens — playing outside the fence. They were rolling in grass. The comparison was so obvious: children of prisoners are as much prisoners as their mothers. Their play ground was concrete and limited. The other children were blessed with green-grass open space to roll in.

In one prison, I asked one of the inmates who was on remand what worried her most. Her prompt answer was:

> My child, she is suffering a lot. She does not like posho and yet it is the only food we are served with; she does not like sugarless porridge and yet I have nobody to give me sugar.

It is only in Luzira where infants are given some kind of special diet. When I asked one of the inmates about the condition of children in prison, she replied: 'When a new woman is brought to prison and we notice that she is either visibly pregnant or has a child with her, we say that she has come with a lawyer.' This is because Luzira prison has a dairy farm which the prisoners look after. The children of prisoners are given milk, and breastfeeding and pregnant mothers are served with a mid-morning meal. Having a child entitles one to extra facilities and is therefore tantamount to having a defender.

In the other prisons, there were no such facilities. In one of the prisons, I met a 31-year-old woman and her 18-year-old daughter who were on remand for arson and murder. In a nearby remand home, another daughter aged 13 years was being held on the same charge. The 18-year-old daughter had a one-year-old child in prison. The 31-year-old mother had also delivered a child in prison but the child had died. Is it possible that the child would have survived had it been delivered outside the prison? The woman told me that her child fell sick and was hospitalised. When it died, she was immediately returned to prison. She never knew where or how her child was buried because, in her own words, 'prisoners are not people'.

The High Court has powers to grant bail to an accused person in all cases including capital cases. However, in capital cases, the court grants bail only if there are exceptional circumstances. It is debatable whether courts ever take into consideration the welfare of an unborn child or an infant before either remanding or imprisoning its mother.

In *Margaret Nakuya v Uganda*,[7] Nakuya was charged with murder together with her two sons aged 14 and 16 years respectively. Nakuya applied to the High Court for bail on the ground that she was a widow and had eight children, the youngest of them being two years of age. The court refused to grant her bail and held that the fact that she was a widow and had small children under her care did not constitute exceptional circumstances.

When the prisoner appeared for further remand in the Chief Magistrate's court at Masaka, she informed the magistrate that she had nowhere to keep the children and was therefore leaving them in the custody of the court. The Chief Magistrate wrote to the Chief Justice, who further considered the application. In his ruling, Chief Justice Kiwanuka held that the existence of a two-year-old in the charge of a widow, plus other young children, constituted exceptional circumstances warranting her release on bail.[8]

In *Uganda v Akidi*,[9] bail was granted, on revision, to a female who was charged with murder. When the accused appeared before the Magistrate Grade 1, a letter from the officer in charge of the prison where she was detained was presented stating that the inmate had with her in prison an 18-month-old child and was expecting another baby any time. The officer was very worried because he had no facilities. The learned magistrate considered the fact that the High Court criminal sessions in Moroto were rare and there was no legal counsel in Moroto to help to apply for bail in High Court. He therefore released her on bail.

When the case came up before the High Court, it was held that, 'indeed, unusual circumstances called for unusual relief.' Although the magistrate's order was held illegal for lack of jurisdiction, it was substituted with the High Court's order granting bail on the same conditions. None of the women interviewed in the course of research for this study had been granted bail either due to pregnancy or to having had an infant child.

Clothing for the children

Whereas the government has the duty to provide prisoners with clothing, there is no duty to dress the infants who are kept in prison with their mothers. On one occasion, I interviewed a woman inmate holding a baby in her arms. The baby was wrapped in a light piece of cloth (a *lesu*). During the interview the baby woke up and as the mother uncovered the baby to feed it the sight shocked me — the two-month-old baby was completely naked and this was during one of the coldest months in one of the coldest parts of Uganda. The woman had come to prison during the late stages of her pregnancy and the child had been born in prison. None of her relatives had ever come to see her in prison.

The state must choose one of two options: either it must provide special facilities for children who stay in prison with their mothers, or it should use non-custodial sentences for nursing and expectant women convicts. One wonders whether it is not even possible for a child in prison to sue the state for denial of liberty, for denial of childhood?

Prisoners' children left outside prison

In answer to the question, 'What worries you most?' most women answered: 'My children'. Several of the women who had killed husbands had no idea who was looking after their fatherless children. Some women were single mothers who had been solely responsible for their children's welfare before imprisonment. There were yet other women whose husbands were alive but had always left the duty of child care and maintenance solely to their wives; for many such men the only pre-occupation had always been alcohol. There were also women whose husbands were also in prison.

In some cases, women had left children in the custody of aged mothers who were 'sick and too old' to effectively cater for those children. There were other women whose children were in the custody of persons whose good will was questionable. Such women were in prison for allegedly killing their husbands' children, or attempting to kill co-wives, and yet these very co-wives were the persons taking care of the children of the those inmates. One of the women accused of murdering her co-wife's child consistently said: 'My children are in the hands of that woman, she will kill them.' Another woman who was accused of arson and murder said: 'My children are with the very woman who led to my imprisonment.'

Most women had been unable to make any arrangements for their children's welfare because as one of them said, 'On arrest I was not given a chance to do anything; I abandoned my children on spot.' Several of the women were upset by their children's failure to go to school as a result of the mother's imprisonment. One of them said: 'My children no longer go to school. I used to struggle and send them to school. ... When a mother is absent from a home, the man cannot think much about her children.' In answer to the question, 'Would like to ask me any question?' she said:

> Is it possible for you to initiate my release so that I can go and look after my children until the 480 days are over and court is

ready to listen to my case? I have been here for six months and my children have since dropped out of school.

It was also not uncommon to meet a woman who had lost her youngest child (usually under two years of age) whom she left in the care of others outside prison. Possibly such children would have lived if they had been in the care of their mothers until a certain age. The stories of some women reflect the gender disparity/ unequal social distribution of child care that exists in our society.

Child delivery in prison

Several women who are detained while pregnant deliver children in prison. The women have to be taken to hospitals nearest to the detention centres to deliver because the prisons have no maternity facilities. This is a heavy responsibility on the heads of the institutions because they have no vehicles attached to those institutions. When the baby comes at night, the woman's life is at risk. In my interview with a prison authority in one of the prisons, it was revealed that the problem becomes even greater when the mother requires an operation.

In Uganda today, hospital personnel expect every patient to have an attendant, and yet the woman prisoner has no such relative available to play that role. While such a woman is escorted to hospital, the warder is not likely to carry out the 'duties' of an attendant — washing for the mother and child. The solution then lies in assigning another prisoner the duties of an attendant. This, however, makes the warder's duty of surveillance more complex — she must not only keep watch over the sick prisoner but also over the attendant prisoner.

It is, therefore, imperative that the criminal justice system reconsiders the desirability of applying identical bail regulations and sentencing considerations to nursing and pregnant mothers, on the one hand, and other suspects and convicts, on the other. The state should also recognise its duty to provide proper natal and post-natal care and treatment, if it must have pregnant and nursing mothers in detention.[10]

Counselling

Many of the women prisoners have a lot of worries about certain aspects of their lives and it is imperative to provide counselling services within penal institutions. I believe that it was partly for this reason that none of the potential respondents turned down my request to talk to her. This was true for convicts as well as remand prisoners. In one case, after I had introduced myself to one of my respondents (Nabisinde), I started to emphasise — just as I used to do in every case — the fact that she had no obligation to talk to me, that nobody would punish her if she turned down my request to interview her. Nabisinde could hardly wait for me to end my introduction. She emphatically informed me that she certainly wanted to talk to me and went on to say:

> Nobody has ever cared to listen to my side of the story. Of course I want to talk to you. Everybody just condemned me from the word go; nobody was interested in my story.

Nabisinde was on remand for allegedly killing her stepson.

Nabwami, another woman on remand, for allegedly killing her grandmother reacted thus: 'Of course I want to talk to you; how can I not want to talk. I am a helpless woman with a host of problems.' Similarly, Mwesigye, who was already serving a five-year sentence for a crime (infanticide) she did not deny, opened her conversation with me thus: 'Yesterday when you came and talked to the others, I kept on praying you would call me also.' In Fort Portal, Luzira, Masaka and Mbarara prisons, I talked to women who were outside the scope of my study, for the simple reason that they asked the prison authorities that they be included in the list of people I intended to talk to.

The need for counselling was brought out even more forcefully through the information that was given to me about Nabalayo, who together with her two sons, was awaiting trial for the murder of her husband. I was informed by the officer in charge of the prison where she was, that Nabalayo had apparently never accepted prison, despite the fact that by the time of my visit, she had spent 280 days on remand. I learnt that when she had first been brought into prison, she would go to the gate and ask the gate-keepers to allow her to go home.

During her first days in prison, she used to wake up in the night, leave her bed and attempt to join other women in their beds. She appeared a very frightened person, too frightened to stay in bed alone. I was also informed that she hardly talked to anybody, but that on one occasion, she attacked another inmate and attempted to strangle her. The authorities had decided that she should not take part in farming because there was a possibility that she could use a hoe to attack other inmates. I was further informed that when she had first come to prison, she refused to take any part in any work and the prison authorities had decided that she should be left alone to do what she liked.

Whereas the other women tried to keep themselves clean, Nabalayo showed no concern for personal hygiene. One time, her bedding and her hair were heavily infested with lice. The other prisoners had cleaned the bedding and persuaded her to shave her head. When her imprisoned sons were asked about their mother's mental state, they said that she had been completely normal before imprisonment.

I still asked for permission to talk to her. I found myself face-to-face with a woman who was carrying a great burden, a heavy load. A short while after I had started the interview, I realised that she was greatly traumatised and each question I asked seemed to open up the old wounds. Since I am a layperson in the counselling profession, half way through the interview I thought it unwise to continue interviewing her.

However, I gathered from her that she had experienced extreme physical and emotional abuse from her husband. I wondered whether she had been traumatised by the life she led before, or by the offence she had committed (if indeed she committed it), or by her experience at the hands of the criminal justice system. It was obvious that prison was not the right place for her condition.

Another case which made it clear that there is need for counselling was that of Nabowa. She was awaiting trial for the murder of her stepmother; a very old woman. Nabowa admitted having killed the old woman and told her story with a smile, as if she was talking about something other than death — death which she had caused. It may be that the law will judge these women legally sane and therefore responsible for their crimes. But the question still stands: Is imprisonment the best treatment to what is obviously a disturbed mind?

Life after prison

Society's duty towards a citizen who has come in conflict with the criminal law should not end with her incarceration. We must ensure that such a citizen is in a position to resume her rightful role in society. Interviews with the women revealed that Uganda does not adequately prepare prisoners for the eventual return to society.

Fear of the 'outside world'
Several women who had stayed in prison for long periods expressed fear about getting back into the now unfamiliar world. In the words of Karugaba, who had stayed six years on remand and was sentenced to eight years imprisonment:

> But being in prison for so long is a problem. One is even afraid to get out; ... where does one start after imprisonment? Getting a job is a problem, because if you tell a potential employer where you are coming from, they will be scared to take you on. Some people do not have relatives to go back to; they have no land to go back to. ... One may even prefer staying in prison since one is assured of a meal, of a place to sleep in. When one has just come in here, it is hard. After some time one gets used to custody and even gains weight. But as the end of one's prison term approaches one is really scared. ... A friend of mine has only three months to go after three years and six months in prison. She has lost appetite as the time for release gets near; she has lost sleep. The other day she said she had fever but when her blood was examined the results showed that she was not infected with anything. She is just scared of getting out. You FIDA[11] people could probably help us; set up

an office where released prisoners can go immediately they are out of prison so that they are helped with a beginning....

Many times the moment of imprisonment robs a woman of marriage: the only role that most women are accustomed to. Thus, when I asked Natukunda whether she was married, she said: 'I was married but I no longer am; I am in prison so how can I be married?' Incarceration also often robs a woman of a home and of all property. Yet her prison experience hardly arms her with the ability to make an independent fresh start.

One woman who was accused of killing her husband's son said: 'After my arrest, my husband gave all that I owned to his new wife — my clothes, my everything.' Similarly, a woman who was awaiting trial for killing a man who attempted to rape her said: 'The villagers sent my husband away from that village; I do not know where he moved to but he went with my children.' Another woman who killed her husband said: 'I do not know where I will go to after prison; my husband's relatives have sold off all his land and my house was destroyed; the iron sheets on the house were taken; everything was taken.'

A 50-year-old woman, who together with her two sons is alleged to have killed her husband said:

> As soon as we were arrested, people took whatever we had, all my property. My sons have no wives; they will need to pay bride price. I had secured myself a future but I do not know where to begin after here. It is hard to begin afresh when one is old.

Even the women who were in prison together with their husbands often gave the same story: 'When we leave prison we have nowhere to go to. Our house was destroyed, everything was taken.'

There is certainly a need to educate society that imprisonment does not rob a person of her right to property and that it is only the courts that have the right to inflict punishment on an offender. It needs to be emphasised that many times these citizens, who are subjected to jungle law, may in fact be innocent of crime and plundering their homes is tantamount to punishing them merely for being suspects and subjects of arrest.

Ill-prepared for the outside society

Asked whether they had learnt any skills since coming to prison, most women answered in the negative. Kagoya, aged 18 years and serving a two-year prison term for attempting to kill her child said:

> When I leave prison, I will look for employment in town. You see I am no longer young so I have to cater for my needs and yet I have no parents. Maybe you could help me get a job....

Kagoya dropped out of school after only five years of formal education. After spending some years out of school, without a job, she became pregnant. The man responsible was married and did not want his wife to learn of his relationship with Kagoya. With no job and burdened with a child she could not support, Kagoya attempted to get rid of the child. Asked whether she had learnt any new skills in prison, she informed me that she had been taught how to make baskets and tableclothes. The question is: Armed with the art of making baskets, would she come out of prison better equipped to face the world than she was before her offence? What kind of job was she likely to get after prison? Would she be able to avoid unwanted pregnancies that were the root cause of her problems or to independently bring up a child in case of motherhood?

There is also the story of 23-year-old Adong, who was serving a five-year prison term for attempting to kill her child. While at school she became pregnant and had to drop out of school. The father of the child was in no position to help her financially and Adong's relatives sent her away from home. The young mother decided to get rid of the child by throwing it in a pit.

Asked whether she had learnt any new skills while in prison, she answered in the negative. As to what she was likely to do after prison, she said: 'I would like to enrol in a course. I would have continued with my education but I have nobody to pay the fees for me. Can you help me get a job?' It would appear from what she told me that she was not receiving any counselling services to enable her to avoid unwanted pregnancies or look after children she may get outside marriage once she is out of prison.

Conclusion

In general, prisons for women in Uganda not only deny inmates basic necessities of life but they also fail to prepare those inmates for their eventual return to society. The few training facilities available may enable women to learn the art of making handcrafts, but the skills acquired may not be enough for those women to secure gainful employment, because the government has not invested adequate resources in prisons' vocational training. Although learning such skills may in itself be a positive achievement, the returns from handcrafts are not lucrative enough to uplift women from dependence on men, a status which often is the root cause of women's criminality. The programmes echo Carlen's (1983:19) criticism of training programmes for women prisoners in Britain and the United States:

> The so-called training programmes are ... linked to traditional conceptions of women's roles. ... Training for domesticity, far from helping a woman develop as a person, can often increase her dependency upon the 'male'; ... women do the laundry, sewing and other 'female tasks'. ... Such programming does nothing to prepare a woman for employment....

Our institutions should reflect the wise principle set out in Rule 58, thus:

> The purpose and justification of ... imprisonment ... is ultimately to protect society against crime. This can only be achieved if the period of imprisonment is used to ensure ... that upon his return

to society the offender is not only willing *but able to lead a law-abiding and self-supporting life* (my emphasis).

As they stand today, prisons in Uganda are primarily custodial and punitive institutions. As Morris (1987:1) has pointed out, the neglect of women in criminology as an academic discipline, and the neglect of the welfare of women prisoners, 'is easy to rationalize. ... Female offenders represent a small proportion of arrested offenders and create few social problems....' Those responsible for penal institutions may therefore reply that only a relatively small number of women criminals is the *problem*; the small numbers of women who offend the law makes it uneconomic to adequately invest in women's custodial institutions in order to provide amenities and basic training facilities to enable them to acquire vocational skills. Such rationalisation is, however, ironical in that it punishes women for being law-abiding as a group. And yet, the goal of every civilized society is (or should be) to prevent commission of crime among its citizens, irrespective of age group, social class or gender.

Notes

1. Adopted by the First United Nations Congress on the Prevention of Crime and the Treatment of Offenders, held at Geneva in 1955 and approved by the Economic and Social Council by its resolutions 663C (XXIV) of 31 July 1957 and 2076 (LXII) of 13 May 1977.

2. International Human Rights Instruments of the United Nations (1948–1982), page 40.

3. Rule 2.

4. Rule 10: All accommodation provided for the use of prisoners and in particular all sleeping accommodation shall meet all requirements of health....

5. Under Rule 88(1): an untried prisoner is allowed to wear her own clothing if it is clean and suitable and if she must wear a uniform.

Rule 88(2) provides that such uniform be different from that supplied to convicted prisoners.

6. Rule 15: Prisoners shall be required to keep their persons clean, and to this end they shall be provided with water and with such toilet articles as are necessary for health and cleanliness.

7. [1971] U.L.R. 53.

8. His Lordship however went on to say that the charge of murder was a result of thief beating and would possibly be reduced to manslaughter. Besides, the Government of the day had publicly instructed the police to shoot and kill robbers at sight and the public was aware of such instruction.

9. 1985 H.C.B. 1.

10. Rule 23(1): In women's institutions there shall be special accommodation for all necessary pre-natal and post-natal care and treatment....
    (2): Where nursing infants are allowed to remain in the institution with their mothers, provision shall be made for a nursery staffed by qualified persons, where the infants shall be placed when they are not in the care of their mothers.

11. The Uganda Association of Women Lawyers.

Conclusion

Where Do We Go from Here?

'How will the courts and people understand how women like myself feel, defeated and in the end helpless?[1]

After emphasising that women in American society usually kill intimates, Jones (1980:xvi) contended that the circumstances that drive a woman into violence tell us something about the ways of that society. In her words:

> [The fact that women kill intimates] is not amusing. But that these homicidal patterns might be shadows of profound cultural deformities — and thus worthy of serious consideration — seems not to have occurred to many.

As noted before, in an attempt to understand a woman's conscious and semiconscious 'choice' of conflict-resolution, it is important to acknowledge that the assessments and decisions she makes take form in specific contexts. They are also shaped by the resources and social controls within those contexts. This book has situated women's violence within the context of patriarchal power.

In this book, I have not only demonstrated that women are victims of oppressive patriarchal ideologies but I have also unveiled violent crime as a type of women's resistance against specific oppressive gender relations within the family. Embodied in women's violent crime is a protest against patriarchal society's oppressive regime: its values and restrictions against women. The victims are usually persons who attempt to confine the woman in enforced roles and the woman's reaction is often a manifestation of a struggle for autonomy and self-liberation. Patriarchal values suppress a woman's personal identity and, in the struggle against self- annihilating roles, a woman may turn to violence.

However, women's reaction to patriarchy is complex and in some instances a woman's violence is a consequence of her accommodation of patriarchal ideals. After she has internalised the values of a male-dominated society and has accepted the roles given to her by that society, she may kill whomever she sees as a threat to those roles: roles she has come to accept as an integral part of her identity.

But whatever interpretation is given to their acts of violence, it is evident that women are trapped in the customary roles fashioned by the male-dominated society and that it is due to the woman's inescapable condition that she resorts to violent crime.

In Uganda, women are forced commit violent crime by our culture, which allows polygamy, which dictates that children 'belong' to their fathers, which permits husbands to physically and psychologically abuse their wives, which creates social situations in which women may be driven to violent behaviour. Socio-cultural values within this predominantly patriarchal society relegate women to an inferior socio-economic and legal status, thus increasing the risk that women will resort to violence as a means of fighting legitimatised inequality and oppression.

Patrilineality has been given as a possible reason for the relative absence of instances where wives kill husbands. For example, Wilson and Daly (1992:208) noted that:

> ... the East Indian and African peoples, ... among whom women scarcely ever killed their husbands, were strongly patrilineal societies with bride acquisition and patrilocal residence (Bohannan 1960). In such societies, ... violence against the husband is futile and almost unthinkable.

I do not contend that women's violence against husbands is high in patrilineal societies. Indeed, research carried out in Uganda has consistently shown that women's contribution to violent crimes in general is very low.

However, my research has shown that in Uganda, husbands are the most common victims in instances where women commit violent crimes. In these instances, as well as in the others where the victims are not husbands, women's violence is often a reaction against specific forms of patriarchal oppression. As Totman

(1978:15) has observed, when women kill, they mostly kill those who are physically and emotionally closest to them — their mates and children — and these victims are 'precisely the people and *part of the social institution which defines woman's primary role and give her her identity; ... her behavior is ... expressive of her status*' (my emphasis).

The results of the present study are in agreement with Totman's observations, for in Uganda, women apparently kill in line with their roles in society; as wives they kill husbands and co-wives and, in their enforced role of child-minders, they kill children.

In a patriarchal society like that of Uganda, the gender relations support men's domination of women and the men are given supremacy over the women within the family. Women are expected to defer to male authority and a husband's use of violence against his wife, for purposes of enforcing conformity to his wishes, is socially permitted. However, a man who subjects his wife to abuse also takes the risk of becoming a victim of her retaliation.

In a male-dominated society, a woman is assigned responsibilities for which she may have neither the interest nor the competence to take up. One such role is child-minding, including children who need not be her own offspring. What is of essence is that the children belong to her husband. In rejecting this enforced role, some women react violently against their stepchildren.

Patriarchal society applies double standards to men and women's sexual behaviour. It gives a man freedom to engage in premarital and extramarital sex and even sire children, while it ostracises his female partner in the same act. The consequent social, economic and emotional burdens that a woman suffers from having a child from such a union, may drive her kill that child.

Patriarchy also results in the male's absolute control of family wealth and denies women any say in the property they help to acquire: a contribution without reward. In contemporary Ugandan society, the position of many women in the family is a contradiction. They have taken up the hitherto men's financial responsibility to maintain the family, but their contribution has not brought them equality, let alone supremacy, with their husbands. The male is still supreme and exercises certain privileges which are oppressive towards the wife. For example, as the controller of 'family' property, a husband may put to use any property belonging to his first wife, with or without her consent. In resisting this societal injustice, some women resort to violent crime against their husbands.

In a patriarchal society, the socio-economic order makes women dependent on men and on marriage. For many women in Uganda, the only economic security they can ever have is a man. Another effect of patriarchy is that a woman's success in society is traditionally attributed to marriage and motherhood. Women recognise the absolute necessity to hold onto a man and it is for this reason that when a man is involved with two women, a very bitter rivalry may develop between these women and may lead to one of the women losing her life at the hands of the other woman. This book has therefore reinforced the view that 'a person's behavior is a fruition of [her] conception of [her] identity, and further that [her] conception of [her] identity derives from the position [she] occupies in society' (H.G. Mead, cited by Totman 1978:27). As Brownstein et al (1994:101) reported, research on women who killed abusive partners effectively suggests that:

> [W]omen's violence is the response of a victim to subordination in a patriarchal society; ... [the research has] convincingly made the case that women who killed abusive partners were responding to that abuse and the system that perpetuated it, ... responding as victims of violence forced out of enforced passivity.

I further opine that even when it is against other members of the family, women's violence is often a response to various forms of patriarchal oppression. Women are driven to despair by abusive societal rules and, in response, they kill whomever they perceive as the (immediate) cause of their distress.

Through the legal concepts of self-defence and provocation, the law acknowledges that an accused person has acted against a particular individual who is threatening her with harm. Through the concept of victim precipitation, sociologists have also recognised the fact that violence is often a reaction against an onslaught on the self by a particular individual.

But women's actions are sometimes against societal repression and the victim may be innocent of violating any of the woman's rights. As mentioned earlier, victim precipitation may constitute no more than the mere presence of the victim in a given situation, no more than a social relationship between the offender and the victim. Such a victim could be a stepchild whom the woman is being 'forced' to look after. The child cannot be said to have precipitated the violence, but society puts children in a situation which predisposes women to react violently against these innocent individuals. In acting violently, women defy societal expectations, but they do so to defend themselves against the violations of the social order. Through the enforced role of child-minder, society has ignored the woman's right to autonomy and the right to limit her activities to areas of her choice. Society has failed to treat women as free persons with interests of their own. The very personhood of a woman is negated and she is treated as her husband's possession.

In the woman's action is embodied the message that she is an autonomous individual who should be given freedom to make decisions. But, as Bardsley (1987:34) observed, a woman (in a male-dominated society) must fight for autonomy of action and female crime can be an expression of that struggle.

A woman's homicide may also be an attempt to preserve her social as opposed to her physical self. Society expects most, if not all women to marry, and an unmarried girl will soon realise that society values her in terms of her marriageability. Anything that lowers her prospects on the marriage market is seen as a threat to her very being. In killing her illegitimate child, therefore, an unmarried woman is getting rid of an obstacle to her status as a potential wife. It is an attempt to preserve what she has been brought up to regard as her proper role in society: a wife-to-be.

In Ugandan society, marriage is a status symbol and it adds value to a woman's worth, not only in the eyes of society but also in the woman's own eyes. A married woman considers herself and is considered to be an appendage of her husband. She will always introduce herself and be introduced by others as her husband's wife. Her whole identity is derived from her marital status. Perhaps this is understandable in a strongly patrilineal society where residence is patrilocal. Marriage submerges a woman's individual identity. A wife hardly considers herself as an autonomous individual separate from her husband. Marriage thus becomes part of the self. The woman's violent reaction against anybody attempting to destabilise her marriage is thus an act of self-preservation. Preservation of the marital status is preservation of the self.

A woman is socialised into valuing her success in terms of marriage. She is brought up to consider herself successful in life if her husband thinks she is a good wife. She values herself through her husband. When the husband — the person through whom the woman attains social status — persistently humiliates and ridicules her, she loses self-esteem. The woman's act of homicide against her husband mirrors an attempt to save herself from the continuous onslaught against her self-worth. She has to annihilate her husband who consistently shows that she falls far below what is expected of a wife.

A woman may, in an attempt to shape and find meaning in life outside marriage, take steps to bring her conflict-ridden marriage to an end. Society, through socio-cultural and economic barriers, will deny her the desired self-autonomy. She is denied the ability to define herself and to determine her own destiny. Her personal identity is suppressed. In response to the disabilities imposed on her by a deeply sexist society, she may commit an act of homicide against her husband.

This book has also revealed that oppressive gender relations within Ugandan patriarchal society operate differently on women depending on their socio-economic class. As observed earlier, nearly all the women offenders I came across during my research tended to belong to the low socio-economic class. Commenting about the fact that while some battered women kill their husbands, others do not, Ewing (1987:61) said that part of the explanation may lie in the relative resource-deprivation suffered by those women who kill. Perhaps the concentration of offenders in the low socio-economic class is an indication that women from the more privileged classes are able to survive without resorting to violence. An educated woman who 'fails' in marriage will suffer social stigma but not the same degree of financial hardship since she is in position to get employment. And there is no doubt that 'an individual's occupation plays a crucial role in determining her life chances' (Evans 1983:5).

It is also generally true that education results not only into economic but also psychological liberation for women as well as men. Education usually leads to greater economic independence and hence gives women relative psychological liberty by endowing them with the capacity to get by, independent of marriage. As a result of relative economic and psychological independence, divorce or separation are viable solutions to educated women faced with conflict-ridden marriages.

When women take the law into their own hands — for purposes of self-preservation — they are processed through the criminal justice system. In the women's encounter with the criminal justice system, it becomes apparent that their perception of crime and of justice is at variance with that of the agents of criminal justice. This is because the standards upheld in the interpretation of the law are representative of fundamentally male standards. The male standard is prevalent in the interpretation of rules governing self-defence and often in the sentences imposed on women who violently react to provocative behaviour.

The discriminatory nature apparent in the criminal justice system is, however, a mere reflection of the social relations between and among women and men, and women's experiences within the system cannot be understood in isolation of the wider concept of gender inequality. Women and men are differentiated and ordered in a given socio-cultural context. Different reactions are expected of men, on the one hand, and women, on the other, by virtue of their sex. Courts have merely followed this pattern and thereby differentiated what is expected of a man and what is expected of a woman. The law's failure to reflect women's viewpoint is an indication of the powerlessness of women in our society.

In line with the unequal gender relations within a patriarchal society, many aspects of Ugandan legislation sanction female subordination. A good example is the law of marriage which allows polygamy and not polyandry; the law of divorce which requires more stringent grounds for a wife's initiated divorce than a husband's, and dispossesses an adulterous wife but not an adulterous husband; the law of succession and inheritance which makes it more likely that a man rather than a woman will inherit land and other property, the criminal law of adultery which more readily punishes an adulterous wife than an adulterous husband, etc. There is no doubt that the law is a reflection of partriarchal social values.

I once again submit that although discrimination against women has its roots outside the law — in socio-cultural and economic conditions — there is still need to amend existing laws to ensure formal equality between the sexes.

The results of this study support the theory that crime has to do with a woman's role, as Richard Ford has noted.[2] Bardsley rightly observed that this is a useful distinction between biology and conditioning. We need not, however, forget that violence is only one, though extreme, way of conflict resolution and that as Tanner (1970:25) stated, it runs counter to human instincts. What Ewing (1987:76) said of battered women's reactions to abuse is equally valid for women's reactions to oppressive gender relations. In her view 'not all [oppressed] women are so seriously threatened [as to kill], and some who are find ways other than homicide to avert the threat [of self-disintegration].'

One may say that a study of a limited number of court records, as well as a limited number of women respondents in particular prisons, is too inadequate to draw definitive conclusions on the subject. Nevertheless, whatever its limits, it throws some light on the patterns of female violent crime and even gives a few hints regarding the situation that tend to push a woman towards such behaviour in Ugandan society.

The results of this study clearly demonstrate that the roots of women's violence in Uganda are found in the power structure of society in general and of the family as a socio-economic institution in particular; a structure which places women in a subservient position and allows men to subject women to various forms of oppression (often enforced by violence) and victimisation. It is often in retaliation against this oppression and victimisation that women resort to violence. Whether the threat is physical, economic, or psychological, the woman's retaliation points to an act of self-preservation. Whether the woman's reaction is viewed as retaliation against physical abuse (by a husband) or against economic and status deprivation (by a co-wife), her act is driven by self-preservation.

As Roberts (1994:8) said:

> Feminism's greatest contribution to criminal law has been to reveal its *political* nature. Feminists have demonstrated that male violence against women is rooted in prevalent power relationships rather than in men's biological or mental aberrations. Scholars should extend this insight concerning male criminality to their analyses of female lawbreaking. Feminists should analyse female crimes within the context of patriarchal power (emphasis original).

This study has revealed that women's familial violence in Uganda is a consequence of their powerlessness in a patriarchal society. It confirms Gelles' (1983:162) report that:

> ... research also finds that violence is more likely to occur in homes where the husband ... has all the power and makes all the decisions; ... if families were helped to change the power structure of their relations and reduce the inequality in decision-making, this would reduce the risk of conflict and confrontation escalating into violence....

Society may be appalled to learn that a significant proportion of women in prison are in for violent crimes they perpetrated against those that they are supposed to love — family members. But mere outrage is not the solution; society must do more: it must alter the socio-economic, cultural, and legal arrangements that deprive women of more humane ways of conflict-resolution, thus driving them into violence. This call is in line with Straus et al's (1980: 222, 223) contention about American society that:

> ... the roots of family violence are to be found in the nature of the family itself; what is needed is no less than a restructuring of the relations between family members. ... The *prevention* of violence in the home and the reduction of family violence involve major structural changes for both society and the family (emphasis original).

Presently, the social reality of many Ugandan women killers was described aptly by Justice Jones in 1969. While presiding over a Uganda High Court case,[3] in which a woman killed a husband who had persistently subjected her to abuse, Justice Jones said that the accused was 'more sinned against than sinning'.

Notes

1. Ahluwalia threw petrol over her husband and set fire to him after being subjected to ten years of brutality. He died of the resulting burns. Ahluwalia was charged with murder before the Lewes Crown Court in England. She pleaded guilty to manslaughter on the grounds that she acted under provocation, but was convicted of murder on the grounds that her act was not a result of loss of self-control; it was a planned act. Through the Southhall Black Sisters, a group which organised a campaign on her behalf, Ahluwalia issued a statement saying that the law should try to understand why she acted as she did (*The Independent*, 2 July 1990).

2. Ex-warden of Britain's only female bail hostel. Quoted by Bardsley (1987:32).

3. *Faisi Apio*, H.C.C.S.C. No. 744/69.

References

Adler F. (1975) *Sisters in Crime: The Rise of the New Female Criminal.* New York. McGraw-Hill.

Avison N.H. (1974) 'Victims of homicide', *International Journal of Criminology and Penology,* vol. 2, pp. 225-237.

Bardsley B. (1987) *Flowers in Hell: an Investigation into Women and Crime.* London. Pandora Press.

Beattie J.H.M. (1960) 'Homicide and suicide in Bunyoro', in P. Bohannan (ed.) *African Homicide and Suicide.* Princeton, New Jersey. Princeton University Press.

Block C.R. (1993) 'The meaning and measurement of victim precipitation', in *Questions and Answers in Lethal and Non-Lethal Violence: Proceedings of the Second Annual Workshop of the Homicide Research Working Group,* pp. 185-193. Quantico, Virginia. FBI Academy.

Blum A. and Gary F. (1978) 'Women who Kill', in L.I. Kutash et al. (eds.) *Violence: Perspectives on Murder and Aggression.*

Bohannan P. (1960a) 'Patterns of murder and suicide', in P. Bohannan (ed.) *African Homicide and Suicide.* Princeton, New Jersey. Princeton University Press.

Bohannan P. (1960b) 'Theories of homicide and suicide', in P. Bohannan (ed.) *African Homicide and Suicide.* Princeton, New Jersey. Princeton University Press.

Browne A. (1987) *When Battered Women Kill.* New York. Free Press.

Brownstein H.H. et al. (1994) 'Changing patterns of lethal violence by women: a research note', *Women and Criminal Justice,* vol. 5, no. 2, pp. 99-118.

Carlen P. (1983) *Women's Imprisonment: a Study in Social Control.* London. Routledge and Kegan Paul.

Carlen P. and Worrall A. (eds.) (1987) *Gender, Crime and Justice.* Milton Keynes. Open University Press.

Chimbos P.D. (1978) *Marital Violence: a Study of Interspouse Homicide.* San Francisco. R and E Research Associates, Inc.

Cipparone J.A. (1987) 'The defence of battered women who kill', *University of Pennsylvania Law Review*, vol. 135, no. 1, pp. 427-452.

Clifford W. (1974) *An Introduction to African Criminology.* Nairobi. Oxford University Press.

Copeland A.R. (1986) 'Homicidal drowning', *Forensic Science International*, vol. 31, no. 4, pp. 247-252.

Cutrufelli M.S. (1983) *Women of Africa: Roots of Oppression.* London. Zed Press.

Dalton K. (1961) 'Menstruation and crime', *British Medical Journal*, vol. 2, pp. 1752-1753.

Del M. (1982) Introduction, in G. NiCarthy *Getting Free: A Handbook for Women in Abusive Relationships.* Seattle. Seal Press.

Duncan J.W. and Duncan G.M. (1978) 'Murder in the family', in L.I. Kutash et al. (eds.) *Violence: Perspectives on Murder and Aggression.*

Eaton M. (1986) *Justice for Women? Family, Court and Social Control.* Milton Keynes. Open University Press.

Evans M. (1983) Introduction, in M. Evans and C. Ungerson (eds.) *Sexual Divisions: Patterns and Processes.* London Tavistock.

Ewing C.P. (1987) *Battered Women Who Kill: Psychological Self-Defence As Legal Justification.* Lexington, Massachusetts. Lexington Books.

Fallers L.A. and Fallers M.C. (1960) 'Homicide and suicide in Busoga', in P. Bohannan (ed.) *African Homicide and Suicide.* Princeton, New Jersey. Princeton University Press.

Fiala R. and LaFree G. (1988) 'Cross-national determinants of child homicide', *American Sociological Review*, vol. 53, no. 3, June, pp. 432-445.

Gelles, R.J. (1974) *The Violent Home: A Study of Physical Aggression between Husbands and Wives.* Beverly Hills. Sage Publications.

———. (1983) 'An exchange/social control theory', in D. Finkelhor et al. (eds.) *The Dark Side of Families: Current Family Violence Research.*

Gelsthorpe L. (1989) *Sexism and the Female Offender: An Organizational Analysis.* Aldershopt, England. Gower.

────── and Morris A. (1988) 'Feminism and criminology in Britain', *British Journal of Criminology,* vol. 28, no. 2.

Gil G.D. (1970a) *Violence against Children: Physical Child Abuse in the United States.* Cambridge. Harvard University Press.

──────. (1970b) *Casebook and Proceedings: Seminar on the Battered Child Syndrome, January 21, 1965.* Topeka. Kansas State Department of Social Welfare.

Gobert, J.J. (1977) 'Victim Precipitation', *Columbia Law Review,* vol. 77, no. 4, p. 511.

Goetting A. (1988) 'When females kill one another: the exceptional case', *Criminal Justice and Behaviour,* vol. 15, no. 2, June, pp. 179-189.

Hawkins G. (1985) 'Prisoners' nights', *Australian and New Zealand Journal of Criminology,* vol. 18, no. 4, pp. 202-203.

Heidensohn F. (1968) 'The deviance of women: a critique and an enquiry', *British Journal of Sociology,* vol. 19, no. 1, pp. 160-175.

──────. (1985) *Women and Crime.* London. Macmillan.

──────. (1987) 'Women and crime: questions for criminology', in P. Carlen and A. Worral (eds.) *Gender, Crime and Justice.*

Isaacman B. and Stephen J. (1980) *Women, the Law and Agrarian Reform.* Addis Ababa. UN Economic Commission for Africa.

James R. (1989) 'The enforcement of prisoners' rights in Papua New Guinea', *The Commonwealth Law Bulletin,* vol. 15, no. 3, July 1989, p. 1033.

Jones A. (1980) *Women Who Kill.* New York. Holt, Rinehart and Winston.

Kaijuka E. et al. (1989) *Uganda Demographic and Health Survey, 1988/1989.* Entebbe. Ministry of Health; Demographic and Health Surveys. Institute for Resource Development.

Kendall K. (1992) 'Dangerous bodies' in D. P. Farrington and S. Walklate (eds.) *Offenders and Victims: Theory and Policy (Selected Papers)*. Volume 7. Leicestershire, U.K. British Society of Criminology.

Kilbride P. and Kilbride J. (1990) *Family Life in East Africa*. University Park. Pennsylvania State University Press.

La Fontaine J. (1960) 'Homicide and suicide among the Gisu', in P. Bohannan (ed.) *African Homicide and Suicide*. Princeton, New Jersey. Princeton University Press.

Lombroso C. and Ferrero W. (1895) *The Female Offender*. London. Fisher Unwin.

Loftin C. (1986) *Firearms violence and the Michigan felony firearm law: Detroit, 1976–1978*. Ann Arbor, MI. Inter-University Consortium for Political and Social Research.

Macdonald J.M. (1986) *The Murderer and His Victim*. Second edition. Springfield, Illinois. Thomas.

Mahfooz K. (1989) *Murder and Homicide in Pakistan*. Lahore, Pakistan. Vanguard.

Maillu G.D. (1988) *Our Kind of Polygamy*. Nairobi. Heinemann.

Mannathoko C. (1992) 'Feminist theories and the study of gender issues in southern Africa', R. Meena (ed.) in *Gender in Southern Africa: Conceptual and Theoretical Issues*. Harare. SAPES Books.

Mannheim H. (ed.) (1960) *Pioneers in Criminology*. London. Stevens and Sons.

Marshall B.C. and Quinney (1973) *Crime in Developing Countries: A Comparative Perspective*. New York. John Wiley.

Mbilinyi M. (1992) 'Research methodologies in gender issues', in R. Meena (ed.) *Gender in Southern Africa: Conceptual and Theoretical Issues*. Harare. SAPES Books.

Meena R. (1992) 'Gender research/studies in southern Africa: an overview' in R. Meena (ed.) *Gender in Southern Africa: Conceptual and Theoretical Issues*. Harare. SAPES Books.

Morris A. (1987) *Women, Crime and Criminal Justice*. Oxford. Basil Blackwell.

Mushanga T. (1974) *Criminal Homicide in Uganda: A Sociological Study of Violent Deaths in Ankole, Kigezi and Toro Districts of Western Uganda.* Nairobi. East African Literature Bureau.

———. (1976) *Crime and Deviance.* Nairobi. East African Literature Bureau.

———. (1978) 'Wife victimization in East and Central Africa', *Victimology: An International Journal,* vol. 2, nos. 3-4, pp. 479-485.

Naffin N. (1987) *Female Crime: The Construction of Women in Criminology.* Australia. Allen and Unwin.

——— and Gale F. (1989) 'Testing the nexus: crime, gender, and unemployment', *British Journal of Criminology,* vol. 29, no. 2, pp. 144-156.

Odoki B.J. (1990) *A Guide to Criminal Procedure in Uganda.* Second edition. Kampala. Law Development Centre.

O'Donovan K. (1991) 'Defences for battered women who kill', *Journal of Law and Society,* vol. 18, no. 2. pp. 219-240.

Pollak O. (1961) *The Criminality of Women.* New York. A.S. Barnes.

Rafter N.H. and Natalizia E.M. (1981) 'Marxist feminism: implications for criminal justice', *Crime and Delinquency,* January, pp. 81-98.

Roberts E.D. (1993) 'Motherhood and crime', *Iowa Law Review,* vol. 79, pp. 95-141.

Rodriguez F.S. and Henderson A.V. (1995) 'Intimate homicide: victim-offender relationship in female-perpetrated homicide', *Deviant Behaviour,* vol. 16, no. 1, pp. 45-57.

Rosen C.J. (1986) 'The excuse of self-defence: correcting a historical accident on behalf of battered women who kill', *American University Law Review,* vol. 36, no. 11, pp. 11-56.

Sampa A. et al. (1994) *Gender bias in the Zambian court system: a report based on research findings, 8 Nov. 1993–6 Feb. 1994.* Lusaka. Women in Law and Development in Africa (WILDAF) – (Zambia).

Schneider M.E. and Jordan B.S. (1978) 'Representation of women who defend themselves in response to physical or sexual assault', *Women's Rights Law Reporter*, vol. 4, no. 3.

Seidman R. (1966) *A Sourcebook of the Criminal Law of Africa: Cases, Statutes and Materials.* London. Sweet and Maxwell.

Smart C. (1976) *Women, Crime and Criminology: A Feminist Critique.* London. Routledge and Kegan Paul.

——. (1983) 'Partriarchal relations and law: an examination of family law and sexual equality in the 1950s', in M. Evans and C. Ungerson (eds.) *Sexual Divisions: Patterns and Processes:* London. Tavistock.

Sommers I. and Baskin D.R. (1993) 'The situational context of violent female offending', *Journal of Research in Crime and Delinquency*, vol. 30, no. 2, May, pp. 136-162.

Southall A.W. (1960) 'Homicide and suicide among the Alur', in P. Bohannan (ed.) *African Homicide and Suicide.* Princeton, New Jersey. Princeton University Press.

Stahly G.B. (1978) 'A review of select literature on spousal violence', *Victimology: An International Journal*, vol. 2, nos. 3-4, pp. 591-607.

Straus J.H. and Straus M.A. (1952-53) 'Suicide, homicide, and social structure in Ceylon', *The American Journal of Sociology*, vol. 58, no. 1, pp. 461-469.

Straus M.A. (1977-78) 'Wife beating: how common and why?' *Victimology: An International Journal*, vol. 2, nos. 3-4, pp. 443-458.

—— et al. (1980) *Behind Closed Doors: Violence in American Families.* New York. Doubleday.

Tamale S. (1993) 'Law reform and women's rights in Uganda', *East African Journal of Peace and Human Rights*, vol. 1, no. 2, pp. 164-184.

Tanner R.E.S. (1970) *Homicide in Uganda 1964.* Uppsala. Scandinavian Institute of African Studies.

Tariq P.N. (1981) *A Study of Female Crime in Rural and Urban Areas of Pakistan*. Islamabad. Printing Corporation of Pakistan Press.

Thompson B.R. and Erez E. (1994) 'Spousal abuse in Sierra Leone: multiple wives in a dual legal system', *International Journal of Comparative and Applied Criminal Justice*, vol. 18, no.1, spring, pp. 27-37.

Totman J. (1978) *The Murderess: A Psychosocial Study of Criminal Homicide*. San Fransisco. R and E Research Associates.

Walker L.E. (1977-78) 'Battered women and learned helplessness', *Victimology: An International Journal*, vol. 2, nos. 3-4, pp. 525-534.

———. (1984) 'Battered women, psychology and public policy', *American Psychologist*, vol. 39, October, pp. 1178-1182.

Warren M. (1979) 'The female offender', in H. Toch (ed.) *Psychology of Crime*. New York. Holt, Rinehart and Winston.

Wilbanks W. (1982) 'Murdered women and women who murder', in N.H. Rafter and E.O. Stanko (eds.), *Judge, Lawyer, Victim, Thief: Women, Gender Roles and Criminal Justice*. Boston. Northeastern University Press.

Wilczynski A. and Morris A. (1993) 'Parents who kill their children', *The Criminal Law Review*, vol. 1993, January, p. 31.

Wilson M.I. and Daly M. (1992) 'Who kills whom in spousal killings? On the exceptional sex ratio of spousal homicides in the United States', *Criminology*, vol. 30, no.2, pp. 189-215.

Wolfgang M.E. (1958) *Patterns in Criminal Homicide*. Philadelphia. University of Pennyslvania Press.

———. (1993) 'Victim precipitation in victimology and in law', in *Questions and Answers in Lethal and Non-Lethal Violence: Proceedings of the Second Annual Workshop of the Homicide Research Working Group*, pp. 167-183. Quantico, Virginia. FBI Academy.

Worrall A. (1990) *Offending Women: Female Lawbreakers and the Criminal Justice System*. London. Routledge.

Further Reading

Allan G. and Skinner C. (1991) *Handbook for Research Students in the Social Sciences.* London. Falmer Press.

Allen H. (1987) 'Rendering them harmless: the professional portrayal of women charged with serious violent crimes', in P. Carlen and A. Worrall (eds.) *Gender, Crime and Justice.* Milton Keynes. Open University Press.

Allot A. (1960) *Essays on African Law.* London. Butterworths.

Allot A. (1968) 'Judicial Precedent in Africa Revisited', *Journal of African Law,* vol. 12, pp. 3-31.

Apodaca L. and Fink L. (1984) 'Criminal law: premenstrual syndrome in the courts?' *Washburn Law Journal,* vol. 24, pp. 54-77.

Ball G.P. and Wyman E. (1977) 'Battered wives and powerlessness: what can counsellors do?' *Victimology: An International Journal,* vol. 2, nos. 3-4, pp. 545-552.

Bandura A. (1978) 'Learning and behavioral theories of aggression', in L.I. Kutash et al. (eds.) *Violence: Perspectives on Murder and Aggression.*

Barnett O.W. et al. (1980) *Family Violence: Intervention Strategies.* Department of Health and Human Services. Washington, D.C. Government Printing Office. Pub. no. (OHD) 80-30258.

Barton T. and Wamai G. (1994) *Equity and Vulnerability: Uganda National Situation Analysis for Women, Children and Adolescents, 1994.* Kampala. National Council for Children, UNICEF, Child Health and Development Centre.

Bernard T.J. (1981) 'The distinction between conflict and radical criminology', *The Journal of Criminal Law and Criminology,* vol. 72, no. 1, p. 362.

Besharov J.D. (1981) 'Toward better research on child abuse and neglect: making definitional issues an explicit methodological concern', *Child Abuse and Neglect,* vol. 5, pp. 383-390.

Bohannan P. (1965) 'Patterns of homicide among tribal societies in Africa', in M. Wolfgang (ed.) *Studies in Homicide.* New York. Harper and Row.

Box S. (1983) *Power, Crime and Mystification.* London. Tavistok.

Box S. and Hale C. (1983) 'Liberation and female criminality in England and Wales', *British Journal of Criminology,* vol. 23, no. 1, pp. 35-49.

Carlen P. (ed.) (1985) *Criminal Women.* Cambridge. Polity Press.

Chan W. (1994) 'A feminist critique of self-defence and provocation in battered women's cases in England and Wales', *Women and Criminal Justice,* vol. 6, no. 1, pp. 39-65.

Curley R.T. (1973) 'The Lango of north-central Uganda', in A. Molnos (ed.) *Cultural Source Materials for Population Planning in East Africa.* Nairobi. Institute of African Studies, University of Nairobi.

Denno W.D. (1994) 'Gender, crime and the criminal law defenses', *The Journal of Criminal Law and Criminology,* vol. 85, no. 1, summer, pp. 80-180.

Dobash R.E. and Dobash R.P. (1977) 'Wives: the "appropriate" victims of marital violence, *Victimology: An International Journal,* vol. 2, nos. 3-4, pp. 462-442.

———. (1984) 'The nature and antecedents of violent events', *British Journal of Criminology,* vol. 24, no. 3, July, pp. 269-288.

Fagan J. and Wexler S. (1987) 'Crime at home and in the streets: the relationship between family and stranger violence', *Violence and Victims,* vol. 2, no. 1 pp. 5-23.

Figueira-McDonough J. (1984) 'Feminism and delinquency: in search of an elusive link', *British Journal of Criminology,* vol. 24, no. 4, pp. 325-342.

Filstead W. (ed.) (1970) *Qualitative Methodology: Firsthand Involvement with the Social World.* Chicago. Markham Publishing Company.

Finkelhor D. et al. (eds.) (1983) *The Dark Side of Families: Current Family Violence Research.* Beverly Hills. Sage Publications.

Follingstad D.R. et al. (1989) *Law and Human Behaviour*, vol. 13, pp. 253-269.

Gaidzanwa R. (1992) 'Bourgeois theories of gender and feminism and their shortcomings with reference to southern African countries', in R. Meena (ed.) *Gender in Southern Africa: Conceptual and Theoretical Issues*. Harare. SAPES Books.

Griffiths C.T. and Nance M. (eds.) (1980) *The Female Offender*. Burnaby. Simon Fraser University.

Hasse Lizbeth (1989) 'Legalizing gender-specific values', in E.F. Kittay and D.T. Meyers (eds.) *Women and Moral Theory*. Savage. Rowman and Littlefield.

Helfer R.E. (1968) *The Battered Child*. Chicago. University of Chicago Press.

Hilary A. (1987) 'Rendering them harmless: the professional portrayal of women charged with serious violent crimes', in P. Carlen and A. Worral (eds.) *Gender, Crime and Justice*.

Hilberman E. and Munson K. (1977) 'Sixty battered women', *Victimology: An International Journal*, vol. 2, no. 1, pp. 460-470.

Hoffman-Bustamante D. (1973) 'The nature of female criminality', *Issues in Criminology*, vol. 8, no. 2, pp. 117-136.

Horney J. (1985) 'Menstrual cycles and criminal responsibility', in F.H. March and J. Katz (eds.) *Biology, Crime and Ethics: A Study of Biological Explanations for Criminal Behaviour*. Ohio. Anderson Publishing Company.

Jensen H.R. (1977) 'Battered women and the law', *Victimology: An International Journal*, vol. 2, nos. 3-4, pp. 585-590.

Johnson E.H. (ed.) (1983) *International Handbook of Contemporary Developments in Criminology: Europe, Africa, the Middle East and Asia*. Westport, Connecticut. Greenwood Press.

Kates D.B. (ed.) (1979) *Restricting Handguns: The Liberal Skeptics Speak Out*. Croton-on-Hudson, New York. North River Press.

Kato L.L. (1960) 'The Court of Appeal for East Africa: from a colonial to an international court', *East African Law Journal*, vol. 7, no. 1.

Kempe C.H. and Helfer R.E. (1980) *The Battered Child.* Third edition. Chicago. University of Chicago Press.

Klein D. (1973) 'The etiology of female crime: a review of the literature', *Issues in Criminology,* vol. 8, no. 2. pp. 3-30.

—— . (1981) 'Violence against women: some considerations regarding its causes and its elimination', *Crime and Delinquency,* January, pp. 64-80.

—— and Kress J. (1976) 'Any woman's blues: a critical overview of women, crime and the criminal justice system', *Crime and Social Justice: A Journal of Radical Criminology,* vol. 5, spring-summer, pp. 34-49.

Kutash L.I. (1978) *Violence: Perspectives on Murder and Aggression.* San Francisco. Jossey-Bass.

Leonard E.B. (1982) *Women, Crime and Society.* New York. Longman.

Mackay R.D. (1993) 'The consequences of killing very young children', *The Criminal Law Review,* vol. 92, no. 1, pp. 21-30.

Marshall B.C. and Quinney R. (1973) *Criminal Behaviour Systems: A Typology.* Second edition. New York. Holt, Rinehart and Winston.

Mill S.J. (1992) 'Legal literacy: a tool for women's empowerment', in M. Schuler and S. Rayasingham (eds.) *Women, Law and Development.* Washington, D.C. OEF International.

Morris H.F. (1974) 'A history of the adoption of codes of criminal law and procedure in British colonial Africa, 1876-1935', *Journal for African Law,* vol. 18, no. 1, pp. 7-23.

—— and Read J.S. (1966) *Uganda: The Development of Its Laws and Constitution.* London. Stevens and Sons.

Naffin N. (1985) 'The masculinity-femininity hypothesis: a consideration of gender-based personality theories of female crime', *British Journal of Criminology,* vol. 25, no. 4, October, pp. 365-381.

Nettler G. (1974) *Explaining Crime.* New York. McGraw-Hill.

Newberger E.H. (1983) 'Child abuse: the current theory base and future research needs', *Journal of the American Academy of Child Psychiatry,* vol. 22, no. 3, pp. 262-268.

NiCarthy G. (1982) *Getting Free: A Handbook for Women in Abusive Relationships*. Seattle. Seal Press.

Nortey D.N.A. (1983) 'Ghana', in E.H. Johnson (ed.) *International Handbook of Contemporary Developments in Criminology: Europe, Africa, the Middle East and Asia*.

Ntozi J. and Kabera J. (1991) 'Family planning in rural Uganda: knowledge and use of modern and traditional methods in Ankole, *Studies in Family Planning*, vol. 22, no. 2.

Odoki B.J. (1994) 'Reducing delay in the administration of justice: the case of Uganda', *Criminal Law Forum: An International Journal*, vol. 5, no. 1, pp. 57-89.

Ogle S.R. et al. (1995) 'A theory of homicidal behaviour among women', *Criminology*, vol. 33, no. 2, pp. 173-193.

Ohlin L. and Tonry M. (eds.) (1989) *Family Violence*. Chicago. University of Chicago Press.

Opio J. (1983) 'Uganda', in E.H. Johnson (ed.) *International Handbook of Contemporary Developments in Criminology: Europe, Africa, the Middle East and Asia*.

Pagelow M.D. (1984) *Family Violence*. New York. Praeger.

Parisi N. (1982) 'Exploring female crime patterns: problems and perspectives', in N.H. Rafter and E.A. Stanko (eds.) *Judge, Lawyer, Victim, Thief: Women, Gender Roles, and Criminal Justice*. Boston. Northeastern University Press.

Pelton H.L. (1978) 'Child abuse and neglect: the myth of classlessness', *American Journal of Orthopsychiatry*, vol. 48, no. 4, October, pp. 608-617.

Rasche E.C. (1993) 'Victim precipitation and social policy: clemency for battered women who kill', in *Questions and Answers in Lethal and Non-Lethal Violence: Proceedings of the Second Annual Workshop of the Homicide Research Working Group*. Quantico, Virginia. FBI Academy.

Read J. (1963) 'Criminal law in the Africa of today and tomorrow,' *Journal for African Law*, pp. 5-17.

Roberts E.D. (1994) 'Foreword: the meaning of gender equality in the criminal law', *The Journal of Criminal Law and Criminology*, vol. 85, no. 1, summer, pp. 1-14.

Rosenfeld E. (1968) *Social Research and Social Action in Prevention of Juvenile Delinquency.*

Sandhu S.H. (1983) 'India', in E.H. Johnson (ed.) *International Handbook of Contemporary Developments in Criminology: Europe, Africa, the Middle East and Asia.*

Sawyer G.F. and Hiller J. (1967) 'The doctrine of precedent in the Court of Appeal for East Africa', in G.F. Sawyer (ed.) *East African Law and Social Change.* Nairobi. East Africa Publishing House.

Schopper D. and Doussantousse S. (1991) 'AIDS-related knowledge, attitudes and behaviours in Moyo district, northern Uganda'. Unpublished.

Silverman R.A. and Mukherjee S.K. (1987) 'Intimate homicide: an analysis of violent social relationships', *Behavioral Science and the Law,* vol. 5, no. 1, pp. 37-47.

Silverman R.A. and Sharma N. (1979) 'Women and crime: does the American experience generalize?', in F. Adler and R.J. Simon (eds.) *The Criminology of Deviant Women.* Boston. Houghton Mifflin Company.

Smart C. (1977a) 'Reply to Paul Rock', *British Journal of Criminology,* vol. 17, p. 397.

———. (1977b) 'Criminological theory: its ideology and implications concerning women', *British Journal of Sociology,* vol. 28, no.1, March, pp. 89-100.

———. (1979) 'The new female criminal: reality or myth?' *British Journal of Criminology,* vol. 19, no. 1, January, pp. 50-59.

———. (1984) *The Ties That Bind.* London. Routledge and Kegan Paul.

———. (1992) 'The woman of legal discourse', *Social and Legal Issues: An International Journal,* vol. 1, no. 1, pp. 29-44.

———. (1995) *Law, Crime and Sexuality: Essays in Feminism.* London. Sage Publications.

Sommer B. (1984) 'PMS in the courts: are all women on trial?' *Psychology Today,* August, pp. 36-38.

Spradley J. (1979) *The Ethnographic Interview.* New York. Holt, Rinehart and Winston.

Steinmetz S.K. and Straus M.A. (1973) 'The family as cradle of violence', *Society,* vol. 10, no. 6, pp. 50-56.

—— (eds.) (1974) *Violence in the Family.* New York. Harper and Row.

Stewart M.J. (1992) 'Legal literacy: a tool for women's empowerment', in M. Schuler and S.K. Rayasingham (eds.) *Women, Law and Development.* Washington, D.C. OEF International.

Stock M. (1985) *A Practical Guide to Graduate Research.* New York. McGraw-Hill.

Suval M.E. and Brisson R.C. (1974) 'Neither beauty nor beast: female criminal homicide offenders', *International Journal of Criminology and Penology,* vol. 2, no. 1, February, pp. 23-34.

Tong R. (1984) *Women, Sex and the Law.* Totowa, New Jersey. Rowman and Allanheld.

Ward D.A. et al. (1968) 'Crimes of violence by women' (reprinted in *The Criminology of Deviant Women: A Critique and an Enquiry), British Journal of Sociology,* vol. 19, p. 110.

Wasik M. (1982) 'Cumulative provocation and domestic killing', *The Criminal Law Review,* vol. 1982, January, pp. 29-37.

Weis G.J. (1976) 'Liberation and crime: the invention of the new female criminal', *Crime and Social Justice: Issues in Criminology,* vol. 6, fall-winter, pp. 17-27.

Weisheit A.R. (1984) 'Female homicide offenders: trends over time in an institutionalized population', *Justice Quarterly,* vol. 1, no. 4, pp. 471-489.

Westhuizen J.V. (1983) 'South Africa', in E.H. Johnson (ed.) *International Handbook of Contemporary Developments in Criminology: Europe, Africa, the Middle East and Asia.*

Wilbanks W. (1981) 'Review of *Women Who Kill*, by A. Jones', *The Journal of Criminal Law and Criminology*, vol. 72, no. 2, pp. 859-863.

——. (1983) 'The female homicide offender in Dade Country, Florida', *Criminal Justice Review*, vol. 8, no. 2, pp. 9-14.

Wolfgang M.E. (ed.) (1967) *Studies in Homicide*. New York. Harper and Row.

—— and Ferracuti F. (1966) *The Subculture of Violence*. London. Tavistock.

Wright, J.D. et al. (1981) *Weapons, Crime and Violence in America*. Washington, D.C. U.S. Department of Justice.

Index

A

abuse 2, 39-65, 71, 77, 85-7, 91, 96, 115-7, 170, 176-9, 188-99, 222, 237-8. *See also* battered women; *battered woman syndrome*; physical abuse; psychological abuse

accumulated violence 160-1, 173-5, 190-1, 197. *See also* abuse; provocation; threats of future injury

acid. *See* weapons

acquittals. *See* verdicts

Adler, F. 73, 76

Adong 109-10, 225

adultery 81, 95, 104-6, 120, 138-9, 169, 178, 204, 236

Affiliation Act, The 110-1

Agaba 45-7, 52, 56, 63, 67-74, 79-87, 92-4, 98, 123, 163-4, 176

age 4-7, 27-33, 43-9, 83, 85, 102-4, 108-11, 119-20, 154, 172, 217, 220, 227

Ahluwalia 238

alcohol 53-8, 78, 145, 219

Alur 17

America. *See* United States of America

American society
intrafamily violence in 9, 40, 76-7, 85, 95, 121, 229, 238
male victims of female criminality in 33
sexist standards of justifiable homicide in 165, 169
victim precipitation in 40, 161-2, 165

Ankole 72, 87-8, 124, 147

anti-social behaviour 7, 195

Asaba 47, 52-3, 56, 79-80, 92, 94

Asiimwe 47-8, 54-6, 60, 69-71, 82, 92, 94, 123, 163

Avison, N.H. 17, 155

axe. *See* weapons

B

Bagisu 17, 37, 39, 62, 192

Bakiga 120, 147, 150, 165

Banyankore 147, 150, 165

Bardsley, B. 2, 78, 233, 236

Basoga 17, 109

Batooro 147

battered woman syndrome 161, 205. *See also* abuse; accumulated violence

battered women 52, 77-8, 85, 97, 161-4, 177, 201, 207, 234-5. *See also* abuse; accumulated violence; provocation

Beattie, J.H.M. 128

bigamy 12, 95. *See also* polyandry; polygamy

Biteete 58

Bituresi Kakurungu 179, 184

Block, C.R. 42, 54, 160

Blum, A. and Gary, F. 28

Bohannan, P. 1, 14, 16-7, 37, 99, 182-3, 230

bride price 68-9, 82-4, 89, 97, 108, 121, 129, 132-3, 145, 224

Britain. *See* United Kingdom

Browne, A. 205, 207

Brownstein, H.H. et al 232

Buganda 67

Bugono village 21, 124

Bunyoro 17, 127

Byamugisha 49-54, 58, 69, 72, 91

Byarugaba 48-9, 53, 60-1, 69, 80, 91, 123, 163

Index

C

Carlen, P. 80, 92, 95, 137, 183
Carlen, P. and Worrall, A. 8, 129
Chacha s/o Wamburu v Rex 209
child homicide 115
child ownership 62, 111-4
children, corporal punishment of 115-7
Chimbos, P.D. 50-1, 62, 70
Cipparone, J.A. 77, 162, 205, 207
civil marriage 82
class 4-10, 66, 84, 95, 153, 166, 171-3, 227, 234-5
Clifford, W. 16, 24, 157
co-offenders 28-32
co-wives 21-3, 32, 36, 58-9, 70, 75, 81, 113-4, 122-9, 136-7, 142-57, 187, 191-3, 205, 219, 230-1, 237. *See also* common-law spouses; junior wives; senior wives
common-law spouses 51. *See also* co-wives
concubines 58, 63. *See also* girlfriends; mistresses; prostitutes
conflict-resolution 8, 80-1, 229, 236-7
conjugal violence 9. *See also* violence
Cook County Jail 40
Copeland, A.R. 99
Cornton Vale Prison 80, 95
corporal punishment of children 115-7
Courts of Appeal 140, 170-3, 179, 186, 189, 209
Crimes (Homicide) Amendment Act of 1982, The 210
criminal justice system 8, 64, 77, 134, 164-7, 175, 200, 212-3, 220-3, 235
criminal law 1, 100, 105, 159, 164, 173, 204, 223, 236. *See also* law; legislation
Criminal Law (Witchcraft) Ordinance of Uganda, The 194
culpability 103

custodial institutions 213, 226-7. *See also* prisons; sentencing
custom 7, 73, 82, 87, 98, 112
customary law. *See* law
Customary Marriage (Registration) Decree, The 97, 157
customary tenure 73
Cutrufelli, M.S. 148

D

Dalton, K. 15
Danish Criminal Code 120, 180, 205
death penalty. *See* sentencing
Del, M. 92, 155
delinquency 4
deviance 157. *See also* anti-social behaviour
Director of Public Prosecutions v Camplin 172, 206
Divorce Act, The 95-7, 104, 137-41
doctrine of self-defence. *See* self-defence
domestic violence 8-9, 50-1, 70-3, 201-2. *See also* violence
Doto s/o Mtaki v Regina 189
double oppression 65-70. *See also* patriarchal oppression
Duncan, J.W. and Duncan, G.M. 51, 99

E

Eaton, M. 153
Edith Nakiyingi v Zadeke 140
education 9-10, 16, 27, 37-8, 105, 110-1, 134, 166, 225, 235
Elizabeth Nyacho 161
Elizabeth Obaro 91, 162, 184
equality 65-70, 74-7, 94-5, 220-38
ethnicity 9
Evans, M. 12, 235
Ewing, C.P. 77, 162, 174, 200-3, 205, 207, 235, 236

Index

F

Faisi Apio 197, 238
Fallers, L.A. and Fallers, M.C. 17
familial violence 31-4, 122-9, 236, 237. *See also* domestic violence; violence
female criminality. *See* women's criminality
feminist criminology 6. *See also* women's criminality
feminists 2, 12, 164, 237
Fiala, R. and LaFree, G. 156
FIDA. *See* Uganda Association of Women Lawyers
first offenders. *See* sentencing
force, use of. *See* self-defence
Fort Portal 18, 20, 221
free will 105

G

Gelles, R.J. 76-7
Gelsthorpe, L. 66, 67
Gelsthorpe, L. and Morris, A. 5
gender 3-9, 13, 24, 37, 41, 62, 173-5, 200, 207, 220, 227-31, 234-7
Gil, G.D. 115-6
girlfriends 117, 129, 136, 146, 152. *See also* concubines; mistresses; prostitutes
Gobert, J.J. 159, 204
Great Britain. *See* United Kingdom

H

Hawkins, G. 211
heat of passion 145, 159, 186-91, 195, 209
Heidensohn, F. 4-5, 6, 18
hoe. *See* weapons

I

Iganga 21
illiteracy 9, 28, 38. *See also* education
imminency 161, 173-8, 201-2
imminent danger. *See* imminency
imprisonment 11, 24-5, 45, 60, 80, 96, 103-4, 110, 114, 153, 168, 174, 187, 191, 195-9, 206, 211-28. *See also* prisons; prisoners
incarceration. *See* imprisonment
Independent, The 238
infanticide 10, 25, 51, 80, 100-6, 110, 118, 182, 221
infidelity 87, 106, 124-5, 149, 152
intrafamily violence 8-9, 70-3. *See also* violence
intramarital homicide 4, 50-1. *See also* violence
Isaacman, B. and Stephen, J. 139
Islamic law 12

J

James, R. 211
Jane Hanagwa 205
Jinja 18, 20
Jones, A. 23, 53, 58, 66, 80, 85, 97, 165, 169, 184, 200, 205, 208, 229
Jones, Justice 238
Joyce Nyakiriti 205
judge made/case law 167, 206
junior wives 144-5. *See also* co-wives
jurisdiction 111, 201, 210, 218
justifiable homicide 169

K

Kabale 97, 214
Kagoya 108-9, 225
Kaijuka, E. et al 21, 124
Kampala 64, 78, 130, 172, 214
Kampikaho 89, 106-8, 176

Index

Kamugisa 128
Kansiime 54, 57, 61-2, 82, 85, 91
Karugaba 43-5, 46, 52, 55, 56, 63, 70, 74-5, 79, 80, 82-5, 88, 128-9, 143, 151, 163, 176, 187, 223
Katungwabusha 115, 199
Kayita 113-4
Kendall, K. 16
Kenjeru w/o Karindori 192-3
Kigezi 71-2, 87-90, 147
Kilbride, P. and Kilbride, J. 147-8
Kinengyere 101-2, 120
knife. *See* weapons
Komugisa 128, 143, 150-1
Kuri 188

L

La Fontaine, J. 17, 39, 62, 192
labour 94, 139-41, 145
land conflicts 70-1, 78
Lango 124
law 24
    customary 12, 42, 80-1, 97-8, 138, 141
    inheritance 72-3, 94
    marriage 11, 95-6, 138, 141, 236
    property 8, 78, 94, 97-8, 138
    succession 112, 137, 236
legislation 1, 7-11, 95-8, 141
leniency. *See* sentencing
Lewes Crown Court 238
Lira 102
Loftin, C. 160
Lombroso, C. and Ferrero, W. 6, 14
love triangles and homicide 124-5
Luo 125
Lusoga 125, 192
Luzira Women's Prison 214. *See also* prisons

M

Macdonald, J.M. 210
Madi 124
Mahfooz, K. 17, 157
Maillu, G.D. 123-4, 127, 148-9, 153-4
malayas. *See* prostitutes
malice aforethought 11, 25, 198, 210
Mancini v DPP 186
manhood 67
Mannathoko, C. 13
Mannheim, H. 7
manslaughter 10, 11, 15, 25, 40-5, 100, 119-20, 123, 144, 164, 169, 174, 180, 186-99, 203, 208, 210, 228, 238
Manzi v R. 179
Margaret Kazigati 168
Margaret Nakuya v Uganda 217
marriage 81-2, 97
    civil 12
    law 11
    legislation 11
    license 85
    monogamous 12, 143. *See also* monogamy
    polygamous 124-5, 152-3. *See also* polygamy
    separation 80-1, 86-90, 138, 140, 234
    status 104, 233-4
    violence in 55, 70. *See also* violence
Marriage and Divorce of Mohammedans Act, The 97
Married Women's Property Act, The 139
Marshall, B.C. and Quinney 24
Marxist theory of crime 25
Masaka 18, 20, 213, 214, 217, 221
Mbabane 206
Mbale 18, 20
Mbarara 18, 20, 94, 130, 214, 216, 221

Mbilinyi, M. 7, 9, 13
Meena, R. 2, 3
menopause 15
menstruation 15-6
mental instability 15, 100, 221-2. *See also* rationality
Ministry of Local Government 97
mistresses 59-60, 78, 128, 153-6. *See also* concubines; girlfriends; prostitutes
mob justice 182, 198, 209
Monika Nagadya and Others 198, 209
monogamy 149, 152-4. *See also* marriage
Moonlight Sengooba Salongo v Administrator General 78
Moroto 218
Morris, A. 4, 8-9, 24, 41-2, 77, 100, 227
Morris, H.F. and Read, J.S. 209
motherhood 7, 63, 92, 156, 225, 232
Mugisa 126
Muhinduka v Kabere 97
Mukandori 117-8
murder 10, 11, 15, 17, 20, 23, 25, 28, 37, 39, 40, 43, 47-52, 58, 63, 80, 106-11, 114, 118, 123, 129, 146, 153, 157, 162, 164, 169, 172, 178, 183-7, 190-4, 198-204, 208, 210, 217, 219, 221, 228, 238
Mushanga, T. 9, 10-11, 14, 17, 33, 38, 39, 40, 51, 55, 71, 79, 87-90, 125, 142, 147, 150, 157, 165, 166-7, 180-3, 204
Mutooro 90
Mwesigye 100, 221
myth of the cruel stepmother 118

N

Nabalayo 69, 221-2
Nabisinde 114, 117, 221
Nabowa 192, 222-3
Nabwami 126, 221
Naffin, N. 19, 164, 169
Naffin, N. and Gale, F. 5
Nafuna 53, 57
Nakyanzi 166
Nalinya 154
Nalukwago 188
Nalwanga 58, 75, 114, 143, 146-9, 152-3
Namanda 143
Namukasa 125-6, 142, 146
Namyalo Dativa 104-5
Natukunda 70, 113-4, 129-41, 142, 143, 150, 152, 224
negligence 204, 210
new female criminal 73
New Vision, The 64
1991 Population and Housing Census, The 38, 72-3
nyieko. See co-wives

O

Odoi 142-3, 146
Odoki, B.J. 195
O'Donovan, K. 158, 190, 202, 210
omission 25, 119-20, 198, 210
oppression, double. *See* double oppression; patriarchal oppression
oweiwali. See co-wives
ownership, of children. *See* child ownership

P

panga. See weapons
partners in crime. *See* co-offenders
paternal property. *See* child ownership
paternity 99-103, 109
patriarchal oppression 69-70, 230-1
patriarchy 12-3, 16, 24, 77, 97-8, 229-32

patrilocality 12, 127-9
Penal Code 25, 78, 105, 119, 167, 172, 180, 186-90, 195, 200, 203
penal policy 212. *See also* Penal Code
People v Garcia 176
perpetrators 1, 51, 174
persecution 174, 176-7, 190, 197. *See also* accumulated violence; battered women; provocation
physical abuse 39-41, 56, 60-7, 71, 79-81, 90, 94, 143, 204, 237. *See also* abuse
PMS. *See premenstrual syndrome*
police 4, 61, 81, 85, 86, 93, 117, 118, 126, 133, 134, 163-4, 173, 175, 196, 228
Pollak, O. 15
polyandry 236
polygamy 12, 21, 81, 122-58, 230, 236. *See also* marriage
pregnancy 15, 50, 61, 101-3, 106-7, 110-1, 120, 132-5, 218, 220
premeditation 2
premenstrual syndrome 15-6
prisoners 22, 31-7, 73, 96, 211-28
  first offenders 214
  non-custodial 104-5, 187, 197, 199, 218
  recidivists 214
  remand 20, 43, 47-8, 53, 61-2, 65, 100, 103, 126, 186-8, 192, 197, 213-7, 221-2
prisons 18-21, 36-7, 64, 70, 96, 99, 212-7, 220-1, 226, 236
  counselling in 221-3
  in Uganda: Fort Portal 20-1, 221; Jinja 20-1; Luzira Women's Prison 20-1, 214, 216; Masaka 20-1, 213, 214, 217, 220; Mbale 18, 20; Mbarara 20-1, 94, 130, 214, 217, 220
promiscuity 41, 70
prostitutes 78, 84-5, 107. *See also* concubines; girlfriends; mistresses

provocation 2, 39-40, 129, 144-5, 159-73, 188-204, 208-10, 232, 238. *See also* threats of future injury; witchcraft
psychological abuse 65, 161-2. *See also* abuse
psychological self-defence 201
puerperal mental disturbance 119
punishment. *See* sentencing

Q

no entries

R

R. v Fabiano Kinene and Others 209
R. v Luseru Wandera 209
Rafter, N.H. and Natalizia, E.M. 6
rape 168-71, 177, 179, 184, 206, 224
rationality 2. *See also* anti-social behaviour; mental instability
reasonableness 161-73, 176, 188-9
recidivists. *See* sentencing
reciprocal assaultive violence 160
Regina v Tamale Grushie 179
rehabilitation. *See* sentencing
remand. *See* prisoners
retaliation 43, 77, 174, 178, 189, 195-9, 202-3, 209, 231, 237. *See also* provocation; victim precipitation
Rex v Hussein s/o Mohamed 171
Rex v Lesbini 186
Rex v Nana Jabu Lukhele 170-1
Roberts, E.D. 54, 67, 92, 119, 237
Rodriguez, F.S. and Henderson, A.V. 59
role theory of crime 14
Rosen, C.J. 171, 176, 206, 207
Rukiga 192
Rwanyarare 57-60, 69, 91

S

Sampa, A. et al 65, 200
Schneider, M.E. and Jordan, B.S. 33, 41, 85, 170, 178-9, 185, 205
Section 182 of the Uganda Penal Code 25, 186, 188, 198-9, 210
Seidman, R. 1, 166
self-defence 2, 39-55, 60, 64, 144, 164-88, 196, 205-10, 232-3
   doctrine of 167-73
   use of force in 44-5, 167-73, 175-85, 201, 205-6
   psychological 201-3; *See also* imminency; threats of future injury. *See also* accumulated violence; self-preservation; victim precipitation
self-determination 76, 211-2
self-preservation 39, 43, 167, 201, 235-7. *See also* self-defence
senior wives 144-5. *See also* co-wives
sentencing 10, 11, 104, 115, 174, 176, 195-9, 205, 215, 220
   and first offenders 213-4
   death penalty 206
   imprisonment. *See* imprisonment
   leniency in 104-5, 135, 153, 164-5, 176-7, 195
   non-custodial 104, 187, 197-9, 218
   punishment in 103-4, 106, 168-9, 174, 180, 195, 206, 211-3, 224-5
   and recidivists 213-4
   reformation through 211
   rehabilitation through 211
separation. *See* marriage
sexual intercourse, deprivation of 41, 63-5
Silivia Barushwa 205
Simba 88
Smart, C. 6, 12, 23-4, 76
social class 7, 227
socio-cultural values 77, 95, 230
socio-economic class 9-10, 234

Sofia Auma 161, 190-1
Sommers, I. and Baskin, D.R. 2, 42
Southall, A.W. 17
Southhall Black Sisters 238
spear. *See* weapons
spousal homicides 59, 96. *See also* violence
Stahly, G.B. 9, 67
State v Kelly 163
State v Little 206
State v Wanrow 185
stepfamily
   brother 109, 112, 122
   child 21, 36, 112-4, 121, 122, 127, 199, 231, 233
   daughter 115
   father 121
   mother 110, 117-8, 122, 125, 157, 192, 223; *See also* myth of the cruel stepmother
   sister 133
   son 110, 187, 221
stick. *See* weapons
strangulation 182
Straus, J.H. and Straus, M.A. 26, 124-5
Straus, M.A. 78
Straus, M.A. et al 119, 238
succession 112, 137, 236
Succession Act, The 98, 121
suicide 25-6, 37, 125, 127, 130, 142, 188, 208

T

Tamale, S. 95
Tanner, R.E.S. 9, 11, 13, 14, 16, 17, 18, 40, 51, 55, 67, 80, 166, 234
Tariq, P.N. 122
Tembo v the King 191
Tereza Nakayima 174, 175, 197, 205
Tereza Namboze 161
Tereza Ngamita and Others 198, 209

Terezina Karawali 173, 196
Thompson, B.R. and Erez, E. 42
threats of future injury 161, 175-80. *See also* provocation; victim precipitation; witchcraft
Thwala, His Lordship 171
Tibamanya 101, 110, 118
Toro 87-90, 147
Totman, J. 14, 27, 36-7, 52, 63, 135, 142, 155-6, 231, 232

U

Uganda Association of Women Lawyers 223, 228
Uganda High Court 165, 179, 238
Uganda Penal Code Act, The 1
Uganda v Akidi 218
Uganda v Gabriel Ojoba 198
Uganda v Kyanda 78
UK. *See* United Kingdom
unfaithfulness. *See* infidelity
United Kingdom 8, 52, 54, 226, 238
United Nations Standard Minimum Rules for the Treatment of Prisoners (1955) 211-4, 226
United States of America 4, 51
US. *See* United States of America
USA. *See* United States of America

V

verdicts 196-9, 203
    acquittals 15, 40, 167-73, 176. *See also* manslaughter; murder; sentencing
victim precipitation 78, 159-61, 164, 195, 233
victimisation 33-4, 36-7, 162, 177, 203, 237
violence 1-6, 10, 14-23, 62-7, 69-77, 81, 87-95, 107, 133-7, 155-7, 183, 200-4, 229-38. See also accumulated violence; intrafamily violence;

violence *(continued)*
    intramarital violence; *reciprocal assaultive violence*
violent crime 1, 10, 14-8, 157, 164, 203, 229-33, 237. *See also* violence; violent criminality
violent criminality 1, 7, 14-5, 20. *See also* violence; violent crime; women's violent criminality
Violet Katungwabusha 199

W

Walker, L.E. 201, 205, 207
Warren, M. 4
weapons 20, 180-8
    acid 44, 125, 142, 143, 146, 154
    axe 7, 8, 106, 186
    bottle 143, 146
    dagger 186, 206
    fire 48, 91, 126, 238
    gun 52, 133, 177, 183, 184
    hoe 49-51, 53, 128, 143, 187, 188, 191, 192, 193, 222
    iron bar 46
    knife 44, 132, 168, 171, 187, 188
    panga 46-7, 133, 145, 161, 184, 187
    pestle 144
    pit 103, 105, 108, 109, 184, 187, 225
    poison 25, 49, 54, 191
    spear 45, 48, 71, 107, 143, 152
    stick 45, 53, 60, 128, 173-4, 182, 187, 188, 196
    stone 188
wife assault 40-3, 178-9. *See also* abuse; battered women
wife-beating. *See* abuse; battered women; wife assault
Wilbanks, W. 10
Wilson, M.I. and Daly, M. 4, 59, 90, 121, 230
witchcraft 107, 145, 148, 191-5, 198-9, 203, 209
Witchcraft Act, The 194

Wolfgang, M.E. 14, 33, 78, 155, 159, 161, 195, 204, 205, 210
womanhood 3, 65, 96, 169
women prisoners 22, 30-7, 73, 212-28. *See also* imprisonment; prisons; prisoners
women's criminality 3-9, 33-4, 226
women's violent criminality 1, 7, 14-8, 20-1, 70, 232, 236-7
Worrall, A. 166, 167

X

no entries

Y

Yoruba 66
Yovan v Uganda 172, 189

Z

no entries